FICTIONS OF
NUCLEAR DISASTER

David Dowling

MACMILLAN
PRESS

First published 1987

Published by
THE MACMILLAN PRESS LTD
Houndmills, Basingstoke, Hampshire RG21 2XS
and London
Companies and representatives
throughout the world

Typeset by Wessex Typesetters
(Division of The Eastern Press Ltd)
Frome, Somerset

Printed in Hong Kong

British Library Cataloguing in Publication Data
Dowling, David
Fictions of nuclear disaster.
1. Nuclear warfare in literature   2. English
fiction—20th century—History and criticism
I. Title
823'.914'09358   PR888.N8
ISBN 0–333–39817–3

FICTIONS OF NUCLEAR DISASTER

For Julian, Jessica, and all the children

Our tragedy today is a general and universal physical fear so long sustained by now that we can even bear it. There are no longer problems of the spirit. There is only the question: When will I be blown up? Because of this, the young man or woman writing today has forgotten the problems of the human heart in conflict with itself which alone can make good writing because only that is worth writing about, worth the agony and the sweat.

William Faulkner, acceptance speech
for the Nobel Prize for Literature,
Stockholm 1950

We are warm, our active
Universe is young; yet we shiver:
For athwart our thinking the threat looms,
Huge and awful as the hump of Saturn
Over modest Mimas, of more deaths
And worse wars, a winter of distaste
To last a lifetime. Our lips are dry, our
Knees numb; the enormous disappointment
With a smiling sigh softly flings her
Indolent apron over our lives
And sits down on our day.

W. H. Auden, *The Age of Anxiety* (1946)

Literature has always belonged to the nuclear epoch . . .

Jacques Derrida, 'No Apocalypse, Not Now'
(*Diacritics*, 1984)

Although we do not know what to do about
nuclear weapons, we should, by now, be
learning how to write about them.

Martin Amis, *Observer* (29 December 1985)

Contents

List of Illustrations

Acknowledgements

I wish to acknowledge the great assistance given to me by Ms Pauline Dickinson of the University of Sydney Library, and the Rare Books Department of that library in making the collection of Mr Ron Graham available to me.

The author and publishers wish to thank the following who have kindly given permission for the use of copyright material: David Higham Associates and Jonathan Cape, for the extract from Russell Hoban's *Riddley Walker*; Weidenfeld & Nicolson, for the extract from Walter Miller's *A Canticle for Leibowitz*; and Mercatorfonds, for the illustrations by A. Dürer, Apocalypse series in Federick van der Meer, *Apocalypse: Visions from the Book of Revelation in Western Art* (London: Thames & Hudson, 1978).

'The Stars Fall', A. Dürer, Apocalypse series in Frederick van der Meer, *Apocalypse: Visions from the Book of Revelation in Western Art* (London: Thames & Hudson) p. 290.

1 The Bomb in Fiction

Do I love this world so well
That I have to know how it ends?[1]

Herman Kahn, the man who gave us the concepts of the 'arms race' and 'escalation', complains that 'it is characteristic of our time that many intelligent and sincere people are willing to agree that it is immoral to think and even more immoral to write in detail about having to fight a thermonuclear war'.[2] The same charge has been levelled at writers about living through and after a nuclear war, but this study is undertaken with the conviction that it is indeed immoral *not* to contemplate the possible nuclear apocalypse.

This does not mean that I shall be assembling *exempla* for a high moral tract about the evils of science and nuclear physics. The nuclear possibility forces late twentieth-century man to confront his human nature and his place in the nature of things afresh; by picturing nuclear developments and responses, he carries on the meditation and debate which was once the preserve of theology and metaphysics. The literature of nuclear disaster is moral in the sense that it ponders what we ought to be and ought to do. When it ponders intelligently, moreover, this literature both rejuvenates mainstream fiction and reminds science fiction of its roots in technological man's investigation of himself. The prospect itself which faces us is absurd: a finger slipping on a button, a burnt out silicon chip, may generate an Armageddon as complete and harrowing as any imagined by the Old Testament prophets. But the framing of that prospect in a plausible fiction can generate imaginative literature of the highest order, confirming F. Jameson's definition that 'science fiction is in its very nature a symbolic meditation on history itself'.[3]

Fictions of man-made disaster have been plentiful from at least the middle of the nineteenth century.[4] Predictions of the

1

carnage of modern warfare were particularly popular in the years preceding the Great War, although even these proved to be inadequate to the technological ingenuity and depravity of the modern technician or soldier. In 1895 R. Cromie (in *The Crack of Doom*) even imagined an explosion caused by one grain of matter containing enough energy, if 'etherised', to raise a hundred thousand tons nearly two miles; but he could conceive of using this weapon only against the French fishing fleet. Still, there was a dawning sense that technology would soon give man Faustian destructive powers: Louis Tracy (*The Final War*, 1896) predicts the need for global disarmament as an expression of the Divine Will, and George Griffith (*Olga Romanoff*, 1894) takes things to their imaginative conclusion. In that novel Natas the Jew, leader of the Great Revolt against all tyrants in 1903, tells his children in 1930 that 'since the sun set upon Armageddon, and the right to make war was taken from the rulers of the nations, we have governed a realm of peace and prosperity'. However the last Czarina wages war from a mountain stronghold, and finally a report from Mars informs us that the planet Earth is doomed to extinction.

In the twentieth century, fictions of global disaster abound. Italo Svevo ends his *Confessions of Zeno* (1923):

> Our life today is poisoned to the root. Man has ousted the beasts and trees, has poisoned the air and filled up the open spaces. Worse things may happen. That melancholy and industrious animal – man – may discover new forces and harness them to his chariot. Some such danger is in the air . . .
>
> When all the poison gases are exhausted, a man, made like all other men of flesh and blood, will in the quiet of his room invent an explosive of such potency that all the explosives in existence will seem like harmless toys beside it. And another man, made in his image and in the image of all the rest, but a little weaker than them, will steal that explosive and crawl to the centre of the earth with it, and place it just where he calculates it would have the maximum effect. There will be a tremendous explosion, but no one will hear it and the earth will return to its nebulous state and go wandering through the sky, free at last from parasites and disease. (411–12)

Often human folly is linked with natural upheavals, as in this cosmic history by Edmund Cooper in *The Last Continent* (1970):

> As if man's inhumanity to man were not enough, Nature herself accelerated the devastation, the trauma, the change. Earth's magnetic field had been constantly weakening and was no longer able to trap the high energy particles streaming out from the sun. As the magnetic lines of force became weaker, the Van Allen radiation belt began to dissipate, and Earth was subjected to increasing bombardment from that vast cosmic nuclear reactor that had hitherto sustained life and maintained relative organic stability. (95)

Such generalised visions of doom, however, soon pall. They are what Ursula le Guin calls 'a pseudo-objective listing of marvels and wonders and horrors which illuminate nothing beyond themselves and are without real moral resonance: daydreams, wishful thinking, and nightmares'.[5] The challenge of envisaging nuclear disaster is an extremely difficult one, for it is, as Warren Wagar says, 'the idea of the end of the world, not as a restatement or exegesis of Biblical eschatology, but as a creative act of the secular imagination'.[6] Le Guin claims that the best fiction is creative in this way, and 'continues to avoid the clean and gleaming sterility of despair'.[7] I will be presenting many fictions which do indeed avoid despair, but I will also exemplify a more common failing for such fictions: the grotesque inappropriateness of the response.

While many writers kept themselves informed of nuclear developments during the early 1940s, ignorance of the nature and effects of atomic explosions persisted well into the post-war era. In 1928 P. F. Nowlan's serial *Buck Rogers* first appeared, with the hero emerging from suspended animation after five hundred years to free the world from despotism by means of disintegrator rays and rocket pistols. The explanation that Rogers had been preserved thanks to the *beneficent* powers of radioactive gas was retained even when the tale appeared in book form in 1962.[8] H. A. van Mierlo's *By Then Mankind Ceased to Exist* (1960) has a Secretary of State whose legs are rotting away, 'being poisoned by the radioactivity' (89). In R. M. Williams's *The Day They Bombed Los Angeles* (1961) a Buck Rogers hero herds beautiful women into the shelters ('Sis, when the

hydrogen starts popping . . .' [9]) and after one day below goes
for a ride sightseeing, cheerily observing, 'Nothing has licked
the human race yet' (123). More alarming than this technical
ignorance is the response which 'uses' nuclear disaster as an
element in some other fiction. For some reason connected with
possible genetic mutation and the 'last man' theme, this other
fiction is often a sexual joke. In Pat Frank's *Mr Adam* (1947) the
whole of America becomes sterile as the result of explosions at
a nuclear fission plant; the one man who remains potent
becomes the object of female attention. In Damon Knight's
'Not With a Bang', the last man is locked in the men's room
and the last woman is a stickler for decency; and in *The Last
Adam* (1952) the last man refuses an apple from the last woman.

   Too often, fictions of nuclear disaster also become, in Brian
Ash's words, 'breeding ground for the fiercest expositions of
myths and religious dogma'.[9] The technological proponents are
among the fiercest, both claiming the accurate prediction of
the bomb as a victory, and seeing the post-disaster situation as
one more challenge for technological man. Isaac Asimov is
right to claim that 'with the coming of the atom bomb, society
could no longer look upon science fiction as childish escape-
literature. The science fiction writer had seen too much to
which others were blind'.[10] But seeing is not believing, and
nuclear fiction must not be confined to the Nostradamus school
of prophecy. Donald Wollheim, at the predictive level,
dismisses Nevil Shute's pessimism in *On the Beach*: 'We science
fiction writers rarely let the world die. We have the farther
vision. It sustains us.'[11] This confusion about the function of
fiction may itself arise out of the ignorance of the 'two cultures'
about each other and the crude, pretended divorce between fact
and fiction, inventions and inventiveness. This divorce has
been perpetuated on both sides, too, as exemplified in the
response of the scholar G. Wilson Knight to Hiroshima: 'The
business of creative literature is, and has always been, the
steady will to the harmonising of earthly experience, the trans-
mutation of war to peace, agony to bliss; the distillation of life
from death. Our mechanised science seems bent on a reverse
process.'[12] Fictions of nuclear disaster are attempts to bridge
the gap, to grasp imaginatively the most hideous assaults on
sensibility caused by the devotion to science. The attempt is
surely better than the fatal retreat advocated by Knight, and it

need not concern itself with the 'farther vision' of Wollheim because, like all fiction, its purpose is to speak to us now. As Frank Kermode cogently argues in his study of endings of all kinds,

> Men in the middest make considerable imaginative investments in coherent patterns which, by the provision of an end, make possible a satisfying consonance with the origins and with the middle. That is why the image of the end can never be falsified. But they also, when awake and sane, feel the need to show a marked respect for things as they are; so that there is a recurring need for adjustments in the interest of reality as well as of control . . .
>
> The apocalyptic types – empire, decadence and renovation, progress and catastrophe – are fed by history and underlie our ways of making sense of the world from where we stand, in the middest.[13]

The distinction between plausibility and predictability is a crucial one, then, because fictions of nuclear disaster must be 'plausible', showing an adjustment in the interest of reality and history, without being simply bets on the future which can be cashed only when 1984 does or does not come about. They are important as coherent patterns because they help us to make sense of where we stand, in the middest. And their degree of plausibility depends not on their affirmation of the values and future of technology or of culture, but rather on their technique of delivery.

How can a writer, then, 'construct an imaginative sketch of the dread but vital whole of things',[14] as Olaf Stapledon puts it? There are various techniques, and because the organisation of this study is thematic rather than stylistic, it is worthwhile to suggest here some of them.

One technique is by indirection, by skirting round the perimeter of the gaping chasm of disaster. The magnitude of the nuclear threat naturally ties the tongue, as the first observers of a nuclear explosion felt:

> Thirty seconds after the explosion came the first air blast, pressing hard against the people and things, to be followed almost immediately by the strong, sustained, awesome roar

which warned of doomsday and made us feel that we puny things were blasphemous to dare tamper with the forces heretofore reserved for the Almighty. Words are inadequate tools for the job of acquainting those not present with the physical, mental and psychological effects. It had to be witnessed to be realised.[15]

This sense of an inadequate language is common in Biblical apocalyptic also, as a commentator on Revelation points out: 'The similes, negatives, parodies and analogies suggest the limits of language. What this finally implies about Revelation as a literary work is that, while it is a stunningly imaginative creation, it contains, in that very imaginative thrust, an enormously important theme in the history of art . . . the limits of human imagination.'[16] Because of this inadequacy, the nuclear fact may be treated as a given, a shadow in the background which colours everything. The two most famous dystopias of our century, *1984* and *Brave New World*, take place under such a shadow: Orwell's state of continuous, contrived intercontinental warfare, and Huxley's dimly remembered Nine Days War. Thomas Pynchon in *Gravity's Rainbow* creates a world where World War II has never really ended, and the development of the V-rocket moves inexorably to the fall of the first missile beyond the last page of the book. The characters long for this apocalyptic release – 'Gravity is the answer, mystical, Messianic – while we are left looking for correspondences in words' (43) – and Pynchon mocks all artistic enterprise, including his own, by ending with us all in a darkened cinema watching the film of history (or the book itself) while outside above us the first real rocket falls. Instead of documenting disaster, Pynchon creates the *climate* of disaster: fear, paranoia, the solitude of despair and panic – 'There is time, if you need the comfort, to touch the person next to you or to reach between your own cold legs' (760). Such reticence is liable to contradictory readings, of course, as can be seen in the following comments:

> There is no holy grail, no pot of gold at the end of the rainbow, only a parodic transcendence, a direct hit . . .

> The rocket falls *after* the book's last words, outside the book's

world (we hear the scream) so as readers, destruction has passed over us, and we have survived.[17]

But at least the unverbalised disaster remains as an atmosphere for the reader to react to without questioning the accuracy of detail or adequacy of language.

'We hunger for ends and for crises', says Kermode of our age, and another way to treat nuclear disaster is as a concept to be satirised. R. A. Lafferty's *Apocalypses* mocks the idea itself by its plural title, and goes on to present a world which does not care about apocalypse. Ennisworthy Sweeny is an American composer whose three operas *Armageddons I, II* and *III*, performed in 1916, 1939 and 1984, have proved to be predictive as well as plausible. But Sweeny's problem is in rousing the nation to make an actual response; even when he slows down the Earth's rotation as a warning of impending doom, 'The people didn't *act* as if the world were ending. But they didn't act quite as if it were going to continue either. They behaved as though they didn't very much care whether it ended or not' (374). Sweeny's fate is that of the sandwich-board man carrying his 'Repent!' sign through a preoccupied crowd. Lafferty's novel, by looking back from beyond 1984 and saying of its present 'The Situation Worsens', challenges us now to formulate an attitude towards disaster which involves an attitude towards life, too. Although it does not describe the disaster itself (Lafferty does not give us the content of Sweeny's operas either), the novel forces us to take up an attitude towards it.

An attitude can also be taken towards disaster if it is framed in some way, usually from a longer perspective of future time and through some pre-existing documentation. John of Patmos achieves his visionary authority in the form of seven scrolls which are handed to him and opened one by one; the modern tradition is established by *A Strange Manuscript Found in a Copper Cylinder* (1888) where the hero Adam More asks that this record of his adventures be passed on to a friend in London. The perspective of 'looking backwards' may be achieved simply by assuming a future time, as in Lafferty, or by resorting to the Wellsian device of time travel, as is demonstrated by Rex Graham's *Utopia 239*, an otherwise forgettable story which has its time travellers learn about the impending Armageddon from a film documentary in a future time:

> Then, with a shattering roar, the screen filled with rank upon rank of planes, all heading west.
>
> Caption: ULTIMATUM EXPIRES AT MIDNIGHT, TAKE-OFF FIVE HOURS EARLIER, RECALL ONLY IF TERMS ACCEPTED.
>
> Another map followed. With horror, they saw that they were going through the same process again. For this, a map showing lines from England, France, and Spain, all leading east, was headed:
>
> AMERICAN BLOWS DESIGNED TO ELIMINATE RED AIR FORCE BEFORE IT HAS CHANCE TO STRIKE.
>
> The night sky again. The bomber's moon. Plane after plane flying high and in almost total silence. . . .
>
> The screen said TIME 2355.
>
> The night sky in the upper air. They recognised the first six bombers now. They were peaceful and even beautiful riding serenely through the moonlight. Below, very faintly in the darkness, could be seen an enormous area of sea with the dark edge of a coast-line jutting into it: the hills of Scotland. The coast-line drew itself quietly and relentlessly forward below the bombers. On it, suddenly, bright red specks appeared; specks which grew, which resolved themselves into rockets which would seek out and destroy the invading force. The guided-missile defences had not been asleep, and Selwyn and Mary and her father sat forward on their couches, hoping, praying although they knew the answer. Red specks were leaving the bombers now with curling streaks of brilliant fire. The battle took place below the bombers, and no pilot was engaged in it. Missile sought missile. The bombers flew on.
>
> And on. (168–71)

Often this kind of global observation requires an appropriate point of view, such as an aeroplane or satellite, and a 'public' form of announcement such as a TV news bulletin or (the most popular) newspaper or radio headlines, e.g.

July 5, 1954:
REVIVED U.N. DEMANDS NATIONS DISARM
June 29, 1955:
STOCKS RISE SHARPLY
RUPTURED? STOP WORRY WITH THIS AMAZING
INVENTION (ADVT.)
June 30, 1955:
U.S. AT WAR!
ATOM BOMBS BLAST CITIES
MacARTHUR DIRECTS COUNTERATTACK
July 10, 1955:
ALL CITIES EVACUATED
August 12, 1955:
GERM WARFARE BEGINS (75)

This example, taken from Lewis Padgett's *Tomorrow and Tomorrow* (1951), supposes a parallel world in order to give the requisite point of view, but the novel also interweaves another popular modern device of plausibility, the inner vision.

Twentieth century man has admired in the works of writers like Beckett, Kafka, Borges and Pynchon an attitude of mind fitting for the times – bewildered, oppressed, fantastical and paranoid. While nuclear disaster is pre-eminently a public occurrence – political, national and 'physical' – the premonition of disaster, the living through and the survival afterwards, are all matters of psychic stress which often seem simply a more extreme form of the continuing modern *angst*. The internalising of the nuclear crisis, then, is one way of effectively writing about it, as in Padgett's paranoid, death-wish-filled hero:

> *Of course, If I were awake, I would never do it. But in a dream –*
> *Do it. It's the release I need*, said the devil at his shoulder. *The release you need. That we need. You're under terrific tension, and you're neurotic and worried for fear this very thing will happen. So get your release. A dream is harmless.*
> Somehow in the dream it was ridiculously easy to do. You merely had to detach the boron dampers and pull them out. But what had happened to their locks?
> He watched the gauges on the walls. Geiger counters began to chatter insanely. Needles rose in jumpy, warning

spasms as the dampers were withdrawn. The critical mass
had nearly been reached.
  But it's only a dream, of course, he thought, as he woke amid
the inconceivable fractional-second beginning of the atomic
blast. (6)

It may not be that the modern writer is like Ellerbee in Stanley
Elkin's novel *The Living End*, who is given a better vocabulary
in order to heighten his experience of Heaven and Hell; but the
focus on the subjective experience through surreal imagery or
the stream of consciousness can convey a sense of apocalypse
without getting bogged down in technical trivia or the
plausibility of prediction. A contrast between a nineteenth and
twentieth century vision of the End may help to clarify this.
Emile Zola's *Work* (1901) describes the final battles before the
rule of science in a journalistic way:

> And the two huge armies of hostile brothers met in the centre
> of Europe, on some vast plains where millions of beings had
> space to murder one another. . . . Each day that dawned
> there still remained human flesh for bullets and shells. The
> combatants did not even take time to remove their dead; the
> piles of corpses formed walls behind which new regiments
> ever advanced in order to get killed. . . . Science had invented
> explosives and murderous engines which carried death over
> prodigious distances, and annihilated a whole community as
> suddenly as an earthquake might have done. And what a
> monstrous massacre showed forth on the last evening of that
> gigantic battle! Never before had such a huge human sacrifice
> smoked beneath the heavens! More than a million men lay
> there in the great ravaged fields, alongside the watercourses,
> across the meadows. One could walk for hours and hours,
> and one ever met a yet larger harvest of slaughtered soldiers,
> who lay there with their eyes wide open, and their black
> mouths agape, as if to cry aloud that mankind was mad!
> (498–9)

Compare this grand description, its Biblical rhetoric and
allusion, its attempts at measurement and objective point of
view, with Kit Reed's tense, paranoid prose in *Armed Camps*
(1970):

Wait till you hear the latest: the scientists have put their heads together (the noble, white-coated intrepid Men of Science, those high minded, I-didn't-touch-it bastards, they look at you and say, Me? Like you? You're a soldier, you *kill* people, I'm an abstract thinker, man. Of course I never put my knowledge to dirty uses, but if you tried . . . Zut: spot radiation burns, disable your victim without damaging any of the surrounding materiel; *voila*: neutron bomb). Our scientists have devised a new system; now we have a lot of important new hardware in the air. They sent it up a couple of years ago and as long as that stuff is up there, zizzing round and round, it will intercept anything ugly that flies, and if something should get through and set off the popcorn, you can rest assured that all that hardware is geared to come crashing in and blow the works, and if the hardware doesn't come crashing in all on its own, we have a way to set it off, so whatever happens, don't worry, we will get the last shot anyway. . . .

It takes a lot of power to keep that stuff up there, an electronic filigree that recharges warheads and gives a zap when an orbit begins to decay and destructs the ones that need destructing and sends up a couple of new ones every day, and if the filigree begins to unravel, if we let down for a minute, They will slip something in on us, They will get the jump on us, whoever They are, and the works will blow, and if They don't slip something in on us then one of those things may go haywire, or one of our pieces of hardware will bump one of their pieces of hardware and the works will blow up anyway, so we have to keep 'em flying. Rest easy, friends, your lives are in good hands. (54–5)

Unlike Zola, we live in an age of constant threat, of potential apocalypse. The magnitude is beyond our reckoning, the technology and perhaps the politics beyond our ken, but what can be explored and dramatised is what it is like to feel in the post-1945 world.

In such a literature, the whole idea of a narrative may seem inappropriate, since the end towards which we drive insanely is not known, only known about. We feel like the passengers on Martin Bax's *Hospital Ship* as it cruises around the rim of a dying world, and yet 'This is only the tenth year of a war that will last at least another half-century' (189). Bax's conclusion is an awful lack of conclusion. Today's writer is like the hero of J. G. Ballard's story 'Now: Zero', who has discovered that when he describes people's deaths in his diary, some of them seem to come true. Convinced of his Godlike powers, he commands the reader to die, 'Now!' Of course we generally do not die (although one day we might) when we reach the end of a fiction; instead, we put the book aside and go and do the dishes. But in an extension of the tendency to focus on the apocalyptic mood rather than the event itself, writers may manipulate the reading process itself to put the reader through a process analogous to apocalypse. By exploding the world of the story, the writer may induce *us* to feel the anguish of real disaster.

Often this involves drawing on post-modernist techniques of reflexivity. In Poul Anderson's 'Disintegrating Sky' (1953), for example, a group of scientists in a highrise apartment muse upon time and history. One of them imagines 'a very young writer. He doesn't know the first thing about the principles of literature. The majority of his characters are dull and stupid. He doesn't have a plot, just a long meaningless narrative broken by melodramatic catastrophes.' (79) Another scientist informs the group that the 'total-disintegration bomb' is now in production and will surely be used. This appeals to the group as a kind of event the young writer might dream up: 'to hell with winding up all the million loose ends in a story that has begun to bore him. Wipe 'em all out, let every blasted one of his characters go up in flames, start on something more interesting.' It remains only for one of the scientists to observe, 'If I'd written that I'd have saved a few characters to realise they were in a poorly written novel'; to walk to the window to see, in the distance, the 'disintegrating sky', and to hear the faint scream of sirens. The apocalypse comes as suddenly and meaninglessly as predicted, and the two fictional levels seem to cancel each other out in the reader's experience until s/he confronts the abyss of a real destruction. What is more, the scientists are portrayed not as illiterate but as astute fictionalists, at once Promethean in their powers of creation and prediction, and fictions in the game of politicians or world history.

Science fiction writers themselves are the subjects of Maxim Jakubowski's neatly titled story 'Just Another End of the

World', where the end comes during a science fiction convention. 'With all our combined literary apocalyptic background', says the narrator, 'we should have known what to expect' (172); but it is only after the survivors have rebuilt civilisation again that printing presses are constructed and the demand for literature prompts a story competition:

> The theme was obvious. It didn't take us long to find it. Every one says he has absolutely great ideas. We've all sworn to outdo ourselves on this one.
> So here I sit, chuckling mischievously, writing my own downbeat end of the world story, writing my life away. (80)

Here, by exposing the fiction, Jakubowski is able to turn the mirror on the mirror and suggest that the real end of the world, outside and prior to the writing of his story, was far more horrific and indescribable than his 'downbeat ending' which we have just read. The last lines about 'writing my life away' grimly suggest a post-disaster setting of slow and agonising death. All implication, the story has an unexpected and haunting power. The same kind of self-reflexivity is explored by Stanislaw Lem in *The Futurological Congress* where the narrator, hiding with his colleagues in the hotel sewer system, dreams of a brave new world of drugged compliance. The profession of futurology is supported by something called 'Trottelreiner's linguistic futurology', a system of morphological forecasting and projective etymology which helps us learn 'what discoveries changes and social revolutions the language will be capable, some day, of reflecting' (109). The limits of my language, as Wittgenstein said, are the limits of my world. But even this apparent affirmation of the power of language and the imagination is shattered when the narrator wakes from his dream and with mocking laughter hurls his colleague's paper into the sewer to 'float away into the unknown future'. Lem simultaneously undercuts the predictive value of his own novel from within and proves that Trottelreiner's theory had at least an element of truth, since Lem's verbal creation may prompt us to modify our behaviour now, even if it has no 'futurological' validity.

Sophisticated fictions like these attempt to locate the experience of nuclear disaster by surrounding the inexpressible with verbal strategies, hemming it in so that our reading experience includes the sense of an ominous chasm of silence and brooding ignorance. They affirm the power of taletelling still to say something about this end to end all endings. Their message is contrary to Nathaniel Hawthorne's in 'A New Adam and Eve', where Adam stumbles on the remains of a library but is barred from opening a book by Eve; for if he had, 'There would have been nothing left for him, but to take up the already abortive experiment of life, where we had dropped it, and toil onward with it a little further' (265). These writers are all saying that if we do *not* open up the book of fictions we will be trapped on the treadmill of history. But perhaps I am being unfair to Hawthorne: Adam's library book was undoubtedly a technical textbook, and moreover Hawthorne did write a story to tell us all about it.

These, then, are some of the styles of post-nuclear disaster fictions. They suggest one possible framework within which to order these fictions; but a thematic one seems more immediate and obvious, and it is the one I have chosen here. The dominant themes can be typified by glancing at lesser examples of the genre, such as Herbert Best's *The Twentyfifth Hour* (1940) with its chapter headings of 'The Man . . . The Woman . . . World Without Men . . . The Silent Land . . . The New Barbarians', or C. E. Maine's *The Tide Went Out* (1959). The unlikely premise of this novel is that underwater nuclear testing causes fissures in the ocean floors which drain away all the water, but the themes are typical: environmentalism versus science; the Faustian over-reaching and responsibility of the scientist; the eschatological reaction of religion ('God in his wisdom decided to challenge the lies told in the name of science. . . . It is the supreme lesson which God in his mercy has seen fit to teach us. . . . The forces of material science have been discredited for all time, and we must turn to God for our salvation' [119]); the pattern of evolution (the hero sees the disaster as a challenge to man's brainpower, and is inspired to melt the polar ice-caps); and the psychological crisis (the hero murders in order to escape and moralises, 'Once you've been touched by violence you lose something for ever' [189]).

Chapter 2 will discuss fictions which address the question of the place of science and the scientist. The nuclear power plant, though not a military threat, represents the apotheosis of the scientist as Promethean saviour, and is therefore included here. Many fictions on these themes either discuss or are examples of the virtues of plain language, the report or diary. But it is worth noting that the mammoth report by the American Office of Technological Assessment called *The Effects of Nuclear War* ended by abandoning empiricism:

> This report cannot predict whether this race for economic viability would be won. . . . There is a controversy in the literature on the subject as to whether a postattack economy would be based on centralised planning (in which case how would the necessary data and planning time be obtained?), or to individual initiative and decentralised decision-making (in which case who would feed the refugees, and what would serve for money and credit?). . . . The recital of possibilities [of the kind of impact on survivors] may fail to convey the overall situation of the survivors. . . . In an effort to provide a more concrete understanding of what a world after a nuclear war would be like, OTA commissioned a work of fiction.[18]

Allied to the scientific approach, then, are the fictional extrapolations of events surrounding Doomsday itself (Chapter 3) and of post-disaster society and eventual evolution, which I will consider in Chapter 4. Many of these fictions are overly optimistic. As I. F. Clarke laments,

> The talk about a 'clean slate' is the customary text for the disaster stories. They are myths of reassurance. They carry the rainbow promise that Homo sapiens will face the evolutionary threat in an exemplary manner. They are deceptive dreams. They pretend that the survivors of the great catastrophe will at last find a harmony and a meaning in their lives – once the complex, incomprehensible, frightening world of the twentieth century has disappeared.[19]

But some of these fictions also offer genuinely utopian or dystopian visions of society, or explore the burdens of living in the shadow of another and more spectacular Fall.

The religious reaction to nuclear disaster and the heritage of Biblical apocalyptic are the subject of Chapter 5 although both themes are implicit in many other fictions considered – especially the conflict between the man of science and the man of God. Finally, before considering in depth two exemplary fictions whose verbal strategies help to maintain an imagined world, I examine the more visionary responses to the nuclear threat. As Warren Wagar says, 'every story of the world's end draws power from, and illuminates in one way or another, the ends and beginnings of the self'; he also quite neatly describes such fictions as 'Grimms' Tales for grown-ups'.[20] In these fictions, authenticity and scientific accuracy are not as important as imaginative truth and psychological complexity. Often, too, these fictions are the most literate and verbally inventive; for, as G. D. Doherty warned, 'The sense of wonder, that Holy Grail for which critics and reviewers search, is enshrined not in the empirical facts of science or in technological jargon, but in the poetic imagination.'[21]

Such a range of themes as I have mentioned – evolution, the philosophy of science, theology, psychology, sociology – surely suggests an area of literature worth exploration, quite apart from the topical interest (and some would say the survival imperative) of post-nuclear fictions. The area has, however, been under attack from respectable critics. Susan Sontag argued that 'the imagery of disaster in science fiction is above all the emblem of an inadequate response . . . the inadequacy of most people's response to the unassimilable terrors that infect their consciousness'.[22] The only purpose of such fantasy literature, she concludes, is to allow people to cope with the twin spectres of 'unremitting banality and inconceivable terror'. Certainly Ms Sontag was addressing herself primarily to the 'pulps' of the fifties, but her attitude is typical of the rejection of disaster literature on the grounds of its inappropriateness or inadequacy. She is in danger, though, of committing her own sin and melodramatising terror until the threat of violence becomes a sacred, Manichean object of fearful reverence. Leslie Fiedler in 1965 also praised the concept of apocalypse at the expense of the nuclear threat: 'the myth of the end of man, of the transcendence or transformation of the human [is] a vision quite different from that of the extinction of our species by the Bomb, which seems stereotype rather than archetype'.[23] Were Mr Fiedler to read more widely or more recently, he would, I am sure, discover fictions which talk compellingly and originally of nuclear disaster and do not fall into the stereotypical depiction of 'inconceivable terrors' and the global 'extinction of the species'. Even Frank Kermode, that eloquent apologist for endings, seems on the defensive when he writes, 'It would be childish to argue, in a discussion of how people behave under eschatological threat, that nuclear bombs are more real and make one experience more authentic crisis-feelings than armies in the sky.'[24] But few of the writers considered here would want to argue that exact proposition; it is simply that, as a fictional pretext, nuclear bombs appear to be more likely than armies in the sky.

All these critics were writing in the sixties, and we have come a long way in the degree of sophistication with which we handle radioactive materials. We know more about the Bomb, and are less likely to imagine that global disintegration of the comic-book 'WHAM!' which was largely the post-war conception of nuclear disaster – a conception which had the attractions of the clean slate and prompted Norman Mailer to talk of 'the middle class rage for apocalypse'. But Mailer also wrote a 1962 filmscript called 'The Last Night', where ecological disaster compels the leaders of the two superpowers to blow up the Earth in order that a few rockets may escape with survivors. The President looks down on Earth from his rocket, and wondering if 'We may destroy the spirit of something far larger than ourselves' he presses the button: 'A scream of anguish, jubilation, desperation, terror, ecstasy, vaults across the heavens. The tortured heart of the earth has finally found its voice' (443). Contemporary writers have translated that new voice into speech. They often use new fictional techniques, but not necessarily; the conventions of disaster fiction discovered in the Bible and redefined in the twentieth century remain potent for as John Barth wrote in 1967, 'If you took a bunch of people out into the desert and the world didn't end, you'd come home shamefaced, I imagine; but the persistence of an art form doesn't invalidate work created in the comparable apocalyptic ambience. That's one of the fringe benefits of being an artist instead of a prophet.'[25]

This book, then, is an attempt to answer the challenge made by J. O. Bailey in his pioneering study of visionary literature

Pilgrims Through Space and Time (1947): 'It is time that this body
of literature, often considered a curious and childish by-way, is
defined, presented in some historical survey, sampled, and
analysed to see what its major patterns and ideas are.'[26]
However, I disagree with Bailey's definition of the atomic age
as one 'on whose threshold we stand chattering the ancient
formulas of Babel'. As early as H. G. Wells in 1913, writers
have discovered languages and forms which will carry their
outrageous fictions. What is more, as Michael Moorcock
observes, 'The visionary impulse has . . . become more
sophisticated since the days of Wells and Huxley. Now writers
assume increasingly the responsibilities of the poet – they seek
to match their techniques to their vision.'[27] It is time to seek out
the forgotten literature of nuclear disaster and to assess it
steadily and seriously, abandoning the academic snobbism
which compelled even Kingsley Amis, in his landmark study of
science fiction, to describe the genre as allowing us 'to doff that
mental and moral best behaviour with which we feel we have to
treat George Eliot and James and Faulkner, and frolic like
badly-brought up children among the mobile jellyfishes and
unstable atomic piles'.[28] There is now, after seventy years, a
distinct tradition within which apocalyptic novelists can work
and against which they can define themselves. The degree of
this self-consciousness is illustrated by Angus Wilson's
apocalyptic novel *The Old Men at the Zoo*, which has a chapter
called 'A Good Old, Rare Old Armageddon'. In his introduction
Wilson says, 'Our future is possibly brighter, probably much
more gloomy.' Certainly the present political situation seems to
be gloomy, and I find little cause for Mr Wagar's optimism
when he wrote in 1982, 'The longer we live with the nuclear
sword over our heads, the stronger seems the thread by which it
hangs.' Indeed, considering the passage of time between
composition and publication, I am tempted to imitate the
America–New Zealand artist Frank Womble who has already
painted the cover for the final issue of *Time* magazine (the one
they won't have time to create), and to post a resumé of my
findings on the nearest wall. But that would not do justice to
the wealth of entertaining, moving and often masterful work
considered in the following pages. Less gloomily, I am perhaps
imitating General Grove who, when planning the plutonium

works at Hanford, USA in 1945, constructed one lane leading to the plant and eight lanes leading away from it. These fictions are our ways of escape, having seen the Minotaur.

'The Four Riders', A. Dürer, Apocalypse series, Frederick van der Meer, *Apocalypse: Visions from the Book of Revelation in Western Art* (London: Thames & Hudson) p. 289.

2 The Scientist and Armageddon

Our ideas have got drunk and drop their H's.[1]

When Oppenheimer, the 'father of the bomb', witnessed the first atomic blast in the deserts of New Mexico on 16 July 1945, he was reminded of the words of a sacred Eastern text: 'I am become Death, the shatterer of worlds.'[2] Twenty years later he was arguing that scientists are, 'like all men, among those who bring a little light to the vast unending darkness of man's life and world'.[3] The irony of that image would not have escaped him, for it was he and his scientists who gave the world a 'light brighter than a thousand suns' which casts a shadow over this century, and which has encouraged the revival of the satanic scientist imaged in Shelley's Dr Frankenstein.

The literature of nuclear disaster has to cope with this paradoxical image of the scientist who, at the top of his bent, at the pinnacle of inventiveness and knowledge, is also perhaps the most morally reprehensible human being on earth. As well, it has to frame a technological world within the humanistic bounds of literary significance. No wonder Anthony Burgess decided that the whole enterprise was forlorn, since 'science fiction is a child of positivism, which rejects catastrophe'.[4] The conflict between the positivist and spiritual or sacramental world view is well illustrated by Perry Miller in his historical survey of American apocalyptic literature. He contrasts two eschatological works of the seventeenth century: Burnet's *The Sacred Theory of the Earth* (1681) and Whiston's *A New Theory of the Earth* (1696). The former looks forward to the Apocalypse, and attempts to identify it with specific geological events such as the eruption of Mount Vesuvius (since the Romish Pope must be Antichrist); the latter book describes a wholly mechanical universe, with stray disasters such as the collision of

21

Earth and a comet and even the possibility of a beneficial future – 'it will perhaps cause a change of heart and bring about a calculus of earthly felicity'.[5] Between the composition of the two works, of course, came the Newtonian revolution and a radical disjunction between religious and secular conceptions of apocalyptic disaster. The former was no longer concerned with specifying dates and causes, as illustrated by a sermon of Jonathan Edwards in 1739 which was frankly vague about the causes of the end of the world ('some way or other . . . by fire from heaven, or by fire breaking out of the bowels of the earth, or both'[6]). As science gave man the opportunity to measure and observe a mechanical universe, it gave him the power to cause his own havoc, too; it also robbed him of the language and imaginative framework within which to make sense of that ruin. Miller concludes,

> When the end of the world was a descent from Heaven, it was also a Judgment; if it becomes more and more a contrivance, it has less and less to do with good and evil. Humanity lusts after the conflagration, even after nature seems unlikely to provide it. The human finger actually itches for the trigger. But then, if humanity has to do the deed itself, can it bring about more than the explosion? Can it also produce the Judgment?[7]

This situation has not been helped by the widening gulf between what C. P. Snow called 'the two cultures'. In his Rede lecture which gave us that term, Snow berated scientists because 'the whole literature of traditional culture doesn't seem to them as relevant, and they are, of course, dead wrong.'[8] But in his second look at the question in 1964 Snow also accused the culture camp for 'making do in our half-hearted fashion, struggling to hear messages, obviously of great importance, as though listening to a foreign language in which one knows a few words'.[9] Snow also illustrated the exhilarating positivism of the scientific outlook by comparing the world-weariness of Eliot's *Hollow Men* with Lord Rutherford's famous rejoinder to the observation that he was riding the crest of a wave – 'Well, I made the wave, didn't I?' The irony is that Snow himself betrays his scientific allegiance by dismissing Eliot ('This is the way the world ends, not with a bang but a whimper') for making 'one of the least likely scientific prophecies ever made'.[10] Whether you consider the fashionable notion of global entropy or the further vision beyond the blast as seen by many writers of nuclear disaster fictions, Eliot's image seems perfectly apposite; it *is* our tragedy that there will be no clean end, and no significant one either. The comment by the father of nuclear physics Lord Rutherford, on the other hand, must surely strike us now as an example of naive, even perverse, optimism. However, Snow's general point remains valid and we must continue to try to place the revelations and advances of science into the intelligible context of culture. J. B. S. Haldane, one of the most civilised of scientific minds, once envisaged the end of the world in these scientific terms:

> It is quite likely that, after a golden age of happiness and peace, during which all the immediately available benefits of science will be realised, mankind will very gradually deteriorate.
>
> Genius will become ever rarer, our bodies a little weaker in each generation; culture will slowly decline, and in a few thousand or a few hundred thousand years – it does not much matter which – mankind will return to barbarism, and finally become extinct.[11]

But he also appreciated keenly the necessity for fictions about science:

> Pictures of the future are myths, but myths have a very real influence in the present. Modern political ideas are very largely the creation of the Jewish prophets. . . .
>
> It is the business of mythologists today to present that idea [the future evolution of man]. They cannot do so without combining creative imagination and biological knowledge.[12]

One example of such a combination is Wells's *The Time Machine*, where the Haldanean vision of biological decay is framed imaginatively by the device of the time machine and the point of view of a group of learned Victorian gentlemen sitting in a living-room. Even the recoil of Henry Ryecroft in Gissing's novel is a useful framing device, because it dramatises an attitude rather than assuming it. Ryecroft declares,

I hate and fear 'science' . . . because of my conviction that, for long to come if not for ever, it will be the remorseless enemy of mankind. I see it destroying all simplicity and gentleness of life, all the beauty of the world; I see it restoring barbarism under a mask of civilisation; I see it darkening men's minds and hardening their hearts; I see it bringing a time of vast conflicts, which will pale into insignificance 'the thousand wars of old', and, likely as not, will whelm all the laborious advances of mankind in blood-drenched chaos.[13]

It was the early science fiction writers who most formidably encountered the problems outlined above. At first there was exhilaration among American writers of the early 1940s who knew of the Manhattan Project and could sense that the scientist would become the lynchpin of military and political strategy. Cleve Cartmill's 1944 story 'Deadline' was so accurate in its technological ideas that the office of the editor of *Astounding* magazine, in which it first appeared, was raided by the FBI. In the story Ybor, hero of the Seilla tribe, manages to foil the evil Doctor Sitruc of the Sixa tribe and his plans to wage nuclear war. Ybor observes to the mad scientist, 'You're like a god here' (170), and eventually defuses the bomb by pouring out the dangerous powders into the atmosphere. Although the Sixa ('Axis' versus 'Allies') are dangerous imperialists, 'They would live because the war would end before Dr. Sitruc could construct another bomb.' Despite this optimism Cartmill certainly understands the magnitude of the new technology ('Our minds can't conceive the unimaginable violence which might very well destroy all animate life') and the theological issues it raises: 'Those religionists who still contend that this war would be ended miraculously by divine intervention would never live to call the bomb a miracle. What a shot in the doctrine the explosion would give them if only they could come through it unscathed!' Three years later the editor of *Astounding*, John Campbell Junior, was reminding his readers of the acute moral problems involved with nuclear weaponry when he wrote *The Atomic Story*, an excellent round-up of the contemporary state of affairs: 'Just as there are unstable radioactive atoms, so there are unstable men. We must learn how to discover and to correct those instabilities in men, and some means of making men more tolerant must be found. . . . The whole pattern of civilisation we have grown up in was blasted to nonsense at Hiroshima.'[14]

There was a tremendous amount of fictional writing about nuclear power in those early years, despite the tight security around research maintained by the military. In 1948 an irate fan wrote to *Astounding* magazine, 'People are getting atomic warfare thrown at them from all angles these days. I for one am heartily sick of it!'[15] Some writers gloried in their vindication as technological prophets: Robert Heinlein praised Wylie's novel *Tomorrow!* because it was set 'in a future no later than tomorrow morning'[16] and was gratified that seven out of the nine specific prophecies in his 1941 story 'Solution Unsatisfactory' actually came to pass. But other writers like Isaac Asimov regretted the euphoria and notoriety, particularly after the events of 1945: 'We were suddenly Cassandras whom the world ought to have believed. But I tell you, I would far rather have lived and died a nut in the eyes of all the world than to have been salvaged into respectability at the price of nuclear war hanging like a sword of Damocles over the world forever.'[17] The example of Hiroshima and the realisation that a nuclear explosion might not produce a global 'clean slate' but rather local horror and lingering radiation contributed to a growing distaste for apocalyptic stories, at least among the science fiction journals: in 1952 Horace Gold at *Galaxy* angrily published his policy of rejecting 'atomic doom' stories.[18]

The history of the literature of nuclear disaster in the decade of the forties is well summarised by two commentators. Here is Douglas Hill on the first phase:

Mankind *can* destroy the world; we have, as the saying goes, the technology; we have already gone a good way towards accomplishing that end. It became the natural duty of the speculators and extrapolators of sf to describe our next steps along that way: it was the bang, not the whimper, that appealed most to sf some years ago. And writers who did not dwell on how we were leading up inexorably to dropping the bomb or the bacilli often made their points instead by showing what would remain, afterwards, for anyone who might be unlucky enough to survive.[19]

Secondly, T. A. Shippey describes the move towards imaginative literature:

> The genre contained its own drive towards making statements about society-as-it-is, which prevented too long a rest on Cartmill and Heinlein's laurels. It prevented also the sort of simple 'extrapolation' of present into future which was in practical terms exemplified by the 'arms race' – A-bomb, H-bomb, cobalt bomb, strategic bomber, submarine missile, ICBM, and so on. Stories about these might work, but they would lose in 'predictability' what they gained in 'plausibility'.[20]

This chapter will examine various fictions which have attempted scientific extrapolation, or which have taken the place of science as their main theme in the context of a plausible future. Sometimes, as in the currently popular future scenarios, or the literature which came out of Hiroshima, the scientific quest for truth has remained a motivating force; more often that motivation itself has come into question in the hideous light of what science has wrought, and science and the scientist become the objects of defence, attack, or painful meditation.

At the centre of most nuclear disaster stories is the scientist himself, especially in the earlier stories of the forties and fifties which were often written by converts to technology who were beginning to re-examine their beliefs. But as early as 1915 we can find this theme in *The Man Who Rocked the Earth*, where a scientist discovers nuclear power by bombarding uranium and then holds the world hostage by threatening to bomb the globe from an aeroplane. He demands that 'war shall cease' (244), planning as a final demonstration of his powers to shift the Earth's axis. Before he can carry out his threat he is destroyed by another scientist, who also has the secret of nuclear power, but puts it to productive use by inventing a 'space-navigating car'. Here we have the archetypal features of the 'nuclear scientist' story: the Faustian over-reacher tries to bend the world to his good (or evil) intentions; salvation is only possible through a higher technology; and nuclear power can be used equally for destructive or beneficent purposes – in nuclear power plants or, very often, as the fuel for space exploration.

The scientist as peacemaker emerges again in Karel Čapek's

Krakatit (1925). Prokop, the inventor of nuclear fission or what he whimsically calls 'krakatit', is aware that matter is 'frightfully powerful' (245) but wishes to pass on his secret in obedience to Love and Goodness, the forces of Nature. At the crucial moment he discovers he has forgotten the theorem, but he will sit down and work it all out again. In *The Absolute at Large* (1927) Čapek extends his confusion of technology and religion by arguing that Marek's atomic boiler or 'Karburator', since it destroys matter, must leave the Absolute in its place – 'What is left behind is pure God' (123). When the entrepreneur sees the machine in operation he has a religious experience: 'He seemed to hear about him the rustle of unceasing and innumerable wings' (15). Unfortunately the reification of God promotes great agitation around the world, and religious wars kill 198 000 000 people leaving thirteen alive. With God reduced to a being 'about 600 metres in diameter, and even then weak towards the edges' (68), people have worshipped things, including (for one African tribe) a Japanese atomic torpedo, and Čapek describes the apocalypse in detail. His two novels seem to be suggesting that whatever the inspired motives of the scientist, his powerful inventions can only lead to global chaos.

In contrast to this there are early stories which see the scientist as the only saviour. Don Stuart's 'Atomic Power' (1934) posits an entropic world slowly expanding like a bombarded neutron and causing disasters and panic. A scientist luckily invents atomic power which releases new energy at the core of the system to counteract the expansion and restore the world's equilibrium. The physics may be suspect but there is a neat symbolism in the Earth itself behaving like a subatomic particle which has been tampered with; and the scientist saves the planet, looking forward to peaceful uses for his discovery: 'He had found the secret of vast power that would warm the frozen peoples and power the industry as Earth thawed out once more' (250). It is interesting to note that ten years later John Campbell (who wrote under the pseudonym 'Don Stuart') was warning his readers about 'unstable men' rather than portraying the scientist as saviour. Another heroic scientist is Bennion in Malcolm Jameson's *The Giant Atom* (1944). His laboratory is taken over by the General Atomic Corporation, which builds a 'reintegrator' despite Bennion's warnings about 'monkeying around with elements up in the nineties and

hundreds. . . . You are playing with cosmic fire' (29). The
invention functions as a kind of runaway reverse atom bomb,
absorbing matter voraciously, killing technicians and eating its
way down inside a mountain. Bennion is blamed for the disaster
but is busy saving the world. He persuades a minister to inspire
his flock to donate money towards a second Ark, as well as
towards Bennion's own research into atomic power. The new
vehicle, to be called 'Star of Hope', will be powered by atomic
fuel and will take the chosen few to a new planet. While
working at the makeshift village of New Eden, Bennion
demonstrates the fuel by firing a bullet with some of the new
substance, prompting an onlooker to exclaim, 'That stuff would
make wonderful ammunition for a war!' (59) Fortunately the
evil scientist is blown up and Bennion with the aid of his Heath
Robinson rocket is able to scoop up the invading atomic mass
and dump it in outer space. He returns to Earth a hero with his
girl at his side and the book version of the story ends, 'I don't
think the world is yet quite ready for atomic power' (128).
Jameson's scientific knowledge may not be ready yet either, but
his story follows the archetypal pattern of the scientist as
saviour and space explorer.

    Even in recent years, stories of noble scientists have been
prolific. Kornbluth's last story 'Two Dooms' presents a physicist
involved in the Manhattan Project who has a dream inspired
by drugs obtained from the nearby Hopi Indians. In the dream
he experiences the occupation of America by Japan and
Germany, so despite his deep fears of his own creation ('He
could see the big dirty one now. Cooked people, fused cathedral
stone, the bronze of the big Buddha running like water' [253])
he wakes and returns to work with renewed patriotic zeal. And
in 1960 C. S. Casewit wrote *The Peacemakers* concerning Rick
Ames, an inventor of the hydrogen bomb who is invited with a
group of eminent scientists to escape the global disaster on a
secluded island run by a fascist General Puckett. Unimpressed
by this leader's advances – 'I like you Ames. . . . You hit the
Russkies with all you had!' (249) – Ames helps a German
Jewish colleague to invent not the required death gas but a
benign drug which finally overpowers the megalomaniac's
army. But nowhere in the novel does the author question the
replacement of one tyranny with another; even the presence of

a Kollwitz drawing in the Jewish scientist's pocket does not prompt a discussion of scientists and morality.

Stories attempting to dramatise the Faustian inner conflicts of nuclear scientists are hampered by the fact that most research is done as part of a team and on detailed components seemingly unrelated to the final explosive effects. L. Sprague de Camp gets around the problem in 'Judgment Day' (1955) by presenting the monologue of a deranged scientist who foresees the development of weaponry. 'It took a long time to decide whether to let the earth live', he begins, then explains that he possesses the secret of nuclear fission and will reveal it to the world because he has led a persecuted life and seeks a personal revenge on humanity:

> So long as these tribes of hairless apes are organised into sovereign nations, the nuclear Ragnarok is not only possible but probable. . . . If I write up the chain reaction, the news will probably get out. No amount of security-regulations will stop people from talking about the end of the world. . . . Once having done so, the knowledge will probably cause the blowing-up of the earth. (252)

He therefore decides to go ahead with his report.

The most remarkable vision of the mad scientist which I have found in this context must be F. H. Rose's *The Maniac's Dream* (1946). It claims to be 'the first novel about the atomic bomb' and arises from the fever of contemporaneous events documented in the opening and closing pages. The story is told by a Spanish version of Conrad's Marlow, who finds himself in the heart of the African darkness watching the experiments of the crazed, Dr Moreau-like scientist: 'Mankind, harnessing to his own uses the power of Atomic Energy, will prove once and for all, that there is no other God but Man, and that he himself is God' (101). Rose uses a prototype of the radio or television news bulletin when he has the narrator look through a magical *camera obscura* to witness the destruction of the great cities of the world:

> We saw first that great Babylon of the world's cities spread below us in the golden hazes of an autumn evening. All the

familiar landmarks, like those of New York, stood out like islands floating in a sea of amber. The great dome of St. Paul's, with its gilded cross, the straight shaft of the Monument. . . .

The atomic Bomb fell somewhere between Westminster and St. Paul's.

Again there was that strange, awful, thrilling hiatus of seconds that seemed like ages. No sound reached us. The silence seemed to us to be more frightful than the most frightful sound. We held our breath, waiting to see. New York was smaller, more concentrated, the Atomic Bomb would the more easily lay it flat.

But London! . . . scarred by the thousand bombs and rockets that had rained down on it during five and a half years of terrific war – London, sprawling its mighty shape not over acres, but over miles and miles – surely London could not be wiped out by that one bomb which we saw flash down upon it through the lovely golden hazes of that Autumn day?

'Look!' exclaimed Thara, with a triumphant cry. 'The power of Atomic Energy in a ball no bigger than your fist will yet be might enough to destroy the world!' (160–1)

The whole show turns out to be a projection of the maniac's fantasies, but the effect is to make the apocalyptic end in the African valley seem the more credible. The native tribes rebel and the maniac hurls his remaining bomb into the mouth of a volcano, natural and unnatural cataclysms uniting to destroy the valley. The narrator describes the 'new Heaven and new Earth' in the colours of Blake and Palmer:

From where we lay in the tunnel I could not see into the cone of the crater. But I could see out into the world beyond. I could see, at the moment of that vast pillar of fire spouting from the mouth of the cone, that a great sheet of flame was suspended in the air, and lighting up the earth below with a brightness and whiteness that would have paled the sun.

It was a sheet of flame that grew in size, depth and intensity of blinding brilliance. The whole face of the heavens was illumined by it. It hung there in the sky like a livid cloud for what seemed to me hours. Then slowly, inexorably, it descended.

I knew then that this was no flame of fire such as ever had belched from the jaws of a volcano. It was the flame of vast, mysterious Atomic radiations which were rushing up from the bowels of the earth and pouring down with terrible and remorseless power upon the world around us . . .

I heard rocks splitting, crashing, thudding; I heard trees cracking and breaking. I heard strange sounds that no human ears had ever heard and no human experience could identify. There seemed to be shrieks of agony, as though the very earth cried aloud in terror of this awful holocaust of destruction which man had unloosed upon it. (224–5)

Although the maniac perishes in his fire, Rose makes his allegory explicit in a postscript which reminds us of 'the ruthlessness with which Science goes forward in its search for truth, brushing aside every obstacle, and caring for nothing but to search and find' (236–7). As for the mad scientist, 'Does not his attitude towards God and Man typify the attitude, and foretell the doom, of all men and nations who exalt Man and despise God?'

Such visions are not new: mediaeval woodblocks showed Antichrist as the 'scientist' Simon Magus calling down fire from Heaven in an ominous parody of Pentecost.[21] Solly Zuckerman has recently restated this vision of the scientist as wizard-king:

It is he, the technician, not the commander in the field, who starts the process of formulating the so-called military need. It is he who has succeeded over the years in equating, and so confusing, nuclear destructive power with military strength, as though the former were the single and sufficient condition of military success. The men in the nuclear weapons labs of both sides have succeeded in creating a world with an irrational foundation. . . . They have become the alchemists of our times, working in secret ways that cannot be divulged, casting spells which embrace us all.[22]

But many writers, like Kurt Vonnegut, stress the group responsibility of a nation which abrogates morality for technology. In *Player Piano* (1953) he shows how the Americans' love for invention actually leads them into a nuclear war. The computer EPICAC (a derisive acronym alluding to the more sinister invention by von Neumann of 'MANIAC' to help invent the H-bomb) wages efficient war, something that 'the reasonable, truth-loving, brilliant, and highly trained core of American genius could have delivered had they had inspired leadership, boundless resources, and two thousand years' (105). The megalomaniacal collusion of power between scientist and politician is satirised in this passage:

> When things were building up to the war, it was recognised that American know-how was the only answer to the prospective enemy's vast numbers, and there was talk of deeper, thicker shelters for the possessors of know-how, and of keeping this cream of the population out of the front-line fighting. (13)

Paul Proteus leads a rebellion against this insanity, and the carnage of technological detritus after the confrontation is vividly described in a mammoth alphabetical list: 'bits of air conditioners, amplidynes, analysers, arc welders, batteries, belts, billers, bookkeeping machines, bottlers, canners, capacitators, circuitbreakers. . .' (281). With his customary, all-embracing irony, however, Vonnegut ends the novel by pointing out that the lust for apocalypse is as misguided for humanists as for technicians:

> And that left Paul. 'To a better world,' he started to say, but he cut the toast short, thinking of the people of Ilium, already eager to recreate the same old nightmare. He shrugged. 'To the record,' he said, and smashed the empty bottle on a rock.
>   Von Neumann considered Paul and then the broken glass. 'This isn't the end, you know,' he said. 'Nothing ever is, nothing ever will be – not even Judgment Day.' (285)

In his 1963 novel *Cat's Cradle* Vonnegut returned to the theme of the scientist to argue that while writers, artists and Bokonists can believe in 'foma' or harmless untruths, the nuclear scientist must at all costs remain in touch with human morality. The narrator pursues the father of Newton Hoenikker who had replied ingenuously to a colleague's shocked reaction at Alamogordo: 'Science has now known sin' . . . 'What is sin?' On the day of Hiroshima, the scientist had been playing with the string from a manuscript sent to him by a man in prison for killing his brother. The manuscript is a novel about the end of the world, and the author wants advice about explosives for the big bomb. Out of the string the father makes a cat's cradle, but the anguished son only remembers, 'No damn cat, no damn cradle.' Eventually it is his father's invention which causes a mass suicide and a general apocalypse. The novel is a shocking portrayal of the irresponsible scientist, but it is also about the power of fictions.

Few writers are as confident in rejecting technology. Edmund Cooper's *The Cloud Walker* (1973) begins with the post-holocaust revival of the Luddite movement. A priest warns the young hero-inventor, 'I have seen a poor washerwoman burnt for devising a machine that would spin the water out of the clothes she washed' (72). Nevertheless he goes ahead and invents an air balloon which proves instrumental in destroying North African invaders. In Jeff Sutton's *Atomic Conspiracy* (1963) too, technology re-emerges triumphant. A repressive post-disaster regime appears to forbid atomic research but secretly it relies on computers and is constructing a rocket to escape to the stars. What is more, the novel's framework of quotations from *Post-Atomic Earthman*, a textbook of the Venusian Press A.D. 2672, suggests that it succeeded. And in John Christopher's *The Priest in Waiting* (1970), though a discovered copy of *Popular Mechanics* is burnt out of terror, the ruling Ezzard and his High Seers are really scientists themselves.

One of the best sustained debates about the place of science in the post-disaster world is Leigh Brackett's *The Long Tomorrow* (1955). It is set in the Mennonite community of Piper's Run, and young Len learns about the war from his grandmother:

> 'There was a rain of fire from heaven and many were consumed in it.' The Lord gave it to the enemy for a day to be His flail.'
> 'But we won.'
> 'Oh yes, in the end we won.'
> 'Did they build Bartorstown then?'
> 'Before the war. The gover'ment built it. That was when

the gover'ment was still in Washington . . . They built a lot
of secret places, and Bartorstown was the most secret of all,
way out West somewhere.' . . .
     'Then,' said Len softly, 'it was real!'
     'But that's not saying it is now. That was a long time ago.
It's maybe just the memory of it hung on, like your pa said,
with children and fanatics.' (29)

The Mennonites have survived well, being self-sufficient, but
other roaming bands have become religious fanatics:

     'And God said, "Even so, I am merciful. Let them be cleansed
of their sin."'
     The howling rose louder, and all across the open field
there was a tossing of arms and a writhing of heads.
     'Let them be cleansed!' cried the preaching man. His body
was strained up, quivering, and the sparks shot up past him.
'God said it, and they were cleansed, my brethren! With
their own sins they were chastised. They were burned with
the fires of their own making, yea, and the proud towers
vanished in the blazing of the wrath of God! . . . But . . .
Satan is still with us.' (19)

At first Len cannot understand this sense of crisis, since he is
overwhelmed by the impression of the world's 'ancientness'.
But he joins Esau tinkering with a stolen radio and some
textbooks – *Elementary Physics*, *A History of the United States* – and
the 'Fall' into both time and knowledge is accomplished. When
he is beaten by his father and his brother commiserates, 'It's
not the end of the world', Len rejoins, 'Oh yes it is. . . . And
that's all people know' (69). Determined to break out of the cul
de sac of fearful apocalypticism he escapes to a town across the
river. There he learns about how the rich and powerful use the
status quo for their own ends; a limitation on the size of towns
(to avoid becoming an enemy target) means big business for
Judge Taylor's transport company.
     At last Len follows the shadowy figure of Hochstetter to the
fabled city of Bartorstown, a subterranean complex where
orderly workers tend a huge nuclear reactor with the dedication
of the Manhattan Project physicists. Their aim is to discover a
forcefield to neutralise the fission–fusion process and so save the

world from further nuclear war. But Len's reaction to this fighting fire with fire is violent:

> The concrete wall loomed up like the wall of hell, and Len's heart slowed and the blood in him turned cold as snow water.
> Behind it is the reactor.
> Behind it is evil and night and terror and death.
> A voice screamed in Len's ears, the voice of the preaching man, standing on the edge of his wagon with the sparks flying past him on the night wind . . .
> 'You're lying,' Esau said. 'There ain't any more of that, not since the Destruction.' (197)

Len's conversion to the new religion is foiled only by the behaviour of one of the scientists who cracks up over the strain, but Len is finally drawn back to Bartorstown by Hochstetter: 'I guess you're right. I guess it makes better sense to try and chain the devil up than to try keeping the whole land tied down in the hopes he won't notice it again' (260).

While Brackett gives us in this novel some extreme symbolism (Len's girl-friend Joan in her red dress, for example, whose first word when he wonders 'what the devil she is doing' is 'Christ'), and extreme advocates of religion and science, she also refuses to make the scientists flawless saviours; the unstable scientist is so because he feels the computer is fallible. But in the quiet simplicity of the Mennonite religion and the quiet dedication of the Bartorstown technicians she finds equally matched antagonists. Len's capitulation is reluctant and wary, especially so when one considers the Orwellian possibilities in the huge word-processor called 'Clementine' ('In a canyon . . .') which is also one of the secret scientific projects. The novel convincingly establishes the parameters of the post-disaster, evolutionary debate. As Gary Wolfe says,

> Like much science fiction on post-holocaust themes, *The Long Tomorrow* is in some sense an encoded parable of the movement from the Dark Ages to the Enlightenment or the Renaissance, with its protagonist the harbinger of the new age . . . .
> Perhaps because it does not focus on the issue of nuclear war itself, but rather on community and character, *The Long*

Tomorrow stands up well a quarter-century after its publication. It remains one of science fiction's more affecting coming-of-age novels, and its subordination of scientific ideas to human themes helped to usher in an age of greater humanism and more sophisticated style among science fiction writers.[23]

The nuclear power plant has proven to be a useful scenario for post-disaster fictions, because it is a familiar yet limited threat which directly highlights the role of the scientist. Robert Heinlein's 'Blowups Happen' was an early consideration of the theme in 1940. A famous psychologist analyses 'recurring situational psychoneurosis' (14) among the workers at such a plant. As well as the risk of mental derangement there is the risk of technical malfunction although in this case a rocket, powered by the same fuel, takes the offending reactor into orbit for man's safety. (In nuclear disaster fiction, outer space operates in contradictory ways as a *deus ex machina*: radioactive waste is blithely dumped there, but rockets carrying future generations also travel there.)

Two other early stories explored the industrial relations at nuclear plants. In Simak's 'Lobby' (1944) a group of Montana businessmen and senators collude to blow up a plant and save their own industries. The story is a plea for business to accept progress and the wise guidance of the saviour–scientist, for 'Men of science will govern, running the world scientifically in the interest of the stockholders – the little people of the world' (158). In Piper's 'Day of the Moron' it is the workers who are at fault. The director of the Long Island reactor complains, 'It is only at the whim of whatever gods there be that the result isn't a wholesale catastrophe. And people like that are the most serious threat facing our civilisation today, atomic war not excepted' (13). Sure enough, while he is at a meeting of union officials who are protesting at psychological screening, the plant explodes because of shoddy workmanship.

In Hans Zeimann's *The Explosions* (1978) various interest groups are in conflict over the proposed 'Helios' plant. There is the antinuclear protester who (while sleeping with the scientist!) laments that when she saw the plant she 'knew what had robbed me and everyone of the hot summer days of childhood' (104); the terrorist group which sabotages the plant; and the professor:

I wish we had never discovered that diabolical thing. I wish God had built a barrier in our brains to block out certain kinds of knowledge. I wish he had made us stupid. And I wish he had turned every single one of us super-arrogant and super-curious men into salt at the right time. (132)

Such *mea culpa* chest-beating does not save the community from radiation fall-out after a bomb explodes; among the victims is the managing director who is frolicking in the nearby woods with his secretary, and who vomits at the orgasmic moment. As documented in the 'Helios Commission Report', the damage in human illness and loss of materials is extensive. The novel is perhaps most notable for its acknowledgement of the increasing possibility of nuclear terrorism for, as the epigraph records physicist Edward Teller, 'Sooner or later some fool will prove to be stronger than a foolproof system'.

The most impressive power plant story is Lester Del Rey's *Nerves*, written 'as a long novelette for *Astounding Science Fiction*, way back in March, 1942.' In his 1975 introduction to the novel the author says, 'If I were to write the novel today I would fill it with the very real dangers of misused or stolen plutonium, the unsolved problem of atomic waste disposal – all the problems that developed over the years.'[24] The power of the novel prompted a *New York Times* reviewer to urge political and industrial leaders, those 'well-intentioned gropers in the dark', to read it also. What engrosses the reader is the personal point of view such as that of the scientist Jorgenson, who manages to extend his life in the midst of the nuclear accident by hiding in a lead-lined box:

But at that moment, as during his whole life, the fates had tricked him. He had located the box, but the lid was at an angle different from his picture. He cursed and screamed to himself in helpless frustration as he realised that the maximum power of his mind had built an imperfect image.

His fingers were moving along the box like little animals with minds of their own, testing it with thumps that carried back messages to his brain. Now he pulled the lid up, grateful that it was on top and the box would need no turning. With the last bit of energy, he let himself inside, solving the problem of the best position to take automatically as he did so. Then he dropped the lid back, trying to force it to a snug fit. He felt the box move under the still active forces of the new matter outside, but he could no longer care. His mind blanked out.

He came to in hell, with the air hot and thick in his suit, and the sweat trickling out of him, though his body felt dried to the bones . . .

But the shock that washed through him didn't come from the realisation of where he was or what must happen to him. The twitching of his muscles and the certain death that must face him meant very little.

The overwhelming fact was that he'd been insane for years! He turned that over in his thoughts, grappling with it – and accepted it. He'd been going insane by the time he reached adolescence. He had been wholly so before he graduated from college. He had lived in an impossible world where only absolute perfection counted, and where he refused to accept perfection as possible, even to himself! (59)

This is a long way from the maniac's dream, and shows the scientist trapped by his own invention, locked literally into his own coffin and realising that his world view of total control and order was a dangerous fiction.

Del Rey also reveals the political mind, as Morgan and the plant director Palmer agree on encouraging nuclear power:

With two more years to go, the plants would be policed, the people would begin to feel safe again, and the whole movement [of protest] would die away like most crazes. It was the answer, of course – the quiet, indirect answer that had saved the country repeatedly from some folly, while the papers screamed at the faults of the system that made it possible. And Morgan was head of the committee that would have to submit the bill with recommendations to Congress. (33)

Emma Ferrel, one of the little people, has been suspicious of media coverage ever since the day she sat on the flood-threatened roof of her Missouri home and heard a radio announcing 'everything was under control, that the river had been stopped' (168); now she buys a newspaper (at an extortionate price) to read:

ATOM PLANT EXPLODES!
Building Demolished, Workers Held by Force, Hint Major Involved.

There was a picture of the plant from the air, looking like a very bad shot made in the early morning, and an arrow that pointed to what was supposed to be the exploded building. She read the story quickly, sick fear inside her. Then anger replaced it. It was all a big guess! They didn't know any more than she did. No wonder the men had picked up the papers. From now on she'd never read it again! (108)

The ignorance of people like Emma forces them to imagine on the basis of popular images and myths. Emma 'had listened to too much talk about the mysterious broken bits of atoms that could come flying out, invisible but deadly as they ripped and mangled the helpless tissues. Sometimes she pictured them as little X-ray "worms" with savage biting teeth, though she knew better' (104). Another man wonders if television movies like the one 'where chrome-plated converters covered with pretty neon tubes were mysteriously blowing up every second day and men were brought in with blue flames all over them, cured instantly . . . helped create the average man's fear of atomics or simply mirrored it' (40).

Del Rey's concern with ignorance and misinformation is relevant and unusual. He shows it extending to government itself, with horrific results. They plan to drop a bomb on the crippled plant although one congressman insists, 'They're still thinking in analogies – fight fire with fire, fight atoms with atoms' (153). In contrast to this misinformed distant viewpoint, Del Rey describes most of the crisis at the plant from the surgical ward on the site itself. While this necessitates some coincidence like the invention of young Jenkins, a surgical whiz-kid who also happens to be the stepson of a nuclear physicist and who solves the crisis, the medical focus insists on the human dimension in the most immediate terms of maimed bodies. On the one hand we see the knowledgeable surgeons, on the other the ignorant workmen who are victims of the radiation leak. Del Rey's final message is that both groups must come together, the wise to disseminate the facts, the masses to learn them in all their complexity:

> But it [the cover up] hadn't been the fault of politicians only. It had started with the plants themselves. They'd given up on trying to explain the facts to the people – tough, almost indigestible facts couched in abstruse mathematics, of course; they hadn't faced up to the fact that some way could always be found to make anything understandable, given time. Instead of hiring the best minds to find the way, they'd made the secrets even more esoteric. And when trouble came they'd been forced to try to conceal it and depend on trickery. Morgan's proposal might work, but not forever. In the long run the only way to fight the bill was to bring everything out in the open. (151)

That theme of public ignorance, so powerfully dramatised by Del Rey, is what is memorable from another otherwise trite portrayal of domestic suffering, *The Nuclear Catastrophe* (1977). After a cloud inversion following an accident at the White Waters plant puts the state of California at risk, a woman gives birth to a mutated baby (the doctor cannot find any legs to hold on to) and experiences the break-up of family and marriage. But from the welter of neo-Gothic clichés, one remembers the image of school children at kindergarten who, upon hearing the news, 'sensing the graveness of the occasion, waited patiently until their teacher returned the day to normal.'

Ignorance is bliss but knowledge is power: the theme common to the idea of the scientist and the factual extrapolation of a nuclear disaster is the disproportionate sharing out of knowledge. On the one hand are the people like Emma, the ignorant victims who, even if they can conceive of the larger dimensions of disaster – in tribal, national or global terms – can cope only by clinging to an immediate circle of friends or family and surviving. On the other hand there are the scientists, usually allied with the military and political centres of power: men in the know, men with the technology both to cause and to survive a nuclear disaster.

The pioneer nuclear physicist Frederick Soddy wrote of scientists in 1932,

If ever they are in a position to transmute the elements at will – it would put into the hands of men physical powers as much greater than those they now possess as these are greater than the forces at the command of the savage. But of this particular contingency there is, perhaps fortunately, as yet no sign whatever.[25]

Hardly a decade later Soddy would have had to eat his words. The nuclear physicist now carries the aura of the ancient priest, for his knowledge is arcane and his power formidable. The crisis of nuclear disaster exposes both his authority and the mass's worship to a harsh light, defining anomaly and paradox. This is nowhere better illustrated than in Fritz Leiber's 1951 story 'Appointment in Tomorrow':

The first angry ray of sun – which, startlingly enough, still rose in the east at twenty four hour intervals – pierced the lacy tops of Atlantic combers and touched thousands of sleeping Americans with unconscious fear, because of their unpleasant similarity to the rays from World War III's atomic bombs.

They turned to blood the witch circle of rusty steel skeletons around Inferno in Manhattan. Without comment, they pointed a cosmic finger at the tarnished brass plaque commemorating the martyrdom of the Three Physicians after the dropping of the Hell Bomb . . . (135)

In Leiber's America, a world of 'juke-box, burlesque and your local radiation hospital', the scientist is remembered and revered as the blameless cause of destruction. In their ignorance and desperation the people need a guru and a period of hatred is soon replaced by a new form of worship. The people are ruled by a group called the Thinkers who in turn worship a huge electronic brain deified by the President and identified by the General with the Second Coming. In fact the brain is a fraud, like Poe's Maelzel from which it takes its name. It purports to distil Martian wisdom for the people, guiding the Thinkers to rule wisely and to colonise the planets – in reality they are doing nothing and rule desperately, pragmatically. One scientist challenges their charade, insisting that they take up their rightful roles and start progress again, but he is banished to

Mars. The Thinkers are the true expression of the people's fear. They need a master, a Big Brother, someone who knows what is going on; but they fear knowledge and change. Their elaborate fiction ensures a steady-state existence, a kind of death-in-life which is at least preferable to the horrors of the Third World War.

The inventor–scientist stands, fundamentally, for change. Nuclear physics is the perfect epitome of this function, since it reveals matter to be composed of endlessly gyrating electronic impulses; the nuclear bomb simply imposes this state of change on the macrocosm, totally disrupting man's thin veneer of system and order. To see the scientist and nuclear disaster as essential harbingers of change is to look forward to Chapter 4 which examines fictional notions of evolution through the nuclear holocaust, but it may also help to clarify the continuing, ambivalent attitude held by the masses and by writers towards the scientist in an age which, above all, seems to worship change in the forms of 'progress'. Before that we must examine attempts to describe the holocaust and its immediate aftermath, and people's reactions to the one great, violent change which seems to imply an end to change.

3 The Day and the Day After

Many have perished; more will.[1]

In 1913, H. G. Wells read about Professor Soddy and the 'Interpretation of Radium' and wrote to his friend Simmons, 'I've suddenly broken out into one of the good old scientific romances again, and I want to know quite the latest about the atomic theory and sources of energy. . . . My idea is taken from Soddy. Men are supposed to find out how to set up atomic degeneration in the heavy elements just as they found out long ago how to set up burning in coal. Hence limitless energy.'[2] *The World Set Free*, dedicated to Soddy and published just before the Great War, accurately predicted the Curies' discovery of radioactivity, even to the year 1933. The novel was also to have a direct influence on the process of scientific discovery, for Leo Szilard read the work in German in 1932 and two years later applied for a patent to cover his method of setting up a chain reaction: 'Knowing what this would mean – and I knew it because I had studied H. G. Wells – I did not want this patent to become public.'[3]

But such happy prediction is irrelevant to the imaginative power of the fiction. Wells begins in the War Control Centre of France and England in Paris; an airstrike destroys the room, the image of an old general crushed against his maps signalling the end of a style of warfare. A 'rather brutish young aviator with a bullet head' flies his plane to Berlin and drops the first atomic bomb over the side, biting a fuse to activate it (98). Soon, armed with their new weapons, the world powers rush to engage in what Wells scornfully calls 'this mere cult of warfare':

They went to war in a delirium of panic, in order to use their bombs first. China and Japan had assailed Russia and destroyed Moscow, the United States had attacked Japan, India was in anarchistic revolt with Delhi a pit of fire

43

'The Great Prostitute', A. Dürer, Apocalypse series, Frederick van der Meer, *Apocalypse: Visions from the Book of Revelation in Western Art* (London: Thames & Hudson) p. 303.

spouting death and flame. . . . By the spring of 1959 from nearly two hundred centres, and every week added to their number, roared the unquenchable crimson conflagrations of the atomic bombs, the flimsy fabric of the world's credit had vanished, industry was completely disorganised and every city, every thickly populated area was starving or trembling on the verge of starvation. Most of the capital cities of the world were burning: millions of people had already perished, and over great areas government was at an end. Humanity had been compared by one contemporary writer to a sleeper who handles matches in his sleep and wakes to find himself in flames. (137)

A world conference in Italy is almost sabotaged by terrorists with nuclear weapons but finally a world government is established and a new world order arises:

The catastrophe of the atomic bombs which shook men out of cities and businesses and economic relations shook them also out of their old established habits of thought, and out of the lightly held beliefs and prejudices that came down to them from the past. To borrow a word from the old-fashioned chemists, men were made nascent; they were released from old ties; for good or evil they were ready for new associations. . . . A new literature, a new interpretation of history was springing into existence, a new teaching was already in the schools, a new faith in the young . . . (234–5)

By the end of the novel, the Russian Marcus Karenin has absorbed the nuclear holocaust into the upward spiral of human history and looks forward to a culmination of heaven on earth in a vague wash of sexual freedom, equality and technological advancement. 'Civilisation was very near disaster when the atomic bombs came banging into it,' he argues (263), and the holocaust was just the right impetus to a new evolutionary path.

Such optimism is, of course, the weakest part of Wells's vision. More powerful is his description of the development of the bomb and the individual witnessing of destruction. From the opening paragraph, Wells insists on the primacy of the word:

And that first glimmering of speculation, that first story of achievement, that story-teller bright-eyed and flushed under his matted hair gesticulating to his gaping incredulous listener, gripping his wrist to keep him attentive, was the most marvellous beginning this world has ever seen. It doomed the mammoths, and it began the setting of that snare that shall catch the sun. (5)

This remarkable opening directly links literacy and nuclear power; 'in the opening pages of his first real tract of social programming,' says critic Frank McConnell, 'Wells makes plainer than ever before or since the ideal relationship between the storyteller's art and the social scientist's public duty. They are not, finally, in opposition to one another, but are rather successive moments in a single, and culturally crucial, process, the process of man's self-definition and self-organisation against chaos.'[4] But McConnell overstresses the mythmaking programme in the novel; what is most memorable is the personal reaction to public event and power, as recorded through words in the diaries of Barnet and Holsten which constitute much of the novel. Barnet's diary ends 'Everything is broken down' (211), while the scientist Holsten records, 'It has begun. . . . It is not for me to reach out to consequences I cannot foresee. I am a part, not a whole; I am a little instrument in the armoury of Change' (39). Wells's description of nuclear destruction, too, amazing though it is as a piece of scientific extrapolation, gains force from his insistence that 'no complete contemporary account of the explosion of the atomic bombs survives', and that he has had to piece together this report on the destruction of Paris with its effective conditional view-point:

Coming in still closer, the investigator would have reached the police cordon, which was trying to check the desperate enterprise of those who would return to their homes or rescue their more valuable possessions within the 'zone of imminent danger.'
    That zone was rather arbitrarily defined. If our spectator could have got permission to enter it, he would have entered also a zone of uproar, a zone of perpetual thunderings, lit by a strange purplish-red light, and quivering and swaying with the incessant explosion of the radio-active substance. Whole

blocks of buildings were alight and burning fiercely, the trembling ragged flames looking pale and ghastly and attenuated in comparison with the full-bodied crimson glare beyond. The shells of other edifices already burnt rose pierced by rows of window sockets against the red-lit mist.

Every step further would have been as dangerous as a descent within the crater of an active volcano. These spinning, boiling bomb centres would shift or break unexpectedly into new regions, great fragments of earth or drain or masonry suddenly caught by a jet of disruptive force might come flying by the explorer's head, or the ground yawn a fiery grave beneath his feet. Few who adventured into these areas of destruction and survived attempted any repetition of their experiences. There are stories of puffs of luminous, radio-active vapour drifting sometimes scores of miles from the bomb centre and killing and scorching all they overtook. And the first conflagrations from the Paris area spread westward half way to the sea.

Moreover the air in this infernal inner circle of red-lit ruins had a peculiar dryness and a blistering quality, so that it set up a soreness of the skin and lungs that was very difficult to heal . . . (201–3)

Writers have been able to extrapolate and caricature the conditions leading up to a nuclear conflict, but when it comes to writing after 1945 about the actual disaster, the imagination is fettered by two things: the inconceivable magnitude of the horror, and the two historical experiences of Hiroshima and Nagasaki. The memory of the Japanese holocaust acts both as a brake and a stimulus to the apocalyptic imagination; the attempt to write about *that* experience commands us to be faithful to the dead and the living survivors, and also exposes the limits of our language and our imaginations.

There have been many official reports on the effects of the Japanese blasts, but clinical details do not crack the shell of reality. To *say* 'The A-bomb experience was brutalising'[5] is not to show it. Only the preface to the official record of damage touches the human dimension in any significant way, when the committee appeals, 'If in this book there is a power that can touch deeply the hearts and minds of readers, it is surely a power that stems from the grievous recollection that the lives of countless people were tragically ended by the blazing inferno and the deeply penetrating, fatally ruinous radiation of the first – and, again we pray, may they be the last – atomic bombs ever used in human warfare.'[6] The researcher R. J. Lifton discovered in the 'hibakusha' or 'psychic numbing' of survivors a metaphor for what even we might feel if we try to live through and react fully to the Hiroshima experience. The barrier between fact and fiction seems to break down, the survivor enters a condition of 'psychic closing-off' because of this enforced 'coming together of inner images of death and outer experiences of virtual annihilation', and he lives in a limbo-land of guilt and horror.[7] For the human mind cannot bear very much of this reality; who can blame the Japanese children who have wiped the past from their minds? And yet the moral imperative remains since, as one survey laments, 'Even among children in Hiroshima and Nagasaki, there are now more and more children who did not know who dropped the bomb or when, who were not worried about political trends that left the peace constitution increasingly void of substance, who even – some of them – thought war is "real cool".'[8] To avoid the reality of the bombings, then, is to attempt to escape from the nightmare of history into a dangerous neverland of ignorance; yet to attempt to understand it is to risk debasing or trivialising it, or retreating into the paralysed shock of 'hibakusha'.

Edita Morris's novelistic treatment *The Flowers of Hiroshima* (1960) addresses us in just these terms: 'I want to tell you, because it is the death that lies ahead of many people, perhaps the end that lies ahead of all of us' (159). The point of view is simple reportage – 'I tell him that this was the spot where our mother became a living torch' – and the reader must do the imagining for himself.

More sophisticated than this approach which, for all its righteousness, risks sentimentality, was John Hersey's *Hiroshima* (1946), with a presentation (as the publisher notes) 'at times almost cold in its economy of words'(9). But for all its apparent naiveté, the book has a sophisticated form. The four main characters represent science (Dr Fujii), domesticity (Mrs Makamura), religion (Kleinsorge) and civil defence (Rev. Tanimoto). We move between these themes within the form of a quartet: 'A Noiseless Flash' announces the theme; 'The Fire' is the scherzo, moving to twelve days after the explosion and the slow movement of 'Details are Being Investigated'; and the book ends with 'Panic Grass and Feverfew', a year later, which recollects the whole experience and restates the main themes. Such design is no affront to the dead or survivors, but a recognition that communication demands artifice.

Occasionally Hersey gives in to interpretation and symbol – Miss Sasaki 'in the first moment of the atomic age crushed by books', the survivors gathered in the park 'because of an irresistible, atavistic urge to hide under leaves' (55), the survivors patriotic in 'a curious kind of elated community spirit' (116) – but on the whole he is a reticent observer and lets possible ironies surface for themselves, as when the lush green growth comes to cover the devastation, or the hospital treating radiation victims is washed away in a flood. What Hersey shows is the characters themselves attempting to erect meaningful interpretative systems: Father Kleinsorge believes that Providence has spared his suitcase; Mr Tanimoto says to a boat bearing five corpses, 'Please forgive me for taking this boat . . .' (57); Miss Sasaki points to her shrunken leg and asks a Catholic, 'If your God is so good and kind, how can he let people suffer like this?' (111) Hersey's reticence extends to religion also, and simple juxtaposition speaks more powerfully than glib eschatological imagery in Mr Tanaka's final moments:

> Standing at the shelter stairway to get light, Mr Tanimoto read loudly from a Japanese-language pocket Bible: 'For a thousand years in Thy sight are but as yesterday when it is past, and as a watch in the night. Thou carriest the children of men away as with a flood; they are as a sleep; in the morning they are like grass which groweth up; in the evening it is cut down, and withereth. For we are consumed by Thine anger and by Thy wrath are we troubled. Thou has set our iniquities before Thee, our secret sins in the light of Thy countenance. For all our days are passed away in Thy wrath: we spend our years as a tale that is told . . .'
> Mr Tanaka died as Mr Tanimoto read the psalm. (85)

Powerful as the investigative journalism of Morris and Hersey is, it inevitably focuses on *survivors* and in that basic way fails to convey the horror of obliteration. But the whole subject is fraught with the dangers of indecorum. R. L. Duncan's *The Day*

The Sun Fell has three westerners attempting to warn the Japanese and avert the catastrophe, therefore approaching the horror with foresight rather than hindsight. But it is difficult to avoid the feeling that the holocaust has become an excuse for sentimentalism and sensation, especially when one finds in a grotesque printing error that the doomed hero's last letter is dated 'Nagasaki, August 9, 1954'! (354) Japanese attempts to render the disaster into art have been more successful. In painting, the series of Hiroshima Panels presents human figures apparently in conventional attitudes of repose or embrace; only closer examination reveals that they are discoloured, covered with sores and contorted with pain – the embraces are last partings, the sleep the sleep of death. The crowded figures have no divine focus but merely peter out in a horizontal progression of shadowy limbs. An accompanying poem in the book of these panels is effective only because we sense an alien voice in a crude translation, the imagery of apocalypse and irony quite unintended:

> A mushroom cloud blown up from the hell
> several thousand feet high up to heaven
> grouped numerous layers of the clouds
> made heavy showers of black rain
> in torrents through the clear sky
>
> Then darkened was the sky
> But lo! a rainbow soon appeared
> brightly shining in the seven colours . . .[9]

Writers since Hersey and the eye witness accounts of survivors of Hiroshima and Nagasaki have, like them, been faced with the three aspects of the day before, the day, and the day after. Wylie, Merle and others achieve great impact by dwelling at length on the peaceful scene, often rural or small-town, before the blast. As for the blast itself, only a few supreme feats of imaginative writings such as the passages in the novels by Wylie, Bradbury and Dick, have been able to suggest simultaneously the vastness of the destruction and the personal sense of stunned horror of the observer. The day after is more easily and popularly dealt with, either as the rainbow of a courageous rebirth, most crudely found in the so-called 'survivalist' literature, or as the cowering uncertainty and slow sickness of those in shelters of one kind or another, or perhaps stumbling about the ruins.

Philip Wylie's *Tomorrow!* (1954) was written out of a practical concern with civil defence. The author was a consultant to the Federal Defence Administration from 1949–54, during which time he became convinced that the authorities were not allowing for the natural human reaction of panic in the event of nuclear attack: 'Most of our statesmen, military leaders and scientific experts have not studied the subconscious mind. . . . There, I believe, is the Achilles heel of an America facing atomic warfare' (dustjacket). This is elaborated in the book by the newspaper editor of the mid-western town of Green Prairie which is the focus:

> We the people of the United States of America have refused for more than a decade to face our real fear. We know our world could end. . . . The medieval lust of men cowering before the holocaust has been exploited by McCarthy. . . . We flubbed the greatest chance for liberty in human history [after World War II] and hardly even noted our blunder, our betrayal. (125–35)

As well as this list of political crimes, Wylie charges the government with underfunding the civil defence system generally.

Surprisingly, his first novel is devoted to realism rather than rant, and for the first two-thirds he builds up a complex picture of this midwestern community. The long, quiet buildup makes the nuclear warning on Christmas Day come as a shock to the reader as to the citizen; a boy whispers to himself, 'It's – *it*' (217). The point of view of Henry Conner, looking down from his God-like position at an office window at the 'ants in an anthill calamity' is brutally dissolved:

> In a part of a second, he was a gas, incandescent, hotter than the interior of any furnace. In that same part of a second the proud skyline of River City and Green Prairie smoked briefly, steamed a little, and no shadows were thrown anywhere in the glare. The façades – stone, concrete, brick-glazed, crinkled, and began to slip as they melted. But the heat

penetrated, too. The steel frames commenced to sag and buckle; metal, turned molten, ceased to sustain the floors upon many floors. Peaks of skyscrapers, domes, steeples, square roofs, tilted sideways and would have toppled or crashed down, but gravity was not fast enough, not strong enough; it was only for that part of a second.

The great region, built so slowly, at such cost, by men, for a second liquified and stood suspended above the ground: it could fall only sixteen feet in that time. Then, in the ensuing portion of a second, the liquid state was terminated. The white in the sky bellied down, growing big and globular, a thousand feet across and more. The liquids gasified: stone and cement, steel and plaster, brick and bronze and aluminium. In the street – if anyone could have seen at all, as no man could in the blind solar whiteness – there were no howling people at all. None. On the sidewalks, for a part of a second, on sidewalks boiling like forgotten tea, were dark stains that had been people, tens of thousands of people. The light went over the whole great area, like a thing switched on, and people miles away, hundreds of people looking at it, lost their sight. The air, of a sudden, for a long way become hotter than boiling water, hotter than melted lead, hotter than steel coming white from electric furnaces. Clothing caught fire, the beggars' rags, the dowager's sables, the baby's diapers, the minister's robe. Paper in the gutter burst into flame. . . . In that second part of a second.

The plutonium fist followed. . . .

The heart of the cities was gone. A third of their people were dead or dying or grievously hurt. A million little fires were flickering, anucleating, to form a great holocaust. And this had required the time in which a pensive man might draw a breath, hold it reflectively and exhale. (268–71)

While this is highly imaginative *and* scientific writing, it does have the unintended effect of dissipating the shock to some extent, working against the polemical point that the people, and we ourselves, are unprepared for this disaster. Where Wylie makes his point most dramatically is in the ensuing panic when the characters we had grown close to in their domestic orderliness are seen storming the airport, looting and pillaging:

Here it was. Here was all that the experts said could never happen. Here was gigantic panic, uncontrolled and hideous.

To tens of thousands of River City people, this was the pay-off. It wrecked such small hopes as they'd cherished, destroyed their trivial but hard-won possessions. In so doing, it broke their link with the rest of the nation, with humanity itself. In reaction, they were turning on humanity, on each other, with a final, mindless venting of their stored-up resentments, their hates, their disappointments. (342)

The firestorm causes more outrageous violence still, since it is now seen in a human context rather than in the twinkling of an eye of the initial blast: 'All the children fell, bleeding. But Irma, the baby, being kissed by her anxious mother, received a point of glass in her back and lungs; she was torn almost apart' (281).

After an awkward change of scene to the Presidential decision to attack Russia, we return to the communal perspective, rendered effective by the details of psychological reaction. Survivors 'walk into the silences' by abandoning their homes, and Coley muses on the amazing power of habit:

Then the Bomb would be no catastrophe at all, but pure benefit. 'End of an era,' they would say. 'Good thing too,' they'd add. 'Can't imagine how they stood those old cities,' they'd assert. 'Barbaric.' 'Positively medieval.' (369)

Wylie's commitment to realism beyond his argument is illustrated by this acknowledgement of human stubbornness and resilience, as Coley adds, 'So it would be here. So it should be.' Early in the novel Wylie was ready to attribute part of the cause of disaster to any social evil, including television sitcoms with their 'utterly savage sound, mirthless and cruel, usually inspired by the sadisms which constitute most popular humour' (28); by the end of the novel the dramatised voices of Green Prairie have taken over, to much more forceful effect.

Wylie's message was one of doom. But, as Coley perceives, nuclear disaster may be cause for rejoicing, especially in the larger view of human evolution to be examined in the following chapter. Even within the immediate confines of the disaster and its aftermath, the human imagination finds fortitude and inspiration. The popular current movement of 'Survivalism' is part of this reaction against intolerable despair, and many fictions portray man as resourceful, obstinate and ennobled by facing this ultimate challenge.

Dean Owen's *The End of the World* (1962) now reads like a fairytale, but at the time was obviously intended as a survivalist document. The Baldwin family is setting off from Los Angeles on a fishing expedition when the bombs start falling. Father Harry's immediate decision is to keep on driving into the wilds, holding up unhelpful shopkeepers on the way to gain provisions. His wife objects to his 'robbing and mauling people, like some kind of cheap hoodlum' (33), but within this American microcosm of the highway (powerfully presented with crazed drivers and clogged main arteries), his actions seem sensible. In one deftly allegorical scene, Harry parts a traffic jam with a wall of fire from a petrol can so that the family can pursue its cross-country course. Like the Old Testament leader that he is, Harry insists on the routines of civilised behaviour once the family have established camp in a cave in the woods: the men will shave, the women will stay pretty, and his precocious son will not take advantage of the exceptional circumstances to point guns at people.

The Baldwins are quite safe from the nearby carnage in their weekend retreat, with no thought of buying bottled water or staying indoors. Their main threat is a trio of looters and rapists who murder some neighbours and eventually kidnap and rape the Baldwin girl. The Baldwin men rescue her and cut down the evildoers, but a sense of regeneration is supplied by the courtship of the son and another rape victim. The novel ends with the rescue trucks of the army. The fact that there is no irony in the last scene suggests the limitations of the novel, which were even more apparent in the film version *Panic in Year Zero* (with Ray Milland). As one critic observed, 'the easy philosophy of becoming barbaric to survive' does not acknowledge the ironical – if not sarcastic – fact that 'the new beginning is the old belief in technology and the ethos of the gun'.[10]

What Owen's novel does capture is the turning point from civility to violence, from community to individual survival. Harry regrets having encountered and let go free the men who later raped his daughter: 'Oh, if he only had it to do over again.

To have stood, shotgun in hand, as they climbed out of the rusted Chevy after trying to run him down. To have cut loose with the shotgun and ended it right there, before it had ever started' (117). But more recent survivalist fictions select their heroes even more carefully as resourceful, technically competent men, ready to replace the decaying official law and order with their own more effective, wiser rule, immediately the bombs start falling.

The hero of *Pulling Through* (1983) is just such a hero – Harve Rackham drives a Lotus Cellular and has a pet cheetah. He is a bounty hunter straight out of a private-eye television series. He rails at his sister for not disciplining her son – 'We've let our kids replace self-discipline with alternatives. No goddamn wonder divorce rates are still climbing, sis' (74) – and his redneck sentiments are galvanised by the holocaust into jingoistic optimism. 'Compared to life expectancy when this republic was young,' he says, 'those odds look bearable' (141), and he and eighty million other Americans set about forging the 'future of this country'.

Nevertheless the author Dean Ing does supply us with some credible psychological reactions to the disaster. The first tentative news flashes ('There has been no official response from Washington to the Syrian claim that the supercarrier *Nimitz* lies capsized in the Mediterranean after a nuclear near-miss by a Syrian cruise missile' ([7]) provoke a desperately crude reaction – 'Oh shit.' Harve's first reaction to the blast damage is that of a private property owner:

A freak shock raced through Concord, making lethal Frisbees of every glass pane and marble false-front in town. My western windows blew in and, with a pistol's report, one of my sturdy old roof beams ended nearly a century of usefulness. (21)

His reactions to the devastated world above his shelter are vividly impressionistic, as he notices the absence of birdsong and highway noises, and feels his flesh sweating and raising goosebumps simultaneously. Harve is also located in history, as shown by his nostalgia for the heady days of youthful revolt ('the evenings when we'd stay by the fire upstairs and toy with the ghastly mathematics of obliteration, comfy and cheerful with our beer and popcorn' [58]) or the way it is the skills of his wife, ironically gained during the counter-culture years, which will help him through the waste land. Even his rough and ready philosophising is sometimes appealing as when he meditates over the body of a woman dead from radiation:

I said: 'Lord, You've heard it all before. You must be hearing it from a hundred million throats today. For which we give no thanks.'

I saw Shar's startled frown, her silently mouthed 'Oh', or maybe it was 'no'. But I saw Devon nod, eyes closed, knuckles white on the fists at his sides. I continued.

'You gave this good woman the terrible gift of free choice, Lord, and she exercised it to keep her son alive, knowing it might kill her.

'And it did. Greater love than this hath no man and no woman, and for this alone we would ask You to cherish her. It's said that you can't take it with you, but Mrs Baird beat the odds. She takes with her our greatest respect, and our hopes for her everlasting grace.

'If I misquote Khayyam, I crave Your understanding:
Oh Thou who woman of earth didst make,
And in her paradise devised the snake,
For all the freely-chosen horror with which
the face of mankind is blackened,
Our forgiveness give. *And take.*
Into-Your-hands-O-Lord-we-commend-her-spirit-Amen.'   I ended quickly. I half-expected a lightning bolt before I finished. I didn't care. (111–12)

But such rhetoric does not fit with the technologist, and the second half of the book, a survival manual presenting in even greater detail the ingenious inventions which helped Harve and his tribe to survive, betrays the heavily rightwing, 'macho' tone of the whole. In an appalling decline from fictional appropriateness, Ing writes, 'Fallout is like lust; it isn't forever, but it colours your decisions.' (152) Then comparing the likely survival rates in Russia (98%) and the US (40%) Ing ends, 'Now do you see why the Soviets marched into Afghanistan with such confidence?' (149)

The survivalist handbooks preach the same kind of

individualistic know-how which characterises the early fictional nuclear scientist. *The Nuclear Survival Handbook* has tips on how to utilise a bicycle and arrange insurance and in desperate understatement reminds us, 'It may be difficult to organise evacuation which involves abandoning the dead unburied' (256). *Life After Doomsday* mocks the fictions studied in this chapter and insists on a realistic frontier spirit: 'Each member of your group should be equipped with a military assault rifle, a reliable combat pistol and a 12-gauge riotgun. You are shooting to *live*.' (112) And the *Survival Option*, setting facts 'against the more common apocalyptic superstitions', is intended for people who want 'to take control of their own destinies' – even though only a tenth of the book is devoted to 'the aftermath and regeneration', and four pages to 'community planning and reorganisation'.

The 'community' seems more involved in David Graham's *Down to a Sunless Sea*, where an enlarged Jumbo jet from New York to London finds itself airborne when the holocaust descends, but this promising *mise en scène* becomes the vehicle once more for the Old Testament technician Captain Scott to lead his people to the Promised Land. At first Graham makes the most of the apocalyptic setting. The 'Airbrit' crew only just make it to the airfield through the urban chaos of New York caused by fuel shortages, and once in the air the global point of view, neatly mirroring the conventional subterranean war-room, allows the captain to call moon craters perhaps 'the fading scars of some vast prehistoric nuclear conflict' (145) and observe the sombre, albeit prerecorded, final instruction of the company director: 'We trust and pray that sanity and tolerance will prevail. We commend all crews and passengers in transit to the mercy and love of Almighty God, this night of Armageddon. Message ends' (115). But once involved in the practicalities of survival, Graham is determined to show science at its best. After choosing to land at the NATO base of Lajes in the Azores where a neutron bomb has wiped out personnel but (conveniently) left the airfield intact, the captain listens to radio reports from around the world cataloguing survivors – usually noble scientists. These include Captain Redfern in the Falklands, who risked radiation exposure to establish that MacMurdo base in Antarctica is able to receive refugees:

WE THINK HE KNEW WHAT IT MEANT WHEN HE
WENT UPSTAIRS. HE WAS A VERY BRAVE MAN . . .
WE ARE CLOSING DOWN HERE NOW AND AFTER A
PRAYER WE ARE GOING UPSTAIRS FOR A LAST
LOOK AT THE SKY. WE WISH YOU A SAFE JOURNEY
AND BELIEVE THAT A BETTER WORLD WILL RISE
FROM THE ASHES. GOD BLESS YOU ALL. MESSAGE
ENDS. (220)

This ecumenical theme is completed by the arrival of a plane-
load of Russian women; a new nation will be established in the
snows, called 'Kubla Khan', because the holocaust has altered
Earth's axis and Antarctica may soon become a secret river of
plenty. Scott intones, 'Out of cold shall come warmth, and out
of the North shall come salvation.' (314) Thus in sentiment and
piety the novel fulfils the technological promise of the new
dawn as seen by the crew when the plane climbed through the
deadly radiation cloud:

> And above us, almost overhead, the blessed wonderful golden
> sun, huge, clean, blazing down upon the remnants of
> mankind. I felt Ben and Jerry at my side, and looked at their
> stained tired faces. They were weeping unashamedly, and we
> locked together in a tripod of thanksgiving, arms around
> shoulders, heads bent, listening to the thunder of cheers and
> rejoicing from those behind, delivered at the eleventh hour
> from the jaws of hell itself. (257)

Fortunately, as if suddenly conscious of the banality of his
ending, Graham appends an 'epilogue/prologue' which reveals
that the radiation cloud is, in fact, moving remorselessly
southward and will inevitably destroy the whole planet.

   This ending typifies the tension in all survival stories between
myths of resurrection and the more 'realistic' appraisals of
lingering but eventual doom. In the post-holocaust world there
is no room for heroes, even if they are brilliant scientists or
Buck Rogers; the disaster denies the possibility of epic as it does
that of tragedy. Some of the most compelling extrapolations of
nuclear disaster or its immediate aftermath, therefore, remain
at the domestic level and often focus on a more manageable,

'domestic' nuclear crisis – the limited war, or the failure of a nuclear power plant.

Judith Merril's *Shadow on the Hearth* (1950) is a novel which takes an unremittingly domestic view of nuclear disaster and – even rarer – does it from a female point of view. The novel begins with Gladys organising babysitters and doing the washing; the destruction of Manhattan passes almost unnoticed by her, until little things go wrong and she finally hears the news on the radio. When her daughters return from school she carries on the eery pretence of normalcy, asking Virginia to clean her room (to keep her indoors) but knowing that her older daughter senses the end of an age which 'wound to a close like an old worn out film' (18). The image is appropriate, because the novel proceeds like a situation comedy, with the living room as the set and many entrances, exits, and visits from neighbours and officials. Gladys is anxious for her husband, maintaining sanity by escaping into memories of him 'down on his back on the floor, mock wrestling with Ginny' (60); speeches by the Governor about enemies 'learning to fear the eagle in its nest' do not comfort her. (This section is weakened by cuts to show the husband well in another part of the city.) Gladys wonders if she might learn something about radiation from her son's science fiction magazines. She asks the warden about boiling the water, copes with a sick neighbour, the accusation that her maid is a spy, the advances of her neighbour's husband, and with looters. Through this escalating violence she learns slowly to think for herself and act independently, and she and her family rapidly but believably become coolly realistic: Ginny asks of the sick woman, 'Will she be dead – like the birdies?' But despite the many realistic touches, like the way Gladys always misses the 'M's' in the broadcast lists of the dead, there are too many solicitous visitors to this household – a squadman, a doctor, a teacher who just happens to be a handsome nuclear physicist as well – and the reader is soon convinced that this all-American family will certainly be re-united at the end.

A bleaker domestic novel is Daniel Keyes's *The Contaminated Man* (1977). Barney is a sculptor, and he and his wife Karen are desperate for a baby. A friend at the motor works unwittingly contaminates Barney, and despite the efficient efforts of the decontamination squad the couple contracts mild radiation sickness. Their psychological reactions are examined in shocking detail. Karen, as a failed mother, is already alienated from her own body, and wakes up scratching at her sores and pulling out her hair. She sneers into the mirror, 'Sculpt me now, darling. Bleeding Venus rising, completely bald, from the radioactive sea' (63). At first Barney is more level-headed, comparing himself not with Hiroshima survivors but with the girls in the watch factory who became sick after putting camelhair brushes used for applying radium, to their lips (an historical event which featured in fiction as early as 1936 in Rudolph Brunngraber's *Radium*). Obsessed with the impossibility of continuing his line, Barney visits his grandfather's grave and wonders,

> Why not? Didn't people make gods of things that could affect birth, modify life, cause death? Why not worship Roentgen, the new god of radiation? Invisible and jealous god who eschewed noise and tumult and who, instead of hurling lightning from the heavens, silently spread his dust. (71)

Karen becomes pregnant, but of course the boon turns into the nightmare prospect of mutation. Barney is slowly ostracised by the town, dismissed from work (because 'the presence of a victim makes people feel guilty' [136]), he makes love to Karen's seductive sister and turns from moulding the Ancient Mariner to images of death and mutation – 'Man was a walking radioactive isotope with a variable half life, decaying a little each second of the day' (192). Crazed by this 'half life' Barney forces the hospital to deliver his child, and the novel ends most movingly:

> Seeing the unliving creature lying there in the basin, he felt something come up from deep inside himself, a wave, a spasm, a contraction that would not be held back, dry at first, but then it broke, and the tears streamed down his cheeks as he cried for his only son. (208)

Fictions of the day after nuclear disaster, then, owe much to the experience of Hiroshima and Nagasaki. Survivalist tracts rarely admit to the 'psychic numbing' analysed by Lifton; the disaster is most often the occasion for an inquiry into the

sociology of groups *in extremis*, the resilience of the human spirit
or the individual passage through a dark night of the soul to a
re-born hope. But some fictions, as we have seen, remain
uncompromising. Perhaps the most striking is Raymond Briggs's
When the Wind Blows, not a text at all but a cartoon strip which
cruelly frames the horror within the conventions of immunity to
violence and assured re-appearance. James and Hilda are two
hardworking middle-aged English folk reduced to disgusting
decay by powers beyond them which they nevertheless try to
understand and regard to the end as wiser masters. James reads
the newspapers in the local library because 'The decisions
made by the Powers That Be will get us in the end.' Over
sausages he and his wife talk pathetically in the argot of the
Second World War ('It looks as if the balloon could go up')
and the announcement of a nuclear alert sends James to his
Guide to Survival. His preparations are shockingly interrupted by
a full-page silhouette of a nuclear warhead 'on a distant plain'.
Briggs represents the blast itself by slicing off the cartoon strip
and leaving the reader/viewer with a blank page which bleeds
to a livid pink and a warping band of red, out of which the strip
slowly re-emerges. This violence wrought on one of the cosiest
and enduring of popular art forms (where no one ever *really* gets
hurt) is extremely powerful, and Briggs underlines his point
that the horror is beyond words when he has James comment,
'Blimey.' In the days that follow the couple waits underneath
their door shelter for the Powers That Be to deliver food. They
even sit out in the sun in deck-chairs, exposing themselves to
fatal radiation. As their bodies decay James insists, 'We'll just
have to acclimatise ourselves to the Post-Nuclear Area. It could
be OK – wiping the slate clean . . . starting afresh – a New
World! perjured of all the Old Vices – like London after the
Fire of London! The New Elizabethan Age will dawn . . .'
Through pastel colours reminiscent of George Grosz, we see the
two creep into their paper bags and go to their final rest
quoting snatches of religious verse and Tennyson's 'Charge of
the Light Brigade'. For Briggs, no language is appropriate to
the holocaust, least of all the political clichés so faithfully
learned by James, the perfect citizen.

Yorick Blumenfeld's *Jenny: My Diary* attempts a similar
documentary realism by posing as a diary, handwritten and
impressively bound by Penguin books (though the blurb on the

back cover betrays the entrepreneurial impulse). The heroine is a rather unintelligent woman working for a theatrical production company, having an affair, and making it to a communal shelter with her two children before the bomb drops. She can describe the scene above ground only as 'incredible . . . unbelievable' and her theological bent inspires her to wonder if God is a sadist. But the author cannot let reticence speak, and burdens his heroine with references to Anne Frank, Beckett, Thomas Aquinas and Limbo. What is convincing is her changing moral values, from prudery ('as if this shelter were some kind of suburban swapclub') through indulgence to disinterest. Her revulsion from 'life forces', especially as a woman, is compelling; but her story must be one of uplifting heroism and, sure enough, she finds a Jewish lover to discuss the Holocaust with and surfaces to a new world where she and her Adam will re-establish the order of Jane Austen's world. A spider weaves a lopsided web, but poison takes care of the rats and glasshouse seeds grow healthily. What authenticity had previously been established is mostly lost in this survivalist flourish. Nevertheless, Blumenfeld can be seen to be following in a British tradition of disaster writing which tends to emphasise the moral and theological implications of the bomb rather than, as in many of the early American stories, the technological challenges of survival. The sense of stunned shock, a sudden calling into question of assumed eternal verities and eternal landscapes, is the more traumatic in a society whose sense of a continuum of history is apparent in every aspect of daily life. St Paul's dome survived the Blitz, but Gustave Doré shocked nineteenth-century London with his illustration for Macaulay's New Zealander pondering a shattered cathedral and derelict Thames, and in *The Maniac's Dream* the narrator is horrified by a similar vision. Similarly, Peter van Greenaway's *The Crucified City* (1962) takes a survivor on a tour of familiar landmarks and laments, 'The guard would never change again, having changed too much' (32). The hero Creston, who survived the war of 1970 by happening to be in a subway, finds that the survivors are embarking on pilgrimages to certain places in an attempt to re-establish a meaningful landscape. The religiously inclined are led by a Doomsayer into the heart of fiery London, while the humanists march to Aldermaston with the instinctive knowledge that if man has a future it must start there (Riddley

Walker makes a similar pilgrimage). Van Greenaway has his representative survivors die one by one during a tedious and familiar theological debate, with a vague symbolic gesture at the end when the hero dies on Easter Monday and a woman asserts, 'We're not survivors from the atomic age any more, but the new beginnings of something else' (215).

The survival shelter, like the war-room, has provided a natural microcosmic setting for the exploration of the post-disaster mentality. It can be a very powerful setting, because like the reader the characters have both lived through and not lived through the horror; they have survived but have done nothing to survive; they are filled with a knowledge of appalling catastrophe which is only second-hand knowledge. As early as 1948 J. J. Farjeon in *Death of a World* explored the philosophical possibilities. Here an alien explorer discovers John Smith's diary: Smith was mountaineering in Wales when he discovered the secret shelter of a group of businessmen, so he joined them and engaged in after-dinner chat about the meaning of life until they all died. The hero of John Griffith's *The Survivors* (1965) survives down a Cornish mineshaft, battling various sexual complications within the group to emerge after the invading Chinese soldiers have died up top of radiation sickness. Griffith's central theme is the survival of human decency. Driving south to the shelter he had witnessed two men ambushing a Mini, killing the parents and driving off 'as though the screaming children in the back seat did not exist' (26). In the shelter he watches 'the veneer of civilisation on these sophisticated scientists begin to wear thin' (81) and the final question is: 'We've survived the holocaust and all the dangers it brought. It remains to be seen if we can survive ourselves' (159).

One of the best 'shelter' fictions is Roshwald's *Level 7* (1959), which takes us 4400 feet down to the command post of the American defence system. The narrator keeps a diary and the four main sections begin: 'April 7 Introduction . . . March 21 Now I begin to understand the problem of 'To be or not to be' . . . June 9 Nuclear war begun and ended . . . October 12 Last entry.' The sense of a real diary is neatly conveyed by the addition of the introduction (which explains how he arrived in the shelter) out of sequence, and the destruction of a month of entries by the narrator's jealous, dying wife. The book ends

I do not think I can write any more. But I must try hard. This is
my contact with – with what was.
  Sunshine was. Does the sun still shine?
  I cannot read the clock across the room. But it is still light.
No. Dark.
  I cannot see Oh friends people mother sun I I
(143)

But there is no framing device explaining how we came to
witness the diary; indeed, we are told that Level 7 is now
impenetrable. Yet the nature of the enclosed, suffocating society
is vividly evoked in a spare prose style echoing the narrator's
technical proficiency (he is able to press the fatal buttons when
colleagues cannot), which alternates with prophetic nightmares
and 'atomic dreams'. In this technological womb with its 'Big
Brother' loudspeakers, a rhythm of life develops, with marriages
and births, lectures explaining the system of an inverted
pyramid with Level 7 the smallest and deepest, and discussions
of democracy and freedom. The children are told stories about
Saint Strontium 90 and his two little devils Alpha and Gamma
who now rule the world. But the radiation gradually leaks
down level by level, as they listen to the broadcast from an
upper level:

> Broadcaster again. 'Hundreds of people . . . lying on floor . . .
> no help at all . . . nobody capable of helping . . . some are
> vomiting . . . diarrhoea . . . horrible stench.'
>   He has stopped to cough and blow his nose.
>   He goes on: 'Some seem to be dead already . . . many
> unconscious . . . perhaps dead too, nobody to check . . .
> makes no difference . . . everyone will die sooner or later . . .
> matter of hours . . . some perhaps a day or two . . . no
> difference . . .'
>   I missed something there, his voice suddenly grew very
> weak. He has turned away from the microphone to be sick or
> something. I can hear groans again, louder.
>   He says: 'I can't go on.'
>   That's all.
>   No, he is trying to say something else. He has to speak
> very slowly.
>   'Our shelter is becoming a grave, a collective grave of

human misery.' Louder now: 'Politicians! Soldiers! From the bottom of our grave we curse you! May you follow our . . .' His voice fails him.

'Steps,' I suppose he wanted to say. But there is nothing coming over except groans and the sound of people vomiting.

Now the station has been switched off. (112–13)

The narrator has a religious sense. He complains, 'If only I had a God to cry to' and likens Level 7 to Hades or Sheol. But this is subservient to a belief in technology, where the plant room supplying oxygen acts as a shrine constantly tended by the whitecoated vestal virgins. A couple who escape to the surface intone Biblically:

She: 'We're a pair of doves, sent out by Noah to see if the flood has gone down.'
He: 'The flood is still around us, the water is deep. We're the doves which *didn't* fly back.'
She: 'But the dove which didn't return to Noah was a sign that the flood was over. It was a sign of life and hope when it stayed away from the ark.'
He: 'How right you are, my dove! We'll stay here, outside the shelter, until it's all over. For this is a much worse flood than the one God made. Men caused this tide of blood to rise and leave no hope for man or dove.' (120)

But the narrator refuses to be drawn in to such melodrama, remaining faithful to his technological vision to the end. That end comes when the nuclear reactor leaks radiation – it is finally the beneficent invention which delivers the coup de grace:

It is strangely ironical that we, PBX Command, should be killed by a gadget making a peaceful use of atomic energy. It does not seem fair. Divine justice, I always thought, was eye for eye, tooth for tooth. It should be bomb for bomb. Instead we are being killed by a piece of faulty machinery. Not really a warrior's death.

Perhaps God intended it as a sort of joke. 'You killed with bombs,' He says. 'You will be killed by peaceful radiation.'

Or maybe he is a Christian God, and Christian charity inspires his acts: 'You killed with atomic missiles,' He says,

'but I shall help you over to the other side with a reactor.'
    What am I talking about? God? Reactor? I feel hot, hot
and cold. I think I had better get into bed, if I can still climb
up to that top bunk. I cannot move X-107. (141)

He accepts the bizarre truce arranged between the warring
control rooms with a devastated globe between them. He dies
content, knowing that thanks to technology Beethoven's 'Eroica'
Symphony will keep playing – for twelve days, anyway. The
master technician, rejecting metaphysics and despair to the
last, Roshwald's narrator is a dramatic embodiment of the
scientific will, whose only humane impulse is the one which
prompted him to write at all:

> I could write just for myself . . . and one day – who knows? –
> my diary might be discovered and published on the surface of
> the earth, up there in the sunshine. Part of me, my spirit, might
> one day see daylight, might be warmed by the sun! . . .
>   I shall go on writing this diary as long as I live. For this is
> the only way in which I can feel the sun. (16–17)

The inverted pyramid system which is the underground world
of *Level 7* is a perfect, Morlock-ian manifestation of the
technological mind, a tunnel vision which thinks that greatest
isolation is greatest safety. The varieties of language in the
book, from the speeches which come through the loudspeakers
to the narrator's low-keyed reporting, indicate the various
frameworks of response possible to the survivor. The device of
encroaching doom gives a sense of finality and conscious
posturing to his tone, while his rejection of all metaphysical
explanations and appeals amounts finally to a kind of courage.
    Courage in the face of impending doom is what made famous
the temporary survival story of Nevil Shute called *On the Beach*
(1957). Like Orwell's *1984*, the novel has become an imaginative
landmark in modern consciousness and appears in subsequent
fictions. The captain in *Down to a Sunless Sea*, explaining the
crisis to his passengers, says, 'We have a similar situation – but
a thousand times worse than Shute could ever have imagined'
(189). A wife in the Hoyles' *Inferno* asks, 'It's only a question of
time, isn't it? Like *On the Beach*?' (145) The sense of remorseless
doom which powers the novel is accentuated by its powerfully

symbolic setting 'on the beach', that same 'terminal beach' where J. G. Ballard sets many of his 'inner landscape' fictions, an interface between man and nothingness, the end of the line. Shute's epigraph from Eliot's 'The Hollow Men' suggests that this sea is also the River Acheron, separating the lost souls from their destined Hell:

> In this last of meeting places
> We grope together
> And avoid speech
> gathered on this beach of the tumid river . . .

Shute also suggested for a dust jacket 'a scene of the main four or five characters standing together quite cheerfully highlighted on a shadowy beach of a shadowy river – the Styx'.[11] And the second epigraph, 'This is the way the world ends . . .', while it may affront C. P. Snow, takes us back to another bungled political act of violence (Guy Fawkes) and reminds us that Armageddon may not be the clean slate we had imagined.

Shute builds up a subtle imagistic pattern from his first lines when Lieutenant-Commander Holmes wakes to see 'the first light of the Australian sun upon the cretonne curtains', discusses sunburn with his wife and wishes he could stay at home for 'a day in the shade'. Only later do we recognise the allusions to the brighter sun from the north with its promise of radiation burns. Anthony Burgess criticises Shute's tone for being like 'some dimwitted archangel's chronicle'[12] but this deliberate thinness and reticence reflects the way the community will stay sane in an absurd situation by clinging to the surfaces of things, little daily rituals and anticipations of a future which does not exist. The men dislocate themselves from the intolerable present in various ways: Osborne devotes himself to finding out things; Holmes lives a fantasy future planting seed with his wife and baby; Towers will return home. Only Moira Davidson expresses her fears openly ('We had nothing to do with it. Why should we have to die because other countries nine or ten thousand miles away from us wanted to have a war? . . . All my life I've wanted to see the Rue de Rivoli' [40]) and scoffs at the scientists' project of leaving a time capsule on a mountain top: 'What sort of books are they preserving? All about how to make the cobalt bomb?' (104)

The trouble with Shute's world is that *everyone* seems to be as sensible and stiff-upper-lipped as his military heroes. Even the bus driver declares, 'I'll go on driving this here bloody tram till I get sick, cock. Then I'll drive it to the Kew depot and go home. That's where I live, see? I've been driving trams for thirty-seven years, rain or shine, and I'm not stopping now' (246). The nearest thing to recklessness is the Grand Prix, and for Osborne this is a triumph over chance – only afterwards does he take suicide pills while seated in his driver's seat. Even the submarine rating who escapes from the cruising craft near his home and insouciantly goes fishing, is quietly noble. There is no mass migration from the north, no panicky looting and mayhem, no building of shelters. The brilliant invention of the submarine, through which Shute can give a credible world view without destroying the stifling sense of a remote Antipodean community awaiting destruction, enforces the symbolic grandeur of the actors too, especially in the final tableau as Moira watches Towers' final, fatal mission head out of harbour: 'Dwight, you're on your way already, wait for me.' (267) Here we understand at an archetypal level that Shute's beach has no use except as an embarkation point for the souls of the dead. But the characters, like Moira, are reduced to posturing rhetorical figures; even Holmes, administering fatal pills to his wife and child, is noble. The thinness at the heart of the novel was exposed in the 1959 film version, which prompted one critic to call it 'a sentimental sort of radical romance, in which the customers are spared any scenes of realistic horror, and are asked instead to accept the movie notion of what is really horrible about the end of the world: boy (Gregory Peck) does not get girl (Ava Gardner).'[13] Yet Shute's reticence may have been a wiser decision than the attempt to realise Armageddon with its problems of scale and language.

A Scandinavian survival book which builds up a similar air of oppressive horror by following a passive group of survivors, is Sven Holm's *Termush* (1969). A university academic's diary recounts the experiences of a privileged group in an isolated hotel. The psychological shock of disaster and the sociological pressures of group living are delicately traced. At first the group expected some kind of saving change ('We put our faith in the disaster' [9]) but at the same time continuity was inevitable ('Did we expect that the molecules of the air would be as sharp as crystals and that our own skin would turn into something dark and glazed, nothing to do with ourselves at all?' [9]). Only a glimpse of the eternal Atlantic Ocean reminds them, paradoxically, that something *has* changed. The 'commodity called survival' which they bought is soon threatened by radiation sickness and marauding bands. The narrator is slowly jolted from a numbed, fantasy world in which bedroom fixtures (especially the mirror) seem out of focus, back into a human quest for companionship and survival. His sick friend Maria describes her feverish vision:

> A faint radiance lay over the landscape, the outlines of the trees, the contours of the mountains, the beach, the stone statues; all this was, as it were, veiled in a watery sheen that seemed to repeat and exaggerate the original shapes. And she saw the hotel residents wandering about in the landscape as if they were part of an old-fashioned painting . . .
>
> The light streamed out of every object; it shone through robes and skin and the flesh on the bones, the leaves on the trees and the moss on the mountains; it seemed suddenly to reveal the innermost, vulnerable marrow of people and plants, the sensitive growth tissue, the chalk, the iron, the blood.
>
> She was aware of this as if the radiation were visible to her alone, as if she, because of some defect, were the only person to have an impression of universal contamination . . .
>
> I could dismiss her fantasies about the management deceiving the guests. But I could not contradict the ideas from which the fantasies had arisen. They contained an insight that could only be captured in a slow, shocked picture. (72–3)

The narrator too has an historical hallucination of elegant guests arriving at the hotel, except that the face of one child dissolves into madness and the grotesque deformities of mutation (74). As sick people arrive at the door the guests band together to defend their castle, but the narrator cannot avoid fears about the lurking menace of radiation:

> One picture in our minds gives us constant anxiety; we see the day when the fish leave the water and push through the sand and earth to the trees, where they bite into the bark

with their skinless jaws and drag themselves up into the branches to live according to new instincts. We see the trees bare of leaves, festooned with fishy skeletons, their skins rustling like a deathrattle.

We see the turtle lay eggs and burrow into the earth, where it dies of thirst; birds fall out of their nests without using their wings; the foal licks stones while the mare's udder is bursting with milk; the goat flays its kid and tries to chew its flesh; the bee turns its sting on itself; the corn starts to grow downward and the roots of the trees rise up to search for water from the air . . .

Our fear is no longer a fear of death but a fear of mutilation. We have not thought this through and cannot talk about it, but in those moments when we are able to escape from our own personal needs the picture becomes clear to us.

It is impossible to sustain this thought. We cut it down; we put a ring around it in order to forget it. And we single out the twelve guests as evidence of our fear which we have not the strength to bear. (96–7)

In passages such as this *Termush* captures the subjective experience of nuclear disaster in visual images which twist and tear in a surreal nightmare, a detailed kaleidoscope of terrors. The visions of the narrator and his companion Maria finally merge in some Dali-like, nonhuman landscape beyond human support; having communicated in glances through the medium of the mirror ('I suddenly met her eyes in the mirror over my shoulder' [75]), they drift apart and the final strategic withdrawal from the invaders into a powerboat is no salvation but the final abandonment of identity and humanity to the hollow land of Acheron.

Robert Merle's *Malevil* (1973) concentrates more on the outward workings of the group than on the isolating, nightmare visions of the individual, and is therefore a more hopeful fiction than those of Shute or Holm. Emmanuel is holding a meeting of his revolutionary club of old childhood friends in an inherited castle, and drawing wine from the cellar, when the bombs land and they miraculously survive by dousing themselves in the vats. The novel documents in excruciating details the slow return to normalcy after the holocaust. Gradually the survivors assemble their senses and observe each other as 'those prehistoric beings who lived in the mammoth cave beside the Rhunes, not far from Malevil, in the days when man had only just emerged from the primate stage' (96). This rebirth is a painful anguish:

> I felt a wave of mortal bitterness towards them . . . like a newly born child howling with pain as the air penetrates into its lungs, each of us had lived such interminable hours since turned in wholly upon himself that it was very difficult to enter once more into contact with others. (91)

Emmanuel assumes command of a mediaeval community and copes with the problems of food, defence, religion, and sex (there is only one female). He reads Genesis to his subjects with a feeling of 'bitter irony', but never loses a spiritual sense, even when the deceiving Abbé Fulbert conducts a mass during the first rains, and everyone else is wondering anxiously if it will bring with it radiation:

> The rain was lashing with such fury of violence and hate that at moments it drowned Fulbert's voice, and yet, however tenuous it now seemed to me, I never lost it altogether. I clung to it; it was a thread I was following through the darkness. (285)

Emmanuel is a good leader; he establishes a primitive agrarian communism, denies his own appetites and is eventually chosen as leader in a contest with the priest. After his death, as indicated by the closing comments of Thomas, the community will continue, assuming with responsibility the path of progress, even to the extent of re-inventing explosives (this, as will be seen in Chapter 7, is an archetypal pattern of evolutionary post-disaster literature). But Merle's long book never quite captures the psychological power of the opening pages and the immediate reaction to the nuclear attack. The image of a dog, whose 'paws had been caught fast in the melted tarmacadam, and it died there, stuck fast, roasted where it stood' (103), remains with us when the intricacies of social planning have faded from our memory. And Emmanuel's brilliant opening disquisition on our conception of Time is never quite replaced by the history of the steady rebuilding of society:

I envy Proust. At least he had a solid foundation under him while he explored his past; a certain present, an indubitable future. But for us the past is doubly past, our 'time past' is doubly inaccessible, because included in it is the whole universe in which that time flowed. (8)

In the documentary fictions so far considered, there has been a clearly defined isolation (whether underground in Roshwald, continental in Shute or fortresslike in Merle) which enables writers to give a realistic perspective on the global horror which is nevertheless limited to radio broadcasts, reconnaissance reports, and victims beating at the door. The central character in the shelter is our representative, unchanged while all about has changed utterly. The demands of scientific accuracy really become demands for psychological plausibility in the succession of reactions and emotions charted from the blast to some kind of equilibrium, either of re-established order or death. Any attempt to document the larger community of town or nation assumes a patently 'false' perspective, and that perspective is justified by the writer's political motivation: he wants to warn, terrify, educate or rally his present audience. The problem of describing a vast disaster may be neatly sidestepped by a writer such as Ray Bradbury, whose 'The Highway' (1951) focuses on a lowly Mexican farmer who watches carloads of American tourists stream past his house shouting, 'The war! It's come, the atom war, the end of the world!' When they have gone, Hernando shrugs, asks, 'What do they mean "the world"?' and resumes his ploughing. But in our time of the 'breaking of nations' writers may wish to adopt a more directly polemic stance. Their creations may serve a real pragmatic purpose.

Wilson Tucker, in a novel (*The City in the Sea*) notable not for its flimsy scenario of a tribe of women in a post-nuclear world led by a man to rebuild civilisation, but for its curious introduction, says, 'The future of the world is a political problem, with statesmen and philosophers holding sway, but the far-future of the earth is a different thing and fairly in the hands of the dreamers and science-fictioneers.' But more and more those politicians are turning to future 'scenarios' and envisaged evolutionary pathways to help them determine even the 'near-future'. For their part novelists must abandon 'art' for this pragmatic goal, according to Jonathan Schell's *The Fate of the Earth* (1982). While not fictionalised, this book sets the context for evolutionary projections, insisting that the effects of any nuclear confrontation will be global, even universal, because 'the totalities in question are now not single cities but nations, ecosystems, and the earth's ecosphere' (45). Schell's demand is for a scientific probability study with an inbuilt element of uncertainty because we can never test these hypotheses and because 'this acceptance of our limited ability to predict the consequences of a holocaust . . . would itself be a token of our reluctance to extinguish ourselves' (25). The irony of the book is that Schell remains wedded to science, rejecting the fictional achievements presented in this study:

> Works of art are undermined at their foundations by the threat of self-extermination. . . . If it wishes truthfully to reflect the reality of its period, whose leading feature is the jeopardy of the human future, art will have to go out of existence, while if it insists on trying to be timeless it has to ignore this reality – which is nothing other than the jeopardy of human time – and so, in a sense, tell a lie. Art by itself is powerless to solve its predicament, and artists, like lovers, are in need of assistance from statesmen and ordinary citizens. (165)

This seems to me to be both high-minded and simplistic. Examples abound of works of art created out of a mood of apprehension or despair – Picasso's *Guernica*, Beckett's *Waiting for Godot* – which are neither mendacious nor powerless. Even the prospect of the end of time has produced such masterpieces as the Book of Revelation or Messaien's 'Quartet for the End of Time'. Of course it is Schell's thesis that nuclear conflict will result in the eventual death of the planet, not simply local misery. But even conceding this, there is surely artistry in books like *Level 7*, *On the Beach* and *When the Wind Blows*, which face unflinchingly the 'jeopardy of human time'.

Lurking in Schell's personification of art ('It') is a nostalgic notion of Renaissance humanism and the optimistic celebration of Man. His premises are more clearly stated by John Gardner in his reactionary treatise *On Moral Fiction* (1977). He argues that 'real art creates myths a society can live instead of die by, and clearly our society is in need of such myths'.[14] He rejects 'art which tends toward destruction. . . . Art is essentially serious and beneficial, a game played against chaos and death, against entropy'.[15] Unless one makes an elementary confusion between content (nuclear destruction) and effect, there is surely no art in our time which better fulfils the demands of Schell and Gardner than the fiction of nuclear disaster. For Gardner, 'the black abyss is merely life as it is or as it soon may become, and staring at it does nothing, merely confirms that it is there'.[16] If Schell is right, no art now can *not* include the black abyss. But we are back with our old distinction between the predictive and the plausible. These fictions do not 'merely' stare at the abyss, but offer plausible myths. Certainly they belong to the art of Bosch and Goya rather than that of Raphael and Leonardo, but their effect *is* serious and beneficial; they play against death by showing us the nobility and compassion in man as well as the stupidity and willing victimisation, the aggression and greed as well as the love and resilience. Even at the most objectionable level, the anonymous victim in a shelter, disaster fiction may also inhabit the high-minded world of these critics.

There are fictions which signal more obviously their intent to conform to these demands; 'scientific probability studies', 'serious and beneficial', exposing the decison-making procedures which bring about disaster, and aimed at warning not only us but the military and political commanders we have accepted. A most recent example of this pragmatic fictionalising is Strieber and Kunetka's *War Day* (1984) whose subtitle, 'And the Journey Onward', indicates its ameliorist perspective. The book is a potpourri of the methods we have already encountered in the fiction of nuclear disaster: official reports, memos, news items, vignettes, diaries, statistics. There is developing a more thoroughgoing, less sensationalised sub-genre of scenarios of nuclear disaster written by qualified scientists, military tacticians and politicians which has a very real purpose in advising not so much the masses as those in power.

General Sir John Hackett's *The Third World War* (1978) and *The Untold Story* (1982) are two better examples. The war, involving nuclear explosions over Birmingham and Minsk, takes place in August 1985, and the report is written in Easter 1987, with difficulty: 'In the chaotic conditions prevailing towards the end, in some key centres of power, vast quantities of records disappeared' (xv). But the author's compromise between fictionality and contemporaneity is illustrated by an acknowledgement in the 1983 reprint of the first volume that the political situation in the Arabian Gulf has changed, and by an 'Alternative Ending' to the second volume which takes account of the peace movement in Europe and the possible non-deployment of NATO missiles. At the same time, both books have the elaborate paraphernalia of a future history, including footnotes from such books as 'Air Vice Marshal Alec Penteith RAF, *Tornados in World War III* (Chatto & Windus, London, 1986), p. 265 (US 203)' and even a reference to the first book in the second – '*The Third World War: August 1985* (Sidgwick & Jackson, London, and Macmillan, New York, 1978), p. 15 (US p. x).' The jargon of Nukespeak also irradiates the books, e.g.

COMBALTAP	Commander, Baltic Approaches
COMECON	Council for Mutual and Economic Aid
CPA	Czechoslovak People's Army
CPSU	Communist Party of the Soviet Union
cw	chemical warfare (*Untold Story*, v)

The second book introduces autobiographical testimony, such as the letters of a Russian soldier Andrei Nekrassov, 'because reflection upon people, and above all, upon the people who get themselves caught up in wars, must lie at the heart and centre of all reflection upon war and peace' (*Untold Story* 7).

That Sir John regards even nuclear warfare as a matter of people 'getting themselves caught up in wars' betrays his soldierly fascination with weaponry and tactics. His main point in both books is that a Russian move of non-nuclear aggression in Europe could be repelled by NATO forces only by good fortune, given the poor nature of their current defences. His message is clear – 'If you want nuclear peace prepare for non-nuclear war: but be ready to pay the price.' (*Untold Story* 66) The books' greatest contribution to the fiction of nuclear disaster is their informed account of the process of escalation, from a skirmish in Yugoslavia to the destruction of two cities. When it comes to describing the bomb fall itself, Hackett is left with the vapid clichés ('enormous . . . tremendous . . . hideous') except when describing the reactions of the controllers in the early warning station on Fylingdales Moor who 'acknowledged this grim news in the disciplined and mechanical way in which they had been conditioned for long to think about the unthinkable' (*Third World War* 371), and the crude ejaculation of the American tracker: 'It sure is going to be hot in Birmingham England.' More effective is the eye-witness account of the familiar found diary, in this case 'Extracts from the Emergency Diaries kept by Three English Communities.' The report from Branscombe, Devon, moves from air-raids to looting to 'district reports nuclear explosion Birmingham area', while the previous day's report had ended, '1400 Cricket match – Village vs The Rest. Village 86 all out, the Rest 87 for 4. 1900 Evening concert, Village Hall.'

Hackett uses other media well, too. But for a resolute Italian television cameraman, the initial skirmish might have faded into obscurity; during the conflict television news is tightly controlled for propaganda purposes; and radio and newspaper reports document the reactions and hostilities in a global context, a context often not achieved by writers attempting to focus on the middle distance, somewhere between personal testimony and stereotypical reports of megadeaths. What Hackett stresses is the *ad hoc* nature of the military conflict: the struggle of the politicians and the military to see things in a global perspective, the ignorance of the ordinary soldier or civilian, the reminder that nuclear war will be a matter not of a single, sudden annihilation but a series of sporadic local disasters with seeping and lingering effects. Informed writers who focus on the military and political activities of the 'day before' remind us vividly of the intolerable responsibility which the human race has placed into the hands of its fallible leaders and, even more horrifically, into the fallible machines of high technology.

Harold Nicolson's 1932 novel *Public Faces* presents impressively in a subdued and convincing form the myriad faces involved in the bungling movement towards nuclear disaster. The Air Ministry of Great Britain has adopted Mr Livingstone's idea that a unique deposit of ore on the island of Abu Saad in the Persian Gulf will prove material for rocket fuel and bombs. Problems arise when the Shah decides to repossess the island in question, and while the hawkish air chiefs engage in shows of strength, Minister of Foreign Affairs Bullinger is insisting 'it would be unwise, nay it would be impious, for us to dabble in the satanic possibilities of the atomic bomb' (20). Personal rivalries and intrigues in the Government ranks push the world to the brink of disaster:

> A cloud, no larger than a man's hand, had risen in the East, and even now it had swollen to a heavy barrier, imminent, dark. . . . Already the situation, with dumb impetus, was sliding away from the scope of calculation to that of force; already a faint shrilling in the air presaged the wind of emotion. In sixteen, in twelve, hours the horrors of open diplomacy would hold Europe in its butcher's grip. There remained but a little hour or so in which the custodians could cope with the danger alone, secretly, intelligently, unharassed by the shrieking of the herd. (112)

The diplomats have not reckoned on the Air Minister Pantry who demonstrates the new bomb in the Atlantic, resulting in the accidental loss of an American ship and the British aircraft carrier *Albatross* in a scalding fog of steam. Eighty thousand people in Carolina are also drowned by the tidal wave. The situation is saved by young Shorland, who tells the whole truth to Reuters and pledges reparations.

Nicolson's satiric butt is the petty squabbling of the bureaucrats and powerseekers, and the confused responses of individuals to global threats. The subplot concerning the romance of two civil servants keeps the whole novel on a domestic level, although the responses of Lady Campbell are not so very dissimilar to those of the leaders of the land. When her daughter tells her, 'We're in for a really first-class crisis', she says, 'Eat your hash, dear, it will be getting cold' (104); and after the explosion she reasons, 'If the bomb is as bad as all that, and if we have several of them, no one will dare to go to war' (224). But Nicolson is also exposing the dangers of secrecy and the virtues of diplomacy. An appendix has Leonid Nikolson, in 1978, explaining his grandfather's motives for putting the record straight in this narrative. The official version by Lord Limpsfield, from which he quotes, praised Pantry and Bullinger and was ignorant of Shorland's actions. In his *Clockwork Orange* style of Russo-English, Nikolson claims that the story demonstrates the 'muddleheadedness of last to kapitalist dekkads'. He apologises for his longwinded grandfather, 'his fawls valyoos, his kompleet lak of enni narrativ gifts. . . . To Limpsfield's emoshonal individualism mi grandfather opposes mental individualism. Interesting see how both ekwalli silli, ekwalli fawls' (251). This playful appendix, then, prompts the reader to carry on the debate about communication and the necessity for free discussion between enlightened individuals. There is a reminder, in the censored second appendix, that a totalitarian system also blocks this kind of necessary communication.

Recognition of the new power of the military is exemplified in David Divine's *Atom at Spithead* (1953), where a Royal Navy Review becomes the opportunity for the 'enemy' to plant a nuclear explosive aboard an impostor ship, and more clearly in Roshwald's *A Small Armageddon* (1962), where a submarine commander holds the world hostage by directing his rockets at major cities and demanding visits from striptease dancers (whose anatomies are likened to atomic reactors in their vibrancy!).

But the dangers of nuclear terrorism are a relatively recent theme. Writers have been more concerned with the dangers from within the military–scientific–political structure itself, and especially from that most bathetic and ironic of possiblities: the technical malfunction. Most famous of these fictions is the cluster of 'countdown' stories focusing on war-rooms and wayward bombers. Peter Bryant began it all with *Red Alert* (1958), a novel about the Cold War and the fact that the American system is based on retaliation, the Russian on aggression. Bryant creates tension by beginning each chapter with a global news report – '10.25 G.M.T. Moscow: 1.25 a.m. Washington: 5.25 a.m.' – but much of the excitement arises from the author's jingoism and fascination for gadgetry. There is no sense of satire in his observation that the bombers 'would have administered a certain amount of punishment' (40) or the airforce commander's 'We're in a shooting war' (17). Although the stray American bomber misses its target, the President, observing that the Russians have bombs embedded in their mountainsides to take the world with them if they go, concludes, 'Latent in all the Slavs is the urge for self-destruction . . .' (75).

Five years later, Eugene Burdick and Harvey Wheeler advanced to *Fail-safe*, a gripping story of escalation with its source in 'a tiny knob of burnt carbon on top of the disabled condenser' (36). One Vindicator bomber passes its fail-safe point on an exercise run, and ironically, the system ensures that its own mistake cannot be corrected: every attempt to contradict the command is taken by the crew as confirmation that their mission must be desperately real. The President's only alternative to all-out war is to bomb simultaneously his own city of New York, as a show of good faith. Despite the easy cosiness of the conversation between the two heads of state, the authors create the hermetically sealed environment of the bunker war-room which has become a staple ingredient in our myths of nuclear war. Not only is the setting accurate; it metaphorically enacts the disjunction between our rational skulls and the physical devastation such 'rational' thinking now threatens to produce. Moreover,

> Now the world was living on two levels. There was an overt public level and a covert secret level. On the overt level the world's business proceeded serenely, innocently, and in its normal fashion: men worked, died, loved, and rested in their accustomed ways. But alongside this normal world, and ignored by it, the covert world went about its huge task of bringing two war plans into readiness. At that moment the covert, counterpoised world of war was in a waiting stage; its war dance had come to a high level of preparation and then stood arrested, held in miraculous balance, a marvellous intricate suspension brought about by suspicions, intentions, information, and lack of information. (179)

In the hawkish scientist Groteschele we find the links with the Second World War and with sexual neuroses which also have become a staple of nuclear war motivation. He remembers his father telling him that 'the first Jews who shuffled quietly off to death camps or hid like mice in attics were instruments of destruction of the rest', and in a crudely imagined episode he is almost raped in his car by Evelyn Wolfe, reminding him that 'he had always feared women because in each of them there was the buried but inextinguishable desire to love a man to death' (110). More convincing are psychological details like the pilot observing his Anglo-Saxon crew and noting, 'No good war novel here . . . what we should have is a Jew in it and an Italian to give colour' (120); or imagining as he flies towards

Moscow 'a stunning montage of old motion pictures of bombs exploding at Eniwetok and Los Alamos and Bikini' (126). All the characters are attempting to envisage the unthinkable, and it is all the more difficult to do so from their unreal insulation at the secret level. The interpreter Buck, for example, imagines a scene captioned 'The End of the World': 'There were rows of buttons on a board – blue, green, and red buttons – and a thick peasant hand with stubby fingers hovered over them, seemingly about to plunge' (236). Less successful is the symbolic overlay the authors try to impose, like the crew of Lowry Air Force Base reading the philosophy of Camus or the President recalling the story of Abraham.

That desire to frame the workaday, clinical rehearsals to Armageddon, was solved by Peter George in *Dr Strangelove or How I Learned to Stop Worrying and Love the Bomb* (which appeared in the same year as *Fail-safe*) by using broad satire. The manuscript is part of a galactic study *The Dead Worlds of Antiquity*, and was discovered in a deep crevice in the Great Northern Desert – that is, the remains of Dr Strangelove's vaunted mineshaft shelter. The framing device therefore mocks the pretensions to grandeur and immortality of Strangelove and his cohorts. The satirical tone is apparent from the first page, as the alien historians observe, 'They [Russia and America] were not on friendly terms, and we find this difficult to understand, because both were governed by power systems which seem to us basically similar' (1). The mad General Ripper sends his boys into battle to foil the 'commie plot' which is diluting his precious bodily fluids by fluoridating the water supply, assuring them, 'There is very little difference between an ordinary bullet and an H-bomb, except possibly a matter of degree, maybe a lot smaller degree than all these *experts* say' (26). The other military personnel are equally deranged and dangerous: General Turgidson clarifying the 'two-point-seven-two megadeaths situation'; Captain King astride his bomb 'Lolita' as it falls; the general protesting at the detonation of the Russian doomsday machine, 'It's wrong . . . it's not right.' At the end George finds time to moralise in the person of the President: 'We trust each other to maintain the balance of terror. . . . Now the bomb has become an even greater enemy to every nation than they have ever been, or ever could be, to each other' (115–16).

Stanley Kubrick's film of the novel (1964) amalgamates George's vision and the Burdick-Wheeler character of Groteschele. As played by Peter Sellers, Strangelove's physical mutilation (his arm tending independently to spring erect into Nazi salutes) and his final plans for a sexual utopia with ten women for every man, alert critic George Linden to the point of the film's title. All Kubrick's men have a 'strange love' for the bomb rather than for each other, and this theme of 'erotic displacement' is present visually from the opening 'copulation' between two refuelling bombers to the final orgasmic spread of the mushroom cloud. The film therefore defines and attacks 'the American pornography of power',[17] a theme discerned by Kurt Vonnegut when he asked, 'How many of you readers will deny that the movie *Dr Strangelove* was so popular because its ending was such a happy one?'[18] The three sets used in the film – the besieged air force base, the control room and the claustrophobic cockpit – also reinforce the idea of determinism, each character performing according to his own inner (Ripper) or external (the dedicated pilots) system. The characters therefore appear 'locked into their "cells", as the fate of the peoples they rule or represent is locked into the events.'[19] Vera Lynn's 'We'll Meet Again' at the climax of the film satirises by its inappropriateness the optimism of those living under the nuclear threat. It also sends the audience out into the light thinking of 'some sunny day' when the sun brighter than a thousand suns may light up the sky. The final effect is a positive one: the song reminds the audience that they are a community sharing the God-given sun on planet Earth who may, by pulling together and acknowledging their humanity and fallibility, avoid disaster. The whole film reminds us of the strength of our individual instincts and the necessity for an overriding social awareness. We need not be passive victims of our aggressive and sexual impulses. We may become self-conscious, able to adapt, and so help the group survive.

This example may help to explain why the most effective of these quasi-scientific documentaries of the experience of nuclear disaster are those which focus on the individual psyche as it reacts to and copes with vast changes. Nicolson's diplomats just manage to rescue the world from the vortex of political disruption, as do the American leaders in the *Red Alert–Fail-safe–Dr Strangelove* trilogy. Philip Wylie's account of nuclear devastation 'comes alive', as it were, when he uses the image of a man's indrawn breath – an image which has its apocalyptic source in Paul's 'twinkling of an eye' when all will be changed. The pressure of inevitable change is the dramatic focus of novels like *On the Beach*, *Termush*, *Level 7*, and *Jenny*. People may be seen to react with stirling courage and resourcefulness, like Jenny, Harve and Mr Baldwin; they may slowly grow to a new maturity, like Gladys and Barney; or their world views may be incapable of accommodating the new reality, as is the case with Briggs's pathetic survivors, or more dangerously with the industrial and political authorities in the power plant stories. In his story 'The Unparalleled Invasion', Jack London foresees the destruction of China in 1982 – 'it was ultra-modern war, twentieth century war, the war of the scientist and the laboratory'.[20] Nuclear disaster may be born in the laboratory, but as Wells claimed, the desires to discover and to tell stories have a common source in the desire to change. Today writers write about change to persuade their community to change, to avoid what Hoban calls the 'Master Chaynjis'; in the laboratories of these fictions we may find some solutions, as they speak of individuals to us as individual readers.

4   The Post-Nuclear Society

Both professor and prophet depress,
For vision and longer view
Agree in predicting a day
Of convulsion and vast evil[1]

A survey of possible global disasters which appeared in 1930
does not mention nuclear war, but a similar book from 1953
includes a lengthy chapter on the subject.[2] The author, himself
a scientist, takes as his authority Albert Einstein. In 1945
Einstein argued that although two thirds of the world's
population might be destroyed in a war, 'enough men capable
of thinking, and enough books, would be left to start again, and
civilisation could be restored.'[3] But by 1950 he was writing less
sanguinely, 'In the end, there beckons more and more clearly
general annihilation.'[4] The Doomsday Clock, an invention of
alumni of the Manhattan Project in their *Bulletin of the Atomic
Scientists*, concurs with Einstein's grim prediction; at present its
hands are at a few minutes to midnight, closer than they have
ever been.[5]

Nuclear capability has given a new edge to what was already
bound to be an 'age of anxiety', in Auden's terms. Technological
progress and the evolution of world politics led George Orwell
to create a fearful new world in 1984, not far off from the
millenial date of 2000 when Yeats's rough beast will slouch into
view. Now mankind has the potential to bring about its own
millenium at any time regardless of the neat symbolism of the
calendar, and the result is an almost insupportable burden of
responsibility. The first accounts of nuclear explosions articulated
this burden:

To know what the end of the world is like one must live
through it, not perish with it. That seeming impossibility is
what is happening to us today – happening, that is, to all

83

'The Four Angels Holding the Winds', A. Dürer, Apocalypse series, Frederick van der Meer, *Apocalypse: Visions from the Book of Revelation in Western Art* (London: Thames & Hudson) p. 291.

except the thousands of Japanese who vanished into vapour. . . .

The only safe and sensible course is to use it [the bomb] now to exterminate or subjugate everybody else on Earth. That would be Hitler's choice, Japan's choice. It is not the American choice. . . . America must join and lead in a worldwide renunciation of this weapon by a worldwide renunciation and prevention of war.

That is one reason why the world is coming to an end, and why we have the chance to share in its rebirth. . . . The dust of creation is in our hands.[6]

Man must shape his own future, because the nuclear possibility has turned the millennial disaster from a theoretical or superstitious symbol into an imminent and immanent threat. The shape of the future is determined by the shape of the present; in the nuclear world, time distinctions become conflated in the overwhelming urgency of each present moment. And yet our image of the future still shapes the present; our hopes for mankind, our conception of nuclear disaster and our appraisal of the present world situation and its tendencies dictate our behaviour as we hover over the fatal button. As Fred Polak concluded in his mammoth study, 'the image of the future is the womb . . . which bears the history of human civilisation.'[7]

To contemplate nuclear disaster, then, one must have a sense of the pattern of human history and future destiny. Only the most simplistic imagination recoils from the ghastly prospect as before a hideous image in a mirror at the end of a maze-like tunnel. Herman Kahn, in the book which gave us the concept of 'escalation', reminds us that his idea is a 'metaphor and scenario', a way for the human imagination to comprehend the outrageous. Only at the top of his escalation ladder does one reach what he calls 'Spasm or Insensate War'[8]: that kind of animalistic reaction, or what in his inimitable prose Kahn calls 'useless and contraproductive destruction', is as useless when contemplating possible nuclear destruction as when actually performing it. Any human response will place the holocaust in a context of human time. Before and after the 'twinkling of an eye', therefore, become crucial elements in our thinking about nuclear disaster. In fictions, indissolubly bound as these are to a linear narrative, these elements are central.

We have already looked at the day before and the day after.

In this chapter, then, I will look at fictions which attempt to place nuclear disaster within the larger before-and-after framework of that other 'escalator', human evolution. In answering the question, 'What then?' these fictions are performing the function of what Robert Scholes calls 'structural fabulation'. This function is particularly appropriate to science fiction, which he defines as 'a fictional exploration of human situations made perceptible by the implications of recent science. Its favourite themes involve the impact of developments or revelations derived from the human or physical sciences upon the people who must live with those revelations or developments.'[9] Because nuclear disaster clears the stage so drastically, the field for extrapolation would seem to be wide open for fantastical futures, particularly when one considers the potential in nuclear explosion for subsequent mutation of organic life. What circumscribes these fictions is the fact, emphasised in the first chapter, that these fictions are directed at us now, before the blast. They are quite unlike millennial writings, which they otherwise imitate in terms of imagery, tone and so on, because they are concerned to avoid rather than to promote the apocalyptic event itself. One commentator wrote of millennialist thought,

> The urge to bring on a day of reckoning – when heaven comes down to earth – is with us still, will always be with us. The lesson of the Revelation seems to be that if we try too hard to hasten that day, we are in peril of losing our humanity. Yet surely we are equally in peril if we choose not to make the attempt at all.[10]

Nuclear disaster fictions attempt to hasten not the horror but the enlightenment, thus – paradoxically – to put off the day. They help us to know ourselves by giving us a new perspective on ourselves, capitalising on the nuclear threat to 'defamiliarise' ourselves, a strategy which F. Jameson argues is common to all fiction but more spectacularly to speculative and science fiction. We can then engage in restructuring our own experience and our own future in the present and out of the womb of the future.[11]

Where these evolutionary fictions vary, then, is in their stance towards the present reader. They may be impartial anthropological investigations into the far future, thinly disguised appeals for tolerance (as in many of the stories about mutant survivors), satires and dystopias, or ennobling parables of heroism and man's indestructability. The two most common themes in all of them are antagonism towards science as we know it, and a tendency towards authoritarian government. The latter usually involves the celebration of an heroic leader but generally it is the group or tribe which is celebrated. We will not often encounter the 'pulps' which prompted A. I. Berger to remark,

> It is frightening to speculate on the degree to which current predictions of social collapse are motivated, consciously or otherwise, by thought patterns which would welcome the war of all-against-all and/or an authoritarian social order built on a fear of personal and social relationships.[12]

What is more common is an alienation of man not from fellow man but from the contemporary symbols of civilisation. As I. F. Clarke puts it, 'The empty worlds of the future are the symbol of an absolute separation between humanity and technology, of a total disjunction between the industrial past and the inchoate future.'[13]

Since Wells, writers have tended to use the post-disaster situation for dystopian rather than utopian purposes. Minor examples include C. Fitz Gibbon's *When the Kissing Had to Stop*, where the peace movement leads the moral decay of England until a socialist leader sells out completely to Russia; Christopher Priest's *Fugue for a Darkening Island* where nuclear war in Africa sends refugees to challenge a racist British government; and Alan Seymour's *The Coming Destruction of the United States of America*, where a newspaper editor presents the scrappy evidence of a dying civilisation and finally becomes personally involved in the racism and self-destruction. The Russian Strugatsky brothers set their *Prisoners of Power* on another planet, but it is recognisably our world. There has been world nuclear war and now the rulers, the 'Powerful Creators', hold sway from radiation towers which blast the people daily into paralytic slaves. The hero finally blows up the centre of power to allow the re-emergence of democracy.

George Orwell's regime in *1984* also uses nuclear war to keep control over the masses. According to the proscribed 'Theory and Practice of Oligarchical Collectivism' by Emmanuel Goldstein, 'atomic bombs first appeared as early as the nineteen-forties, and were first used on a large scale about ten years later.' (157) Since then, the world's three super-states know that mutual survival is necessary for individual survival, so they wage conventional warfare only. This absorbs surplus production and expends labour, while the people are kept amused with films of victory like 'the very good one of a ship full of refugees being bombed somewhere in the Mediterranean' (10). Orwell's anti-apocalyptic, 'steady state' nuclear age was based upon his observations of the superpowers after 1945. In an essay of that year, 'You and the Atom Bomb', he argued that the sheer cost of such weaponry meant increased power for totalitarian states and a deliberate avoidance of final solutions: 'It is likelier to put an end to largescale wars at the cost of prolonging indefinitely a "peace that is no peace".'[14] Two years later Orwell attacked James Burnham's predictions of nuclear war between Russia and America, arguing that 'history never happens quite so melodramatically as that.'[15] For forty years Orwell has been correct.

Upton Sinclair's *The Millennium: A Comedy of the Year 2000* (1929) supposes that a glass jar containing a purplish gas has leaked 'X-radiumite' and reduced the Earth's animal life to dust. The only people to survive this version of what would now be called by the military a 'clean' bomb are a group of wealthy celebrants at New York's new Pleasure Palace, who fly aloft for six hours. They return to Earth and in the struggle for survival – burning priceless antiques for warmth – the old social order is reversed: the pilot marries Helen Granville and Tuttle the butler oversees the production of food pills. After moving rapidly through the historical phases of social evolution – slavery, feudalism, capitalism – the survivors revolt and join Helen in her pastoral arcadia. Tuttle, like the mad scientist, dies of starvation amid the disused machinery of megalopolis. More interesting than Sinclair's satire of consumerism and capitalism is his novelistic understanding of the importance of free communication and imaginative literature to the health of society. De Puyster the journalist tries in vain to interest the ruling class in literature; like the rulers in Orwell's *1984* and so many post-disaster dystopias, they sense the claims of freedom, truth and individualism inherent not just in scientific text books but in all literature. Sinclair also finds room to satirise contemporary journalism when he has a survivor discover a newspaper from the last day of the old world: the front page is devoted to a sensational murder, the back to the evils of smoking in bed, and 'practically the rest of the paper was devoted to an advance account of the great ball at the Pleasure Palace' (234).

L. P. Hartley's *Facial Justice* (1960) also takes us to 'the not very distant future, after the Third World War' (9) and also explores the recoil to totalitarianism after such a disaster. When the subterranean survivors are finally led out into the open by a child, they gratefully submit to the 'Dictator', whose theme song 'Every valley shall be exalted . . .' has been grotesquely reflected in the grey, muddy waste land of the post-nuclear landscape. The Dictator institutes a campaign of 'Facial Rearmament' designed like the class systems of Orwell and Huxley's dystopias to establish a steady state. There are *alpha* and *beta* faces and at the bottom of the social scale patients and delinquents who have the names of murderers. The world which 'needed a new language' (116) has been given the simplest of labelling systems to go along with the psychological and physiological levelling of plastic surgery. The heroine Jael is inspired by the spire of Ely cathedral to challenge the system and the language – 'a storehouse of dead metaphors' (115); but in an awkward denouement she is won over to the philanthropic theories of the 'Darling Dictator' and perpetuates the system herself. Despite Hartley's retreat from liberalism at the end of the novel, however, *Facial Justice* is important for 'facing' the issue of how we are to regard one another after the holocaust. Our old faces might remind us too painfully of what we have lost, or the evil in us which caused the loss, and a literal face-lift promoting an evolutionary fiction may be a very real demand.

Many writers of nuclear disaster reflect on man's present situation not by envisaging future utopias or dystopias, but by placing the present age and the impending disaster within the larger evolutionary process. Whatever may be Jonathan Schell's objections to this turning of nuclear apocalypse into an event which does not end the world and time but simply sends it in a new direction, these evolutionary fictions form a major part of the literature of nuclear disaster. George Stewart's ecological parable *Earth Abides* (1949) is a classic of the type, with its sole survivor (Ish, after Melville's Ishmael) achieving mythic and Biblical status as leader of the tribe, saviour of the race and the consummate 'adaptable man'. It exposes the tension in all such writing between, as one critic put it, 'cultural shock versus cultural inertia',[16] with Ish devoted to making arrowheads rather than teaching, rediscovering the arts of the Red Indian rather than attempting to continue the upward spiral of history by salvaging what he can of a technological age. But even by 1950, shortly after publication, the reviewer Frederick Pohl could say, 'There is nothing to be said in this story that has not been said in a hundred sf stories before.'[17] Indeed as far back as 1941 one *Astounding* reader was complaining, 'Why must we always have Rousseau's Noble Savage, with his biceps, his stone axe and his mate, crawling around the ruins of mighty Nyawk or Chikgo? After all, don't you think a post-Euro-American Age would at least start on the level of, say, Rome?'[18] Being bombed back to the Stone Age is not the only scenario.

The direction of evolution after the bomb must certainly be impossible to determine, given the magnitude of the psychic and physical disruption. The question of the far future is made doubly imponderable by the immediate question: how far 'down' the evolutionary tree will the disaster cause man to slide? Writers give their answers according to their own faith in technology or else in their preference for an alternate life style altogether, the post-disaster landscape serving as a convenient testing ground for the old, forgotten virtues of self-reliance and simple living. Many writers content themselves with a static vision soon after the disaster when the desirable new order is in place. While these fictions may be compellingly complete, there are only a few which look beyond the period of re-adjustment to further evolution of the society. Often the society becomes rigid or must fight against other societies which represent different phases of evolution. Whatever the nature of the pressures, any evolutionary study of society under nuclear stress must be an advance on the vague, contradictory musings of futurists like Magnus Clarke, whose study of the fate of Britain collapses into contradiction: in thirty years he says, 'if society has not collapsed in the meantime, existence in Britain should not be unpleasant. There will be limited industry and food should not be a problem. . . . Overall, long-term British prospects are not good'.[19]

Some of the earlier post-nuclear fictions are remarkable for their optimism, based on an ignorance of the effects of radiation. Pat Frank's *Alas, Babylon* went through thirty-one printings between 1959 and 1975, and must have played an important role in shaping the American imagination towards nuclear weapons. The setting is Fort Repose in Central Florida, and Randy Bragg (another obvious, 'macho' name) receives a coded message from his Air Force brother – 'Alas, Babylon.' The brothers learnt it from a hellfire Baptist preacher and for them it means imminent nuclear war. All the town learns of the message from the gossiping telephone operator but only the librarian deciphers it; she reacts by asking a friend over for the weekend – 'If it came soon, she would have a friendly hand to hold' (25). The breezy ignorance of the radio news bulletins ('The Navy has just ordered preventive action against unidentified jet planes which have been shadowing the Sixth Fleet in the Eastern Mediterranean. At Tropical Park today, Bald Eagle won the Coral Handicap . . .' [58]) contrasts with the military debriefing of Mark Bragg; the son's insouciance ('Sounds like the kick-off') contrasts with Randy's confused, panicky preparations. He does not fill his bath with water and only at the last moments has the daring to spend his money.

The Braggs watch the falling missiles as if they are enjoying a fireworks display and the fallout seems confined to military targets. Radiation appears only in a moral guise: a greedy looter gives away contaminated jewellery and the wearers receive neck and wrist burns. There is the occasional blind patient, and panic at the hotel, but most of the citizens flock to the library to read about survival, and Randy stops to assist at a car crash because 'he could not shuck his code, or sneak out of his era' (98). The novel does not sneak out of its era, either: Randy explains radiation as nature's way of protecting the race, sets up a vigilante group, quotes from Benjamin Franklin and learns with relief that although now a 'second-class power' America has enough nuclear fuel left to rebuild a once proud nation. The people flock to church, affirming that 'faith had not died under the bombs and missiles' (258), and the novel ends, despite the more realistic afterthought, on a jingoistic note: 'We won it. We really clobbered 'em . . . not that it matters.'

Despite the comical optimism, Frank does have moments of insight into the post-nuclear trauma. A retired general puts away his war games and sighs, 'We inhabit the same purgatory, the dark level of not knowing' (142). Frank notes the change in language after 'The Day': 'how quickly you picked up the jargon of the post-Day age. It was like entering a totally new environment, like joining the Army' (309). Although it is unlikely that the newspaper would continue to publish quite so easily, the advertisements do evoke the painful transition from a consumer society:

> WILL SWAP – Late model cadillac Coupe de Ville, radio, heater, air-conditioned, battery run down but undamaged, for two good 28-inch bicycle tyres and pump. DESPERATELY NEEDED evaporated milk, rubber nipple and six safety pins. Look over our house and make your own deal. (189)

There is also a superb vignette where the bank president reacts to the sudden abandonment of money by blowing out his brains, with the thought, 'Well, let them try to go on without dollars. He would not accept such a world' (122).

The hero of Stephen Minot's *Chill of Dust* (1964) has a more difficult time retaining order and civility within a cluster of twenty-one Catholic families surviving a harsh winter. The teacher Adams (who else?) insists that the children attend his school, believing that any learning, even the four-page fragment of *Paradise Lost*, will help stem the slide into barbarity. Unfortunately the priest Leblanc who lives parasitically on the community stirs up the youngsters and hires a hobo, Luke, to spy for him. A ruthless raid by a marauding band leaves some children raped or dead and a mother accuses Adams of making the children helpless in a savage land. While Adams sees the error of his ways and tries to immolate himself in the holocaust of his own precious books, Luke takes his adoptive daughter and follows the new community of Leblanc. After three phases of society – humanist, religious, pagan – Luke is seen teaching his grandchildren the required domestic virtues and hardihood to get through the difficult years ahead. Elements of church piety, humanist learning and pagan 'know-how' are all needed for survival. Minot's novel is broadly sympathetic and reconciliatory, and only our own age is truly condemned:

She looked at the dark, leathered backs of her hands and had the feeling that in her life she had been sinking like a shell in the deepest sea, drifting through progressively darker zones – gliding back through epochs of human effort toward the darkest age. But why? How petty, narrow, shortsighted, self-centred, and brutal men must have been the year they smashed so much for reasons no succeeding generation would ever understand. She wondered if perhaps theirs, not hers, was truly the darkest age. (316)

Following the Darwinian theory of a struggle between competing tribes or individuals for survival, many fictions move beyond one community to dramatise in tribal conflict the debate over how humanity really should be organised. Alfred Coppel's *Dark December* (1958) is a simple prototype of this kind of story, pitting a humanist against a madman in a Californian waste land. Major Gavin, a missileman who escaped the holocaust in Alaska, flies home over what looks like Earth 'before the first bacterium came to be in the primeval sea' (31). He survives radiation, rescues a girl from rapists, and refuses to kill – even his donkey. In this way he resists the challenge of the satanic Captain Collingwood who, although an ostensible figure of authority, betrays by his brutality and bloodlust that he has descended the evolutionary ladder. His argument with Gavin that he has at least taken fewer lives than the missile-man has by directing bombs from his silo, deserves more attention than Coppel gives it; but our sympathies lie with Gavin as he faces a more realistic representative of the survivalist hero. Says the captain,

'You button pushers. For a while you had it all your own way. You could hide in your holes and let the computer and the rockets do your fighting for you. But not any more, mister. Not any more. . . . You've made us important again. A man with a bayonet and a gun fighting for a piece of ground –'
My God, I thought sickly. The world smashed and burned and bleeding and here it was ready to start all over again. Here was the face of the real enemy. The man with a bayonet eager to kill. (47)

Having disposed of the captain on Golden Gate Bridge the hero returns home with a new lover and foster son to ensure the perpetuation of the new race 'as Cro-Magnon did over Neanderthal', moralising thus: 'History has to begin somewhere. With us, now, because we're here. That's what I think it means to be a survivor' (118).

It is a short step from this kind of ideological struggle to fictions which popularise a present-day ideology, particularly that over which nuclear conflict may be fought. The political motives of Ryder Stacy, the latest contributor to survivalist fiction, are clear from the outset of his two novels *Doomsday Warrior* and *Red America* (1984). An unmotivated pre-emptive Russian strike of 1990 has destroyed two thirds of the world's population and given the Russians possession of the United States, largely because of the effectiveness of their secretly installed 'killer sats' (an obvious comment on the 'star wars' debate). Those Americans not killed or enslaved have established communities in the waste land, chief of which is Century City led by the 'Ultimate American' Ted Rockson. Rockson doesn't need to change into a Superman suit; like Harve Rackham he attains his immunity through technical skill and by believing in America. He and his Freefighters wage a war of resistance (with the German Gestapo replaced by the KGB), slaughtering Russian soldiers and surviving the usual gamut of threats in the nuclear wasteland: mutant wild dogs, radiation storms and mud slides. Their aim? 'We're trying to restore the dream the way the people back there failed to do. The original dream' (128). After freeing America of the red curse, says Rockson in a tone neither ominous nor ironic, 'we'll spread freedom to them'. Although this is the stuff of pulp fiction, Stacy does sketch in cartoon form the traditional elements of post-disaster fiction: thanks to a time warp the Freefighters are treated to a mirage of Salt Lake City, the 'before' perfectly preserved in the 'after', while a scientist talks of 'de-evolution' (193) and the whole planet 'was sinking back into the Middle Ages' (235). Rockson discovers an enclave of survivors for whom time has stopped – the 'Macy's folk' of a large shopping mall, who prowl the stocked shelves in ignorance and dress up their Russian victims as dummies. Another enclave, the Technicians, are taught by Rockson how to hunt game. In return for the skills of animal survival, the scientists give the Freefighters a secret weapon which they use to decimate a Russian convoy:

> The freefighters looked at what they had done and at each other. They felt no guilt, no shame. Nor happiness. They had accomplished what they set out to do. Had done it beyond their wildest dreams. Now at last they had the weapon they needed. A weapon as powerful and awesome as the atomic bomb itself, the twentieth century's gift of extinction. But now the twenty-first century as well had its weapon of superdeath. (*Red America*, 37)

Unlike the Spenglerian cynics such as Miller and Hoban, neither Stacy nor Rockson seems aware of the ironic implications in matching technology with technology, superdeath with superdeath. Even when Rockson encounters a band of motorcyclists in the desert in a scene reminiscent of the excellent if one-dimensional 1981 Australian film *The Road Warrior*, his faith in technology is not weakened. It is a matter of evolving technology rather than standing still; being American, the heroes of these survivalist tracts have nothing to say about the finger which pulls the trigger except that if it is on the side of democracy and capitalism it is beyond good and evil. In the post-holocaust jungle the individualist excels, but questions of authority, the production and availability of weapons, and the quality of daily life, await Harve Rackham and Ted Rockson beyond the last page of their novels. After all, even Superman serves his society.

Tribal warfare in a decaying world was a staple of fiction from as early as 1905 when Van Tassel Sutphen wrote *The Doomsman*, set in the twenty-first century when 'the highly civilised North American continent had relapsed, within the brief period of ninety years, into its primeval state' (17). Various tribes – the Doomsmen or ex-convicts, House people and Stockaders – struggle for supremacy until a priest explodes the 'Shining One' (an electric dynamo which anticipates the nuclear power plant) revered by the doomsmen, and antarctic rescuers come in an 'electric cruiser' to establish an era of technology and happiness. Piers Anthony shows the debt of this theme to Wells's Eloi and Morlocks by envisaging underground thinkers who supply weapons to the Samurai-like warriors above ground, like *Sos the Rope*. He and his comrades work to keep the tribes apart, precisely to avoid the kind of concentration of power and resources which led so fatally to nuclear weapons. In Poul Anderson's *Vault of the Ages* (1952), set in the Allegheny Mountains, the peaceful Dalesmen survive by discovering the secret of dynamite, formerly hidden in the taboo vault; as the hero Carl explains to his people, 'There is no evil in the vault. There is only evil in the hearts of men' (207). Anderson also wrote an anthropological story in 1962 called 'Progress', where the post-disaster centre of world culture is in the South Pacific. A Mauri (Maori?) delegation visits an island searching for a nuclear reactor. They are gentle and telepathic, but the Brahmards are imperialistic and warlike, and their leader Dahnanda ('Down Under'?) must be stopped. Evolution demands change, and Anderson projects the conventional sf future of space colonisation as a reaction to the boredom of the 'global village': 'Some day, in spite of everything we do, Earth will have grown unified and dull. Then it will be time to try for the stars' (129).

In 1983 Anderson returned to the question of the place of atomic power and space exploration in a post-disaster society and worked out his ideas fully in the novel *Orion Shall Rise*. His assumption is that hundreds of years after the 'War of Judgment' the world will reassume its basic tribal groupings: the Mong in Asia, French descendents in Uropa, Northwesterners in America and Maurai in Polynesia. Because N'Zealann escaped the nuclear wars, the Mauri are pre-eminent as diplomats and ecologists. They berate the Northwesterners for secretly building a nuclear power plant, but Anderson suggests that the ecological and moral arguments are a cover for the old motivations of greed and lust for power. In the more civilised Europe a 'Skyholm' or orbiting weather station, one of the last achievements of technological man, remains to suggest the peaceful use of science. However war does finally break out around the globe, waged with chemical weapons and those nuclear warheads either left over or cobbled together by tribes seeking the ultimate weapon. Anderson, like Wells, avoids the problem of describing a workable world democracy by inventing a class of superhuman right-thinkers who belong to a kind of Rotary Club called the Wolf Lodge. The hero and heroine, politically independent, launch Orion, a spaceship powered by nuclear explosions but bearing an even more deadly solar weapon. Anderson's imagination is here archetypal for science fiction: peace is imposed by a Big Brother in the sky who wields the ultimate weapon which, with its solar power, has more ecological appeal than the tainted power of nuclear fission. The hero, in fact, finds time to meditate on how history seems to conform to just such archetypal imaginings:

> What I feel upon us is a gigantic conflict of . . . mystiques – a conflict so deep-going that human beings and whole civilisations are turning themselves willy-nilly into archetypes and re-enacting memorially ancient myths . . . (268)

Mankind's lust for atomic energy is a lust for self-destruction according to this large pattern, for 'an obsession about the atom is built into them, into our entire culture' (432). For Anderson, the Orion's combination of solar and nuclear power is the last whip necessary to hold man to the evolutionary path which leads to space. As the hero informs the world at the end of the novel:

> Let Orion rise, but not as a weapon – no, as a tool. . . . Yes, it will release radiation, but the time is overpast to be reasonable about that. The contamination will be slight, bearable and temporary until we have a permanent foothold in space. (460)

In the fictions of the fifties and sixties in particular we see writers responding to the global nature of nuclear disaster to address evolution in global, rather than local, terms. N. B. Williams's *Atom Curtain* (1956) has the world literally divided by a curtain of radiation after the Third World War. The hero who flies through the curtain discovers that the Americas are inhabited by two Wellsian races, the subterranean one living in the nuclear shelters and dominated by a Big Brother figure who every so often carries out the Malthusian exercise of sluicing away his population, saving a few males to breed again. O'Hara becomes the new leader, and returns to the narrator in his Bloomsbury apartment with a plan for world government which involves asking the 'Twelve Old Men of Geneva' to supervise an armistice. A notable virtue of this otherwise derivative novel is its recognition of the evolution of language. The primitives speak 'a decadent English, elided and bastardised and purified of abstracts. . . . The trick of understanding it was not to attempt to get it word for word – the words themselves no longer had their English identity – but by complete sentences. . . . Much of it depended of course on inflections . . . and yet, slurred in his mind's ear, repeated rapidly, it suggested the more complex English structure' (53). Very few fictions, we shall see, take advantage of the inevitable mutation of language to create an imaginative world.

Global evolution leads, of course, to thoughts of the stars, thereby re-affirming the link between the pessimistic science fiction of nuclear disaster and the optimistic science fiction of space exploration. Several of the stories examined in previous chapters involved nuclear powered space-craft saving the world from nuclear powered weapons. Camille Flammarion's classic of 1894, *Omega: The Last Days of the World*, set the trend, with the sole survivors of the human race (after another five centuries of war and mismanagement) being raised by an Egyptian god into the heavens, there to begin life afresh; the author salutes the cosmic evolution – 'there is neither end nor beginning.' Olaf Stapledon, an English writer with as grand a vision, reduces the earthly apocalypse to a trivial incident in galactic history as seen from the point of view of a Neptunian, in *The Last Man in London* (1932). Ray Bradbury gently satirises our global allegiance in *The Martian Chronicles* (1946), where the new Martian settlers return to Earth at the news, 'AUSTRALIAN CONTINENT ATOMISED IN PREMATURE EXPLOSION OF ATOMIC STOCKPILE. LOS ANGELES, LONDON BOMBED. WAR. COME HOME. COME HOME. COME HOME' (180). Their return only ensures the destruction of the planet, and we are left with one family on Mars preparing to start it all again. In Poul Anderson's *After Doomsday* (1965) and Roger Zelazny's *This Immortal* (1966), intergalactic fighting also reduces Earth's apocalypse to a footnote: Anderson's hero 'realised with a shudder how little difference Ragnarok had made' (17), while Zelazny's victorious aliens use Greece, unharmed among the 'Hot Spots', as a tourist resort.

Cosmic evolution is one perspective from which to dwarf man's achievements and follies. Another perspective is that more cynical appraisal of Darwin's theory of terrestrial evolution embodied in Conrad's *Heart of Darkness*. The unutterable rites which Kurtz engages in have been translated into the researches of the nuclear physicist in *The Maniac's Dream*, and notions of the primitive and the advanced become generally problematic. In an early parable on this theme ('I Am Eden' [1946]), H. H. Kuttner has the scientist Jacklyn enter an Amazonian valley where he discovers the mineral necessary for the splitting of the atom. His experiment ends in failure but later explorers discover an Edenic valley dominated by a curious trinity: a diamond cave, a giant orchid and the scientist's long lost daughter. The daughter is rescued but the valley disintegrates in a cataclysm, ending Jacklyn's pious hope that 'two thousand years from now, there may be an allegory about this Eden, an allegory which will be read by a race not human, the race that is beginning in this valley now, the synthesis' (31). For Kuttner nuclear power symbolises a new way of being, perhaps a symbiosis of mineral, plant and animal life, but the surviving explorers quit the valley quoting the Bible: '*He placed at the East of Eden . . . a flaming sword . . . to keep the way of the tree of life*' (35). Like Kurtz's, Jacklyn's quest is doomed. At a tribal level, this see-sawing of the cultured and primitive societies pivoting on the discovery of nuclear power has been noted already in several fictions. In Margot Bennett's *The Long Way Back* (1965) a group of African archeologists visits the devastated wastes of Britain. Their own religion is overly cool and abstract (one's 'vital article' obeys the 'Noble Abstraction') and the wise men have outlawed books. They find giant frogs, man-eating ants and sand fused into precious stones, all evidence of what 'our own primitive forebears called the Big Bang' (14); the natives are thrown into a panic by the recorded sound of a nuclear explosion. But under the influence of the wise guide Brown, the hero learns to be humble also. Brown recalls garbled versions of the Christian Creation stories; in one, two people were underground in a place called Eden, 'so far down that the bang was not even heard. Then they came up and had children' (230). And in the last lines of the novel, Brown looks forward to the day when Britain will again 'become a nation that would conquer the Earth' (228). Set against this linear, Judaeo-Christian view of history is the hero's dawning appreciation of the Spenglerian cycles of history, as he gazes at the ruins of London 'in sad exaltation' (219), or misreads a weathered inscription on the ruins of a cathedral: for the Africans, '. .e p.a.e. o. .od pas. . . . a. . und. .sta. . .ng' becomes 'The place of God's passage and understanding' (223). For them London is a place of enlightenment, even if they miss the ample opportunities for satire concerning the earlier tribe's vanity.

J. Leslie Mitchell touches on similar themes in *Gay Hunter* (1934), where the eponymous hero, an American woman visiting London who indulges in a time-travelling experiment prompted by J. W. Dunne's *An Experiment with Time* (1927), finds herself in a post-disaster England leading a tribe of noble savages. A recorded voice in the Chiltern Dam powerhouse recounts a history of atomic attacks by the 'Transatlantics', the union of the Great Hierarchies into War States, the War Plagues, the revolt of the Sub-Men and finally the destruction of a tyrannical regime by the Army of the Communes (135). Gay learns about the savages' world through Rem, who communicates telepathically and warns her against other voices such as the 'song of the mad men' which still radiates from a huge communications reflector. Gay's companion enters the Shining Place (the ruins of London) and establishes an empire ruled by death rays. The novel descends to pulp fiction at this point, with Gay being tied to a phallic tower and threatened by man-eating rats. Nevertheless, Mitchell has a light and philosophical touch and introduces themes and techniques which were later to be used by more sophisticated writers of disaster fictions. The last line of the novel, for example – 'There are other songs' – nicely exposes the fictional basis of all such enterprises without undercutting them; indeed, the sentence sums up a compelling theme in the book, that of communication through 'radiation'. Gay Hunter's world is full of messages on the ether, a confusion of tribal chants, transmuted history, and radio and electronic impulses still emanating from the fatal high technology of the previous civilisation. There is an acute sense of literary tradition, too: Gay quotes Blake and Swinburne, accuses her companion of 'snivelling here like a thing in an Edwardian novel – being Wells-ish and save-humanitarian and oh-dear-planetish' (216), and is mindful as she explores this new world of 'the early Wells, of Flammarion, of their hosts of imitators' (47) (which include, of course, her own creator). Mitchell is even able to suggest for a moment a point of view antagonistic to the dominating Spenglerian one, when Gay observes to Rem,

'Here, in this evening quiet, you could sit and doubt even the endurance of change' (221).

If Sutphen's novel is the American *locus classicus* for evolutionary disaster fictions, the English equivalent would be G. A. England's *Darkness and Dawn* (1914), which features an Adam and Eve beating off apemen in the jungle to restart civilisation after devastating wars involving 'pulverite bombs . . . poisonous gases were thrown off, to impregnate the entire atmosphere of the world' (303). But half a century later, that Darwinian optimism had clearly been abandoned for a confusing relativism, nowhere better illustrated than in Angela Carter's *Heroes and Villains* (1969), a world of warring viewpoints where no one seems to win. The heroine Jewel grows up in the sterile 'ivory tower' of the learned men:

Before the war, there were places called Universities where men did nothing but read books and conduct experiments. These men had certain privileges, though mostly unstated ones; but all the same, some Professors were allowed in the deep shelters with their families, during the war, and they proved to be the only ones left who could resurrect the gone world in a gentler shape, and try to keep destruction outside, this time. (11)

But 'the melancholy whimsy of Professors gathered together over their after-dinner, home-brewed blackberry brandy when they would discuss apocalypses, utopias and so on' (132) seems etiolated compared to the lusty physicality of the savages who invade and 'rescue' Jewel. Out there in the real world Jewel meets the people who are battling to discover a new way of life, epitomised by Doctor Donally PhD, a crazy organ player who abuses his son, paints Adam and Eve on Jewel's back ('He wants to do the Last Judgment on my chest' [121]) and is obsessively aware that nuclear war has mocked evolutionary assumptions and even the notion of time itself: 'Time is going backwards and coiling up. Who let the spring go, I wonder, so that history wound back on itself?' (123)

Perhaps wisely, Carter gives no solution to this conflict. Evolution, natural or man-directed, is a precarious enough force at the best of times, and nuclear destruction seems to destroy the former and mock the latter. For these extrapolators of the farther effects of nuclear destruction, there seems generally to be a no man's land of warring principles and claims, with the signposts of religion, morality and humanism removed as effectively as the physical theories of Einstein removed the comfortable parameters of a Newtonian universe. Unlike many of the fictions discussed in Chapter 2, or to be discussed in the chapter on religion, these fictions subvert the notion that the irruption of nuclear war into the fabric of human history will have any one, overwhelming significance – the end of time, the end of man's vainglory, the end of science. Instead, time dribbles on in that horrific waste land so thoroughly envisaged for us already in the works of Eliot and Beckett. Mark Geston's *Out of the Mouth of the Dragon* (1969) is the clearest expression of this world view, implicit but often hidden beneath the layers of conventional 'goodies and baddies' warfare which are the vehicle for so many of these fictions. In Geston's world, the explorers of the stars have returned to Earth only to be attacked by the primitives who stayed behind. After an attenuated series of nuclear conflicts the land is blighted by contamination; hideous wolf-spiders disembowel themselves and the weary armies pray for an Armageddon. The hero plants his bayonet on the terminal beach which haunted the imaginations of past writers – Ballard (in *The Terminal Beach*), Wells (in *The Time Machine*), and even Arnold (in 'Dover Beach'). In this entropic end the human memory glows and fades, time endlessly lost and regained, played and replayed:

> Even the memories of what some men had seen faded; eventually they passed from the stage of memory to lapse back into the form of scriptural allegory, back into the turns of phrase they had worn before assuming concrete form, for a little while, on earth. (150)

The epigraphs from Revelation and the Book of Eric are mocked by the refusal of Geston to supply any kind of closure. Even as the hero slumps towards death, a technological glimmer appears – 'but then, perhaps some sort of echo-ranging apparatus might be lifted up by his eye and arm . . .' (156). So the mad carousel spins.

When one considers the biological aspect of future evolution, distinct from its philosophical implications, one is struck by a single phenomenon: mutation. Essential for any future history is reproduction, yet the 'last man' theme is a real, not only an imaginative, possibility. In James Elroy Flecker's *The Last Generation* (1908), for example, the 'Mutual Extermination Club' successfully practises self-imposed sterility, and Stephen Vincent Benet's poem 'Nightmare for Future Reference' (1938) focuses on the declining birthrate since the Third World War ('the one between Us and Them'):

> Well, we had a long run. That's something. At first they
>   thought
> There might be a nation somewhere – a savage tribe.
> But we were all in it, even the Eskimos,
> And we keep the toys in the stores, and the coloured books,
> And people marry and plan and the rest of it,
> But, you see, there aren't any children. They aren't born. (461)

When there are births, the possibility of mutation gives a new twist to evolutionary and religious concerns. The tourists to Zelazny's Greek resort discover mutant beasts reminiscent of the fabulous beasts of Greek legend, suggesting 'the convergence of life and myth, here, during the last days of life on this planet' (101). Generally, however, the results are less picturesque.

The early mutant stories were often pleas for tolerance of the exceptional. Lewis Padgett (alias H. H. Kuttner) wrote 'The Piper's Son' (1945) about Burkhalter, a 'Baldy' or telepathic mutant who, two generations after the Blowup, is helping a psychologist to write a book called *Psychohistory*. He sees himself as one of Nature's experiments ('After the deluge, me') with no spiritual advantages – 'We don't have horns or halos' (13). He avoids a fight with a neighbour, but reconciliation cannot work against a paranoid rabble-rouser who has been taking over children's minds with fascist doctrines such as 'God made us to rule lesser men.' In the novel version of the story, *Mutant*, Burkhalter leads the Baldies in a fight against these fascists, avoiding the easy solution of an 'Operation Apocalypse' which would destroy all non-telepaths. The spirit of reconciliation – 'we are one' – extends to the Baldies' explanation of their own affliction: 'God wouldn't have given us our power if He hadn't intended us to use it' (62) – a high-sounding moral which doesn't quite explain the nuclear holocaust itself.

A less qualified liberal message informs 'Tomorrow's Children' (1947) by Poul Anderson and P. N. Waldrop. The narrator, returned from a worldwide search for nuclear survivors, philosophises about how Spengler did not foresee nuclear bombs and their radical disruption; how the word 'pre-war' cuts like a sword 'across history with a brutality of murder, hazing everything in the past until it was a vague golden glow through drifting, red-shot black clouds' (18). The hero's next assignment for the President, ostensibly for the Census Bureau, is in fact to identify and destroy mutant children. Alarmed at the 75% live mutant birth rate, the President insists that 'the frustration of parenthood is . . . a cancer at the root of society' (36), but when his own wife gives birth to a mutant son he abandons his drastic solution. Anderson recalls that at the time of writing this story, 'the atom bomb was on everyone's mind. Few people questioned the dogma that a nuclear war would bring at least an eclipse of civilisation if not an extinction'.[20] In the expanded version of the story (*Twilight World*) the mutant heroes actually lead the tribe to the stars to a chorus of quotations from the *Elder Edda*.

Mutant children are often seen as the true inheritors of the world. In S. Martel's *The City Under Ground* the breakout from the underground world thousands of years after the Great Destruction is led by children; in H. M. Hoover's *Children of Morrow* two telepathic children escape from a repressive post-disaster regime; and in W. H. Shiras's *Children of the Atom* (1953), from a series of stories of 1948–50, an explosion at the Helium City power plant produces a race of masterminds who are concealed by their teachers from a crazy lay preacher who incites the people against them by calling them 'Satan's offspring' and witches. André Norton's *Star Man's Son* (or *Daybreak 2250 A.D.*) is the most well known of these fictions, with a million copies sold since 1952, suggesting to Donald Wollheim that 'a whole generation of Americans must have taken it for granted since their childhood.'[21] Here a mutant boy roams far from his eyrie through the deserted cities with his mutant cat Lura, fighting off giant lizards and rat-men, reconciling the warring tribes in a new brotherhood. There are some fine moments of what Douglas Hill calls the 'living-in-the-rubble theme', such as the discovery of a bank teller's skull amid the rusty coins of a decaying bank, but most of the story is adolescent adventure. There is little of the oppression of mutants which dominates in other such fictions: 'Mutant! For more than two hundred years – ever since the black days of chaos following the Great Blow-Up, the atomic war – that cry had been enough to condemn without trial' (2).

Perhaps the best-known story of child mutants is John Wyndham's *The Chrysalids* (or *Rebirth*) (1955). The religious folk of Waknuk have cleverly incorporated evolution into an apocalyptic view of the nuclear disaster or 'Tribulation', because after God's punishment for 'a phase of religious arrogance at the time' (40) the people are now 'in the process of climbing back into grace'. Deviationists are banished to the Fringes or badlands beyond, which is where the narrator David and his telepathic friends also escape to. Although Wyndham presents David's father's views with sympathy, his blindness to relativity and the insignificance of physical deformity (a captured Fringes raider is a mirror image of David's Father) is insupportable. The novel ably documents David's growth towards fuller knowledge of himself and the world beyond the town. His sense of relativity and possibility ('Nobody really *knows* what is the true image. They all *think* they know' [64]) helps him beyond the oppressions of his father's regime. The book is full of nets – the Sealanders use them as weapons, the Fringe leader 'Spider' seems associated with them, and David must escape the nets of conventional wisdom and classification – and Wyndham tries to match this complexity in his novel. Although the fleeing children are finally rescued by the highly evolved Sealanders, they are seen to have their human weaknesses: David's lover patronises his little sister Petra, perhaps the most accomplished telepath in the group, in the last lines, and we cannot help but admire the lusty bravery of the physical mutant Sophie. The Sealand woman speaks for the author in insisting on endless evolution:

Sometime there will come a day when we ourselves shall have to give place to a new thing. Very certainly we shall struggle against the inevitable just as these remnants of the Old People do. . . . The essential quality of life is living; the essential quality of living is change, change is evolution: and we are part of it. (195–6)

Still, it is hard to imagine a more perfect human spirit than the Sealander, and her tolerance is in fact based on a notion of the proper direction of evolution. As Gary Wolfe notes, the last pages, while not replacing 'the fundamental concern with attitudes towards those who are different, certainly raise questions that Wyndham does not offer to resolve'.[22] In addition, the rather lifeless prose style does little to suggest David's alienness from ourselves, even though in the course of the book 'he is supposed to become more like us in knowledge but less like us in kind'.[23]

There are, however, many fictions which explore the human reaction to mutation more as an imaginative challenge than as part of a theory of evolution. One of the simplest statements of a normal person's reaction is Judith Merril's 'That Only a Mother' (1948), for once focusing on the emotions of the bearer of that new life. A worried mother gives birth to what seems to her a normal, precocious child, but when the father enters he cradles his child and feels no skeleton; the shocked reader vividly admits the desperate self-delusion of a loving mother. Another early story, Fritz Leiber's 'Coming Attraction' (1950) has the narrator escorted by a masked girl into a New York nightclub where the anti-radiation clothing of the recent war has become fashionable. Railing against the superpowers ('Mutilated by each other, yet still strong, they were crippled giants poisoning the planet with their dreams of an impossible equality and an impossible success'), he witnesses the masked wrestling bouts between men and women, the sexual warfare of the club itself, and finally the raw wound beneath his hostess's mask – all symbols of a mutilated, decadent, '*Cabaret*'-style of lingering but deathly society.

The experience of being a mutant, particularly a psychic mutant, is a challenge for the imagination to which several authors have risen successfully. In his story 'Emergence' (1981) David Palmer presents the diary of an eleven year old girl trapped in her foster father's shelter, trying to cope by throwing a party for her parrot: 'gala party to celebrate passing of 2nd month. Was smash, high point of entombment, sensation of sepulchral social schedule' (30). She is a child prodigy and as such is immune from the germs triggered off by the nuclear explosions; as she explains it: 'Only difference between harmless tourist and pathogen: soothing counsel transmitted from pacific gene in DNA helix to cytoplasmic arsenal by radiation-vulnerable RNA messenger. Enter energy particle flood, exit restraint: hello Attila the Germ. Clever these mad scientists' (28). In this story, the child is exceptional before the blast and this very fact renders her immune to change, but Palmer adequately captures the mental processes of a genius in the extremity of nuclear disaster.

In *Freak's Amour* (1979) Tom de Haven imagines a psychedelic suburb suffering the effects of the Blofeld Blast, an accidental radiation leak:

77,000 had their chromosomes mugged. . . . Human fingers reshaped themselves into rasorial bird claws, skulls ballooned or stretched until they resembled butternut squash. Arms – like Da's right one – grew as long as boa constrictors and then became paralysed. Flesh thickened into pachydermal hide or cloaked itself with monkey fur. Teeny blind eyes (some human and some not) burst through cheeks and palms and (just like Mary Shelley's nightmare) the nipples of breasts. And, like what happened to Ma, and was passed on to me, pores gave birth to fish scales and gills. (15)

While the physical setting is firmly established (Antichrist Newsboys parading with nooses around their necks) and life goes on normally elsewhere in the city, de Haven cleverly mingles hallucination and reportage until the dividing line between real and imaginary, normal and mutant, is blurred. People are leaving the area either in space-rockets or in their spaced-out minds – 'The world's got skin cancer . . . it's got lung cancer. Brain cancer. It's dying. We want to survive, we take our leave' (240) – and all meaning to the event is possible and impossible:

Things are more like comic books than Rosetta Stones. . . . There were also, of course, the more bizarre hypotheses, full of such cosmic characters and sentiments as God, the Devil and Reckoning Day. Da would smile, then twist his mouth out of shape. 'Reckoning Day, shit! Why should we've been singled Out?' (240, 18)

One of the most successfully sustained visions of mutation is

Daniel Galouye's *Dark Universe* (1961). Jared lives with other
survivors in the remains of one of the US Survival Complexes.
They harvest 'manna' in an underground orchard fed with
cricket and bat manure and watered by underground springs.
The people cannot see, but find their way using echoing 'click-
stones' as a crude radar. The Great God Light Almighty will
return one day, for once he dwelt in vessels like the Holy Bulb.
Priests conduct ceremonies like the Excitation of the Optic
Nerves, laying fingers on people's foreheads so that they can see
the Almighty. The twin devils, cobalt and strontium, wait to
carry people off to the depths of Radiation. The remarkable
text is purged of all reference to sight. Jared believes in whatever
he can hear, taste, smell or feel, and he struggles towards the
upper world in a blind terror. When he finally encounters light
he can describe it only in these terms: 'a great cone of roaring
silence . . . a tremendous burst of sound . . . something that
wasn't sound or smell or touch' (31). Consistent with Galouye's
ironic reversal of the usual religious imagery of light, Jared feels
that the light was more like a nuclear explosion: 'The light was
not in paradise. It was in the Infinity of Radiation with the
Nuclear monsters . . . for men there was no paradise' (150).
Jared is finally rescued by surface dwellers but he and his clan
retain an extra-sensory perception as a result of their sensory
deprivation for so long. The story is resonant with mythical
overtones. For one critic the shelter is Plato's cave and the
journey reveals 'a kind of reverse *Heart of Darkness* where the
Light may be simply a larger cave';[24] for another, 'the birth and
related sexual imagery of *Dark Universe* is an excellent means
of reinforcing the innocence-to-experience theme of the novel',[25]
with Jared's pilgrimage a harrowing of hell as well as a birth
passage. More importantly, once the reader realises what is
going on, there is the pervasive irony that Jared's predicament,
his temporary mutation, has been caused by human beings
seeking the light of knowledge only to plunge themselves into
the dark in one apocalyptic illumination which is a travesty of
spiritual enlightenment.

    Philip Dick's *Dr. Bloodmoney* (1965) takes place above ground
in San Francisco following Dr Bluthgeld's ('Bloodmoney')
nuclear accident in 1972. This Strangelovian character is
overshadowed by the mutants his experiment has created,
especially Hoppy Harrington, a 'phocomelus' confined to a

wheelchair but skilled in technology and, like Jared, developing extrasensory powers in compensation. When the actual nuclear attack comes Hoppy is safe in his basement refusing to go up immediately ('That was the mistake those Japs made; they came right up and smiled' [69]), while Bluthgeld sees the disintegrating world as if in a dream:

Good Christ, he thought. What is it? He peered into the sooty fog; the sky was gone, obscured entirely by the rain of dark.

And then he saw, picking about in the gloom, among the split sections of concrete, in the debris, little shrivelled shapes; people, the pedestrians who had been there before and then vanished – they were back now, but all of them dwarfed, and gaping at him sightlessly, not speaking but simply poking about in an aimless manner.

What is it? he asked himself again, this time speaking aloud; he heard his voice dully rebounding. It's all broken; the town is broken up into pieces. What has hit it? What has happened to it? He began walking from the pavement, finding his way among the strewn, severed parts of Berkeley. It isn't me, he realised; some great terrible catastrophe has happened. The noise, now, boomed in his ears, and the soot stirred, moved by the noise. A car horn sounded, stuck on, but very far off and faint. (60)

This high quality of writing is maintained throughout the novel. Dr Stockstill's reaction, internalising the cataclysm, is in keeping with the psychological emphasis: 'The impersonal has attacked us. That is what it is; attacked us from inside and out. The end of the co-operation, where we applied ourselves together. Now it's atoms only. Discrete, without any windows. Colliding but not making any sound, just a general hum' (67).

Gradually the society reforms. Air Force planes drop leaflets directing survivors to Burlingame for water, anti-plague shots and treatment for burns. Eldon Blaine the optometrist does a roaring trade in spectacles, and makeshift pharmacies spring up everywhere. Horses pull carts, and electronic vermin traps are made out of unexploded Russian rocket parts. Finally Bonny the earth mother reunites the scattered remnants of the tribe and leads them back to the city. Bluthgeld's insane ranting is only ended by Hoppy's 'mind-murder' of him:

> My job is to wait here, tending my sheep, waiting for him who is to come, the man appointed to deal out final justice. The world's avenger. . . . The high altitude bombs which I set off in 1972 find reinforcement in the present act, sanctioned by God himself in his wisdom for the world. See the Book of Revelation for verification . . . have you cleansed yourselves . . . are you prepared for the judgement which is to come? (138)

In a bizarre assortment of misfits, Dick's supreme creation is Dangerfield, who was shot off to Mars years ago with his wife and got stuck in orbit round the earth. From there he broadcasts to the world, acting as a voice of and for the people: he gathers medical advice and disseminates handy hints ('Things you can do with the timer out of an old RCA washer dryer combination' [109]), reads regularly from Maugham's *Of Human Bondage* and dispenses homely wisdom – 'Want to know the reason I wasn't in the war? Why they carefully shot me off into space a little bit in advance? They knew better than to give me a gun . . . I would have shot an officer'. Doomed Dangerfield is nothing less than the voice of man, resilient yet fated, individual yet bonded to our planet and cipher for the world.

Within the exactly rendered experience of Dick's mutant terrestrial survivors there is a pattern and message. As discerned by the critic Jameson and approved by Dick himself,[26] *Dr. Bloodmoney* traces the re-alignment of the human axis from Bluthgeld/Hoppy (symbolising the theory and practice of technology) to Dangerfield/Bill (the sender and receiver of information). Bill is the homunculus twin of Edie, carried within her own womb, who communicates telepathically with his sister and with Hoppy. It is he who perceives Hoppy's megalomaniacal ambitions (including the murder of Dangerfield) and exchanges places with him, leaving Hoppy to wither and die in the tiny host body. Everyone in the novel lacks something physical or spiritual and is therefore mutant in some degree, and only the communicators are able to bridge the gaps and restore wholeness, both to individuals and to communities. The novel, then, has a positive message, especially in its focus on the traditional do-it-yourself virtues and Bonny's pastoral simplicity. As Jameson says, Dick looks forward to an 'artisanal world . . . some genuinely Jeffersonian commonwealth beyond the bomb . . . [Dick is] the unseasonable spokesman for an historical consciousness distinct from and superior to that limited dystopian and apocalyptic vision so fashionable in western science fiction today.'[27]

One other sub-species of mutant fiction must be considered here, the satirical treatment which lurks close to the surface of so much disaster fiction. In William Tenn's 'Null-P', for example, the future evolution of man comes to a bleak end when, in the conservative fear following disaster, scientists discover George Abnego, miraculous embodiment of the statistical average. He is soon elected President of a banal land whose 'outstanding cultural phenomena' include 'carefully rhymed and exactly metred poems addressed to the nondescript beauties and vague charms of a wife or a sweetheart' (134). Finally *homo abnegus* is superceded by a race of dogs. In an equally grotesque genetic reaction to nuclear disaster Aldous Huxley gave us *Ape and Essence* in 1949. The framework is the discovery by a Hollywood hack writer of a script which (literally) fell off the back of a truck. The author was a romantic doomed to uncover life's sordid reality, and the tension between idealism and disillusionment plays over the rest of the book. The nuclear war is disposed of in one jeering image of two warring tribes of apes and we enter the American post-disaster society from the objective viewpoint of a New Zealand expedition. Because their loins are blighted by radiation, the ragged mass worships Satan: 'What is the chief end of Man? Answer: The chief end of man is to propitiate Belial, deprecate his enmity and avoid destruction for as long as possible' (68). The essence of the new religion is misogyny: the womb is the focus of all hatred, women wear blouses printed with 'NO NO' and the men pray for detumescence. Sexual activity is confined to a horrific session of satanic worship where mutant babies are sacrificed and a general orgy ensues. The expedition's leader Poole falls in love with Loola and, via Shelley's 'Adonais', discovers true love in an optimistic second half which answers the depraved evolution-denying, futureless dystopia of the first. Poole has travelled the same journey as the duke in *Measure for Measure* from which Huxley takes his central image:

> . . . man, proud man
> Drest in a little brief authority,
> Most ignorant of what he's most assur'd,
> His glassy essence, like an angry ape,
> Plays such fantastic tricks before high heaven
> As make the angels weep . . .

We are left with the transcriber's moral (he is called 'Tallis', near enough to the Hebrew word for 'prayer shawl'[28]): 'Only in the knowledge of his own essence has any man ceased to be many monkeys.' Huxley, like his imagined scriptwriter, utilises the convention of fiction to help the reader see himself as in a mirror. By opening the novel on the day in 1948 when Ghandi was assassinated, he keeps us from losing ourselves in the future or in fantasy, and challenges us to apply our vision to the here and now, to escape the escalator of mindless evolution or devolution.

That, of course, is the message of most of these fictions of evolution. There are the pulp exceptions (like Clark Darlton's *Mutants vs. Mutants*, an excuse for a good shoot-out, or A. M. Lightner's *The Day of the Drones*, where an African expeditionary force discovers European survivors of the holocaust dominated by huge mutant bees), but on the whole these various futures are proffered in order for us to clarify just what we think is man's essence, and where our next step should take us, as we ourselves were taken beyond the apes. The fiction of nuclear disaster has capitalised on the fortuitous 'side-effect' of genetic deformity and mutation to foreground the evolutionary question. Very few of these visions have been as sanguine as that of the nuclear physicist Edward Teller, who protested against the 'fall-out scare': 'Because abnormalities deviate from the norm, they may be offensive at first sight, but without such abnormal births and such mutations, the human race would not have evolved and we would not be here.'[29] To regard nuclear war as an evolutionary step would be abhorrent to most of the writers considered here; it is, rather, an interruption of evolution, a denial and even a destruction of the very concept. What we must do, here and now, is to incorporate into our understanding of ourselves the capacity to destroy on a vast scale. That alteration and enlargement of our conception of humanity is helped by our incorporating minority groups and exceptions such as those symbolised by mutation. Having enlarged our 'biological' conception, we must then face the moral issues, a question which the next chapter focuses on more directly. Edward Shanks's early disaster novel *The People of the Ruins* (1920) could imagine only a familiar England 150 years hence, with civil war raging. But, at the end, the hero points a gun to his own head. That is the central question posed by these evolutionary fictions: what is our reaction as readers to the end of mankind as we know it? How fiercely do we believe in community and the fragile continuity of human experience? Brian Stableford, considering stories of atomic holocaust, writes, 'In the final analysis, what these stories have in common as their fundamental assumption is the argument that we do not – and perhaps cannot – care enough about one another. We are all estranged, and even when we do not find it all too easy to hate one another we still find it far too difficult to care much one way or the other what happens to people.'[30] Nuclear disaster, the intended extinction of one tribe by another, is indeed a problematic baseline for a vision of man's evolution: is it a survival instinct or a death instinct? But while these fictions may set up a tribal backcloth, the focus is individuals, and from Merril to Huxley, even to Stacy, love is celebrated; and with love, childbirth. Children dominate this area of disaster fiction because the womb of the future appeals to the womb of the present; in talking about the end of Man we are talking about our children. A short story by Edward Bryant called 'Jody After the War' may therefore epitomise the central concerns of this chapter. A young couple lie on a clifftop about to make love, but the half-Indian girl cannot rid herself of the nightmare of pregnancy with radiation sickness – the future renders the present impotent. That, for all the fertility of invention displayed in these stories, is their final warning.

'Satan Thrown into the Bottomless Pit', A. Dürer, Apocalypse series, Frederick van der Meer, *Apocalypse: Visions from the Book of Revelation in Western Art* (London: Thames & Hudson) p. 304.

5 Apocalypses and Revelations

We would rather be ruined than changed,
We would rather die in our dread
Than climb the cross of the moment
And let our illusions die.[1]

The word 'apocalypse' comes from the Hebrew word meaning 'to reveal' or 'what is revealed . . . a revelation'; it is a word, as David Ketterer observes, 'as fashionable and relevant to our times as it is carelessly and inconsistently employed in critical discourse'.[2] From Tom Lehrer's song of the fifties about the GI gaily marching off to Armageddon, to Coppola's 1982 film about the Vietnam experience (*Apocalypse Now*), to Schell's *The Fate of the Earth* where the word 'holocaust' is used alongside scientific terminology – the language of Biblical apocalypse has been transferred effortlessly and wholesale to the description of late twentieth century angst and, in particular, the secular menace of nuclear destruction.

Science fiction, within whose dimly defined borders the earliest fictions of nuclear disaster were formulated until the early fifties, has always had a metaphysical and eschatological dimension, so Biblical imagery came naturally to it. The development of nuclear technology seemed merely to fulfil the implication of these allusions:

> Gunther Anders has said that since 1945 the axiom that 'all men are mortal' has acquired a sinister corollary, to the effect that 'all men are exterminable'. The change of consciousness brought about by this new axiom has been one of the principal forces shaping post-war science fiction, making it a literature of anxiety, often apocalyptic in tone and content.[3]

115

The politicians and military theorists came more recently but as inevitably to the same imagery. At the first nuclear testings Winston Churchill talked of 'this *revelation* of the secrets of nature long mercifully withheld from man' (my italics);[4] President Truman in a speech of 1945 said, 'It is an awful responsibility which has come to us. We thank God that it has come to us instead of to our enemies, and we pray that He may guide us to use it in His ways and for His purposes';[5] and Major G. F. Eliot said at the same time:

> This is no repetition of the warnings which have been written before the publication of the first use of atomic force as a weapon. Those warnings were based on the known nature of pre-atomic war. They were warnings of chaos and terror, but they were not warnings of the end of the world, only of the end of a particular phase of civilisation.[6]

Survivalists and many other critics of such extreme language have argued that such talk of global annihilation is simplistic, erroneous and perhaps even a deep kind of wish fulfilment. But the Biblical imagery remains tenaciously appropriate since what is contemplated is not so much the end of the physical world as proof of man's degeneracy and the end of the Christian era. Again, the nuclear threat was seen in these terms as early as 1945, when Chancellor Robert Hutchins of the University of Chicago said:

> A French philosopher referred to the 'good news of damnation' – doubtless on the theory that none of us would be Christians if we weren't afraid of perpetual hellfire. It may be that the atomic bomb is the 'good news of damnation', that it may frighten us into that Christian character and those righteous actions and those positive political steps necessary to the creation of a world society.[7]

Before going further, it is perhaps best to refresh our minds concerning 'apocalyptic'. It is the form of recorded revelation in Judaism from around 200 B.C. to A.D. 200, inspired by a feeling of despair about present circumstances and a belief that direct revelation of the affairs of God is possible, through dream, vision or divine intermediary – usually a prophet. The revelation usually involves an assurance of the intrusion of the divine will into human affairs with the subsequent redemption, in some form or other, of the chosen people. Pierre Grelot distinguishes four apocalyptic subject matters: the mysteries of God, Heaven and Hell; the mysteries of the divine plan for the universe; the mysteries of the origins of the world; and the mystery of the individual destiny.[8] The subject matter is therefore extremely wide, extending from theology to science, mankind to the individual; the common element is that such secret knowledge must be revealed in a special way, usually 'to some hero of the faith of past days'.[9]

Although Biblical apocalyptic talked of 'last things' through the mouthpiece of an historical figure its impulse was acutely contemporary, namely 'the feelings of eschatological anguish which are brought to a climax by the bloody conflict with the totalitarian empire of Antiochus Epiphanes (170–164 B.C.).'[10] The anticipated judgment was likewise related to the immediate context of crisis:

> The court of judgment was about to be set up, and sentence about to be executed on the great world empires, and the Golden Age was about to burst in its glory. It was no distant hope that they held out to the faithful, but one on the point of being realised, and because it was set forth in association with the recognisable past and the recognisable present, it forcefully declared that it trafficked not in the things that should some time come to pass, but in things that were right here . . .
>
> The prophets foretold the future that should arise out of the present, while the apocalyptists foretold the future that should break into the present. . . . The apocalyptists had little faith in the present to beget the future.[11]

As for the nature of that future, there was generally a transitional period of great strife before the Day of Judgment, but developing Jewish notions of an afterlife did not completely supplant the notion of a future new Jerusalem established here on Earth:

> Throughout this whole process, from Daniel to II Edras, we find evidence, then, of a tension between a this-worldly kingdom and an other-worldly kingdom. In the earlier period

especially the former of these predominates and even when, in later years, the influence of the latter makes itself increasingly felt it does not oust from people's minds the earlier hope whose roots can be traced back to ancient prophetic expectations. In their teaching concerning a millennial or a temporary kingdom to be followed through resurrection and judgment by the 'age to come' they were expressing a compromise which witnesses to the strength of that traditional faith which looked forward to the establishment of the rule of God not only over his own people in their own land, but also over all people throughout the whole earth.[12]

The history of millennial thought and of Biblical exegesis shows the gradual adaptation of these apocalyptic notions which were applicable specifically to the historical plight of the Jewish nation, to other and more personal forms of religious conviction. Northrop Frye distinguishes the historical apocalypse of 'staggering marvels' from the apocalypse which converts the reader, 'a vision that passes through the legalised vision of ordeals and trials and judgments and comes out into a second life. . . . The apocalyptic is the way the world looks after the ego has disappeared'.[13] Yet D. H. Lawrence, while acknowledging the intention of apocalyptic to 'wake the imagination and give us at moments a new universe to live in',[14] is suspicious of the motivation underlying it all; he identifies that motivation as 'the undying will-to-power in man and its sanctification, its final triumph'. Lawrence's point seems to be supported by the history of millennial movements, at least according to Norman Cohn:

> So it came about that multitudes of people acted out with fierce energy a shared phantasy which, though delusional, yet brought them such intense emotional relief that they could live only through it. . . . It is a phenomenon . . . not irrelevant to the growth of totalitarian movements, with their messianic leaders, their millennial mirages and their demon-scapegoats, in the present century.[15]

Frank Kermode, another 'literary' commentator, also feels that the ideological expression of apocalyptic is fascism, 'its practical consequence the Final Solution.'[16]

Clearly, when writers and readers adopt a system of imagery from another time and place, they may be doing so for a variety of motives, not all admirable. There is also room for much confusion when the imagery of apocalyptic is adopted into a secular context and the already confused notions of an interim period of strife (the thousand year reign of the Devil), Judgment Day and the new Jerusalem, struggle to find some secular counterpart. Nevertheless a basic symbolic pattern common to millennial thought and the fiction of nuclear disaster, is noted by W. H. Oliver:

> In the early nineteenth century, if one called the Revolution, or popular democracy, or the Napoleonic Empire Antichrist, one added a great deal. Today's apocalypses appeal in their own right – their mythological shoring up, if it exists, is as likely to come from science fiction as from Christianity.
>
> Yet, as science fiction, the U.F.O. hypothesis and related beliefs show, many of the old symbols are transmuted rather than eliminated. Very frequently . . . one finds a scenario essentially made up of three acts – original purity, intervening disorder, restored purity. Purity, both original and restored, comes from elsewhere. . . .
>
> Few contemporary apocalypses, except those still reproduced by Christian fundamentalists, retain the intimacy and comfort of a prospective providential rescue, except the markedly post-Christian versions of science fiction. No one else appears to believe that we can save ourselves from the bomb, or from people, except by our own arduous effort. Whether this is gain or loss is quite another question.'[17]

What Oliver does not consider are fictions which 'play with' these various apocalyptic schemata within the context of an undeniable disaster which has much in common, imagistically at any rate, with Biblical apocalyptic: nuclear disaster. These are the most vivid examples of what Brian Stableford has correctly identified as a tendency of modern literature to confront the 'last things' which were the subject of the similar Jewish period of tribal crisis; and as he observes, 'A remarkable phenomenon associated with the boom is the resurgence of images which are obviously analogues of religious notions but which are disconnected from religious doctrine.'[18]

It is no coincidence that several of my references here have been to creative writers or literary critics, for we are dealing primarily with a system of images. For us, at any rate, questions of Jewish history and Biblical exegesis are not as important as questions of symbol, voice and the expression of the inexpressible. In the field of free play which is art, the rhetoric of the religious zealot and the secular millenarian converge. This is how Melvin Laski concludes a chapter called 'The Metaphysics of Doomsday':

> *Thunder and lightning . . . overturning days . . . teetering and tumbling affairs . . . blood will have blood . . . doomes-day drawing nigh . . . the rule of the just . . . a true reformation . . . a flood tide of change . . . audacious men and dark prophecies . . . words are actions . . . the minds of men . . . purge the nation . . . overthrow the rotten structures . . . the holy destruction of the evil of oppression and injustice . . . the golden age is at hand . . . the fire and the sword.*

For three centuries these accents, with a few historic variations, would remain the basic elements in the world of the radical temper. They are the constant links in the great chain of human hope. A modern cycle of revolution would begin with its saints and would end with its scientists. But there is a meeting-point – and it is, as we shall see again and again, an emotive as well as a semantic convergence – between the new radical who would dream of secular solutions in terms of religious forms or phrases and the old rebel who envisioned an eschatological end to his this-worldy struggle for the good cause. One man's metaphor was always another man's reality.[19]

Of course there are extremes in the literary expression of 'last things', ranging from the deliberately purged and sterile vision of J. B. S. Haldane in his essay ironically entitled 'The Last Judgment'[20] to the flood of apocalyptic imagery in the work of Norman O. Brown.[21] Of course, also, there are fictions of nuclear disaster which look forward to an establishment of a new Jerusalem as the author would like to see it, or even to the disaster itself as 'something good in itself'.[22] But there is still room for an engaging apocalyptic literature, one which, as Ketterer defines it, is 'concerned with the creation of other worlds which exist, on the literal level, in a credible relationship (whether on the basis of traditional extrapolation and analogy or religious belief) with the "real" world, thereby causing a metaphorical destruction of that "real" world in the reader's head.'[23] This function of what Darko Suvin elsewhere calls 'cognitive estrangement'[24] is the essential feature of all science fiction, and is exactly what F. A. Kreuziger is describing in his book *Apocalyptic and Science Fiction* when he talks about 'disjunctive expectation . . . a radical dehistoricising of the present, this in-between time'.[25]

The fiction of nuclear disaster, then, shares many of the concerns of Biblical apocalyptic, if not a specific historical and eschatological one. In literary terms, it also encounters similar problems and often mimics the strategems of solution found in the Bible.

One issue is the limitations of language. Biblical apocalyptic resorts to similes, negatives, parodies and analogies in its attempt to describe the indescribable, leading one commentator of Revelation to say, 'While it is a stunningly imaginative creation, it contains, in that very imaginative thrust, an enormously important theme in the history of art . . . the limits of human imagination.'[26] When it does use symbolism, Biblical apocalyptic borrows from a wide variety of mythologies (including Greek and Oriental) and does not enlarge upon the symbol, preferring to leave the text as a juxtaposition of images profoundly enigmatic. While we have already seen descriptions of the nuclear holocaust and aftermath which take the imagination some way down the scientific, descriptive path, they often fail to dislocate the mind sufficiently to suggest the vastness and enormity of the disaster; only a few writers have learnt from the studied reticence of the Biblical apocalyptists.

Another issue is the notion of voice. Unlike the prophets, the apocalyptists recorded their own visions but borrowed names from ancient heroes – Enoch, Abraham, Ezra, Daniel and so on – to use as mouthpieces transparently fictional but also authoritatively transcendent. This tradition of 'pseudonymity' includes the personal testimonies of Paul and John of Patmos to the extent that they seldom identify individuals in the apocalyptic drama, choosing instead to describe outstanding features so that the characters become enigmatic, somewhere between reality and symbol. The apocryphal Apocalypse of Paul, however, retains a vivid sense of an eyewitness (the scene could have come directly from the streets of Hiroshima):

> And I saw other men and women covered in dust, and their faces were like blood, and they were in a pit of tar and brimstone, and they were running in a river of fire, and I asked: Who are these, Lord? And he said to me: They are those who have committed the iniquity of Sodom and Gomorrah.(39)

Associated with voice is the notion of secrecy. Much is made of the speaker's secret sources, either to heighten dramatic tension (as with the unrolling of the scrolls in Revelation like 'the anticipatory raising of the curtain to display the final scene'[27]) or to suggest terrible truths best kept hidden ('But you, Daniel, must keep these words secret and the book sealed until the time of the End' [Daniel 12:4]). The prophet Ezra dictated to five scribes 'in characters which they knew not' (2 Ezdras 14:42) and God directed him to publish twenty-four books and keep seventy for the wise (14:45). The final words of Revelation, indeed of the whole Bible, concern the sacred secrecy of the text: 'If anyone cuts anything out of the prophecies in this book, God will cut off his share of the tree of life and of the holy city, which are described in the book' (Rev. 22:19). This foregrounding of the text itself is a technique often used by writers of nuclear disaster fictions (for example Roshwald, Blumenfeld, Gee, all the found diaries). Another common technique is the manuscript found in a bottle, or more commonly in a fall-out shelter. Often books from the pre-disaster world take on this sacred mystery, particularly when an oppressive regime wants to limit knowledge of history or science.

Finally, the imagery of Biblical apocalyptic is ubiquitous in the literature with which I am dealing, often so ingrained into our habits of thought and turns of phrase as to pass unnoticed. There are at least seventeen books in the Bible which are 'apocalyptic', but they share common patterns of imagery.[28] The first period of trial on earth generally involves destructive warfare. Joel describes an enemy army sweeping across the countryside in a path of devastation: 'In their van the fire devours, in their rear a flame consumes. The country is like a garden of Eden ahead of them and a desert waste behind them' (Joel 2:3). The waste land is purged by fire, with all religious icons or 'holocausts' (a powerful complex of images to be discussed shortly) destroyed (e.g. Maccabees 4:46, Psalms 74:8–9). After John's red rider of war come biological and environmental horrors. The riders of John's first four seals are given authority over one quarter of the earth 'to kill by the sword, by famine, by plague and wild beasts' (Rev. 6:8). Disease is a staple of apocalyptic, as in Zechariah: 'Their flesh will moulder while they are still standing on their feet; their eyes will rot in their sockets; their tongues will rot in their mouths' (Zechariah 14:12–14). If this is suggestive of nuclear radiation, John is even more prophetic:

> The third angel blew his trumpet, and a huge star fell from the sky, burning like a ball of fire, and it fell on a third of all rivers and springs; this was the star called Wormwood, and a third of all water turned to bitter wormwood, so that many people died from drinking it. (Rev. 8:10–11)

By the time of the sixth seal, physical upheavals occur, the sun going black, the moon red, and the stars falling down. Isaiah is particularly vivid:

> Yes the sluice-gates above will open,
> and the foundations of the earth will rock.
> The earth will split into fragments,
>   the earth will be riven and rent.
> The earth will shiver and shake,
> The earth will stagger like a drunkard.
>
> (Isaiah 24:18–20)

One finds here a ready-made description of the micro- and macro-cosms of a nuclear detonation. And the firestorm soon follows, as the Christian Sibyllines foretold:

> Woe to thee wretched, woe malevolent sea!
> Thou shalt be wholly consumed by fire, and with brine shalt destroy a people.
> For there shall be as much fire raging upon earth
> As water, it shall rush and destroy all the land.
> It shall burn up mountains, set rivers afire, empty the springs.

The world shall be no world, when men are destroyed.
Dreadfully burning, then shall the wretches look
To heaven, lit no more with stars, but with fire.
Nor shall they perish quickly, but dying in the flesh
Yet burning in spirit for years of ages
They shall know that God's law is not to be deceived.[29]

After these 'quick' initial upheavals there usually follows a drawn out, agonising and lingering death like that of radiation sickness, usually described in terms of fire, disease, and the persecution of wild beasts. It is a time of private suffering, and while one can trace the more public prophecies of doom throughout English literature, from Milton and Blake to Shelley and Tennyson,[30] it is perhaps typical of fiction and of the twentieth century that these apocalyptic patterns of imagery should be internalised into the landscape of nightmare, or even controverted for effect, since they are so familiar. This is what happens in D. H. Lawrence's *Women in Love*. Lawrence, deeply familiar with apocalyptic literature, sees as modern man's darkest fears not the possibility of apocalypse, but the possibility that there will *not* be an apocalypse – and he describes it in imagery the opposite of the blinding flash of fire:

As for the future, that they never mentioned except one laughed out some mocking dream of the destruction of the world by a ridiculous catastrophe of man's invention: a man invented such a perfect explosive that it blew the earth in two, and the two halves set off in different directions through space. . . . Or else, Loerke's dream of fear: the world went cold, and snow fell everywhere, and only white creatures, Polar bears, white foxes, and men like awful white snow-birds, persisted in ice cruelty.[31]

The best fictions of nuclear disaster adapt apocalyptic imagery in a similarly sophisticated way.

Just as the imagery is ubiquitous, so is the narrative reference to religion: people turn naturally to forms of religion before, during, and after the holocaust, because it provides a framework – imaginative, ethical, spiritual – within which they can comprehend the grotesque events around them. Because of this, it is difficult to isolate in this chapter those stories with a religious component. We have already come across preachers in *The Long Tomorrow*, and in most pre-disaster narratives there is, as in Jameson's *The Giant Atom*, a background crowd of zealots waving banners which read 'PREPARE FOR THE EVIL DAY THAT COMETH' (49). But in this chapter I will examine fictions which have religious ideas as a central theme.

Before looking at these fictions I should give some modern examples of the literary techniques which were the special invention of the apocalyptists. The importance of 'the word' is illustrated Pierrepont Noyes's *The Pallid Giant* (1927), where a manuscript discovered in a cave tells of the discovery of Klepton-Holorif, from which nuclear weapons are made. The world is subsequently devastated, 'the human species abandoned, forgotten by that departing sun, and left by a pitiless God to pay the penalty alone for sins of a self-destroying race' (282). But the manuscript itself is laid out typographically like a Bible and the reader is meant to feel that he is reading not fiction but prophecy:

¶ 'Preserve this record,' thus my father spoke, 'as warning to mankind. Here may all future generations read how pride and intellect uncurbed by fellow-love brought low the human race, – brought man to this, – ' He pointed through the window where our 'nar-'lights faded to the gloomy darkness of the sea, and monstrous shadowy forms moved to and fro. 'More cruel than those monsters there have men become. The few still left alive now skulk in dark recesses of the sea, hiding from dangers, which their cruel fear alone creates. To you and Promil's son belongs the task of saving these. What I have written here, I leave with you.'
¶ This is the tale my father told: –
¶ War raged through all the world. Yet 'twas not war alone but preparation for its gruesome harvests drove man from that early paradise he had attained through countless centuries of toil and misery. . . . At first devices for defence kept pace with new machines for killing men. But in the end these lagged and war grew ever more calamitous. For two long generations then, none dared to fight; fear kept the peace. Yet that same fear made war inevitable . . . (194–5)

The opposition of book and fire, or thought and action, is

collapsed only at the final apocalyptic conflagration in the Bible when the 'word' of God, and the word of the apocalyptists, becomes flesh, or rather fire. Books like Noyes's document can be preserved from the fire, but if what they say is true they will be consumed by the fire they prophesy. Through this ironic consummation runs another symbolic thread, that of the book being destroyed by ignorance – which is why the apocalyptic books are so secretive in source. In the twentieth century imagination it is the burning of books, rather than the burning of people, which symbolises tyranny and the brutish, man-made apocalypse.

We can see rising out of this concatenation of images a group of fictions which explores the relationship of the word to power, and find there a profound expression in secular terms of the religious debates and claims of apocalyptic. Elias Canetti's *Auto da Fé* (1946) ends with his bookish hero immolating himself in his precious library as the Nazis begin their holocausts of imaginative literature in the street outside. While not specifically nuclear, Canetti's novel points directly towards Bradbury's *Fahrenheit 451* (1954) where the imaginative 't's are finally crossed. In Fireman Montag's brave new world, which has waged two successful nuclear wars since 1960, the Promethean mastery of fire in the form of nuclear power requires also the domestic mastery of books by fire to maintain the totalitarian regime (as Orwell predicted, only totalitarian states can afford to wage nuclear war). Montag finally escapes from the hellish city (which is replete with a mechanical Hound straight out of the pages of Revelation) and joins a band of booklovers. The leader Grainger greets him with 'Welcome back from the dead' and, of course, assigns to him the Book of Revelation – but also part of Ecclesiastes, the book which preaches 'All is vanity' and ends, 'Of making of many books there is no end.' Montag learns humility and also the necessity of making no end to books. He vows to absorb the world by observing it and so he watches the nuclear destruction of his city across the river. It is one of the best descriptions of disaster that I know of, for Bradbury captures the sense of utter change in the twinkling of an eye, alluding to apocalyptic symbolism but never deserting the precious, personal viewpoint:

Perhaps the bombs were there, and the jets, ten miles, five

miles, one mile up, for the merest instant, like grain thrown over the heavens by a great sowing hand, and the bombs drifting with dreadful swiftness, yet sudden slowness, down upon the morning city they had left behind. The bombardment was to all intents and purposes finished, once the jets had sighted their target, alerted their bombardiers at five thousand miles an hour; as quick as the whisper of a scythe the war was finished. Once the bomb-release was yanked it was over. Now, a full three seconds, all of the time in history, before the bombs struck, the enemy ships themselves were gone half around the visible world, like bullets in which a savage islander might not believe because they were invisible; yet the heart is suddenly shattered, the body falls in separate motions and the blood is astonished to be freed upon the air; the brain squanders its few precious memories and, puzzled, dies.

This was not to be believed. It was merely a gesture. Montag saw the flirt of a great metal fist over the far city and he knew the scream of the jets that would follow, would say, after the deed, *disintegrate, leave no stone on another, perish. Die. . . .*

For another of those impossible instants the city stood, rebuilt and unrecognisable, taller than it had ever hoped or strived to be, taller than man had built it, erected at last in gouts of shattered concrete and sparkles of torn metal into a mural hung like a reversed avalanche, a million colours, a million oddities, a door where a window should be, a top for a bottom, a side for a back, and then the city rolled over and fell down dead.

The sound of its death came after. (151–3)

Kurt Vonnegut's *Slaughterhouse-Five* (1969) continues this apocalyptic meditation on fire and the book. In hospital, Billy Pilgrim talks to a history professor who is reading President Truman's announcement of the Hiroshima bomb as well as accounts of the fire-bombing of Dresden, in which Billy had been caught. The professor concludes ruefully, 'The advocates of nuclear disarmament seem to believe that if they could achieve their aim, war would become intolerable and decent. They would do well to read this book and ponder the fate of Dresden' (167). When Billy replies quietly, 'I was there', we find juxtaposed the theoretical and the experimental, the political and the spiritual. Vonnegut takes pains to avoid the usual terms of reference – nuclear warfare, Biblical apocalypse – and indeed invents his own mythology of Tralfamadore. By focusing on Dresden he hopes to turn our minds away from one kind of warfare to warfare in general and to man's degeneracy. Yet the holocaust of Dresden, real as it was, is also perfect apocalyptic symbolism as is Vonnegut's bookish apparatus: the lengthy autobiographical introduction, the subtitle 'The Children's Crusade: A Duty Dance with Death'. Vonnegut simply replaces the content of Biblical apocalyptic with his own vision.

Finally, Robert Coover's *The Public Burning* (1976) rewrites the history of the Rosenberg trial, reclaiming the 'truthful' version of history through the excesses of fiction and so, once more, bearing witness to the primacy of the word. The Rosenberg's 'crime' was smuggling secrets of the H-bomb to the Russians, so the book has a connection with nuclear holocaust as well as with religious holocaust through the tradition of witch-burning and through the false religions which Coover sees as motivating the American people. They live at an apocalyptic fever-pitch, and in the finale Uncle Sam himself appears to oversee the orgasmic proceedings of the execution in Times Square, carrying a blinding fireball which is at once the flame of the Statue of Liberty, the blinding light of racial and religious prejudice, and the atomic bomb itself:

> For a moment Uncle Sam seems to hover flickeringly above them, his craggy features lit eerily from beneath by the fiery glimmer in his cupped hands, his coattails flapping blackly behind him – and then he plummets suddenly down upon them like a falling star! The people, interrupted in the mind-shattering throes of what might have been some ultimate orgasmic fusion, are as yet unable to cope with this new information – they cry out, shield their eyes, and fall back in slippery confusion, tumbling out of some linkages and into others, but generally shrinking back into their old isolate and terrified selves . . . .
>   '*Philosophers have explained the world,*' he cries, '*it is necessary to CHANGE the world! So hang on to your hats, folks, cause jist as that old astronomicalizin' Prophet Nate Ames soothsaid nigh onto two hundred years ago, the Coelestial Light directed here by the Finger of*

God is gonna drive out the long! long! Night of Heathenish Darkness!
I shit you not! Stand back! it's the NEW New Enlightenment!'
The little orb of blinding light hovers for a moment on the palms of his hands, slowly expanding, pulsating like a living heart, so bright that even the people with their eyes squeezed shut see it there – then suddenly it flashes outward, cutting through the Square like a sheet of sun, inundating the streets and all the city and nation and oceans beyond with glaring light, with white heat, like some kind of super flashbulb, as suddenly contracts back in on itself, dragging people to their heads, knees, and elbows, and whipping them as in an orange whirlwind toward the stage, and then – WHOOSH! – the darkness lifts up off the Square like a great mushroom cloud, rising high into the lightening sky and sucking all the fears and phantasms of the people's nighttime up with it – and a lot of the people as well, for a foot or two anyway, before dropping them back on the sweaty pavements in an exhausted bare-bottomed heap. (604–5)

This, I think, is the nearest we shall come to modern apocalyptic, at once satiric and horrifyingly realised, re-interpreting authorised history and making of the book itself a bomb to change people's minds. It is a remarkable achievement, especially when compared to the attempts to render another central component of apocalyptic, the physical destruction of the globe, in imaginatively powerful terms. Books like Balmer and Wylie's *When Worlds Collide* and Niven and Pournelle's *Lucifer's Hammer*, while replete with apocalyptic quotation, leave the imagination totally unilluminated.

It is now time to look at those fictions which consciously couch the nuclear apocalypse in religious terms.

Isaac Asimov's 'Hell Fire' (1956) is a simple, straightforward little gem of a story which does in miniature what Coover accomplishes in his vast novel. A slow motion film of a nuclear explosion is examined, and reveals that 'in that moment of stasis the expanding ball of fire had shown dark spots for eyes, with dark lines above them for thin, flaring eyebrows. And where a hairline came down V-shaped a mouth, twisted upward, laughing wildly in the hell-fire. And there were horns' (98). Brief visions like this are often more effective than narratives of religious practices during the period of crisis, which often seem to have little point beyond the borrowed frisson of their apocalyptic sources. In D. A. Moore's *Mirrors of the Apocalypse* an eastern financier wages war on Russia with solar rayguns, and his demonic regime centred in Jerusalem is curtailed only by the reincarnation of the prophet Enoch. In Shaw Desmond's *Ragnarok* or 'The Armageddon of the Gods', an American aviatrix scoffs at Doomsday during a trip to Europe ('Telling me that the Book of Revelation with the skids off is one day going to fall on America out of the sky' [81]) only to witness the Japanese attack on New York with liquefied gas. A selfstyled Antichrist leads mass orgies in Westminster Abbey but the narrator sees it as merely another turn in 'the eternal cycle of evolution' (349). R. H. Benson's *Lord of the World* is a disguised Jesuit polemic culminating in the bombing of Rome and an English priest's claim to be God incarnate, followed by a dimly realised Antichrist. F. T. Jane's *The Violent Flame: A Story of Armageddon and After* (1899) has the Finis Mundi Society welcoming the Antichrist Dr Mirzabeau, who vaporises Waterloo Station and the Albert Hall and destroys civilisation, leaving a new Adam and Eve. R. Pape's *And So Ends the World* and F. Wright's *Deluge*, while both conceiving physical catastrophes, end with Biblical flourishes: 'and neither shall they learn war any more', and 'Though he slay me yet will I trust him.' H. C. Asterley's *Escape into Berkshire* epitomises these lacklustre tales, with the hero escorting his girlfriend with a 'nuclear pistol' to discuss last things with a padre in Berkshire. A tortuous theological debate is light-years from the holocaust itself, momentarily dramatised in a Cockney's observation, 'This ain't an 'oly world no more, laidy – if ever it was' (57).

More interesting are those fictions which frame their apocalyptic claims equivocally. In Wilson Tucker's *The Year of the Quiet Sun* (1970) a cynical futurologist who has translated a Qumran scroll called 'Eschatos' only to argue that all Jewish apocalyptic is simply fantasy or 'midrash' is transported forward in time to discover a post-nuclear age. His former belief – 'Don't fall into the trap . . . don't try to take those prophets out of their age and fit them into the twentieth century. They are obsolete' – is contradicted, though he achieves a happy ending. In this novel time-travel is not merely a clever device but 'a metaphor for a process of redemption'.[32] P. Anderson Graham also uses time-travel in *The Collapse of Homo Sapiens* (1923) in which the hero, 2000 years from now, travels up a clogged River Thames and learns of the coloured invasion, the bombs and plagues, and the boy who learned the Book of Common Prayer by heart and established a new religion. The novel remains interesting because of the sceptical attitude of the narrator himself: 'Some who wrote in the chronicles believed that the whole world had been desolated when England fell. They were reduced to guessing because ships had disappeared from the waters' (33). The perspective of time is used in a different way by Robert Silverberg in *Vornan-19* (1970), set in 1998 but viewing the world from the perspective of an alien who arrives in Rome one Christmas Day on an anthropological mission (his first question is, 'Where may I find a house of intercourse?'). While the narrator reads Blake's Prophetic Books, Vornan finds himself surrounded by apocalyptic followers anticipating the end, although he himself writes in *The New Revelation* that the planet will continue for another thousand years. When Vornan finally vanishes, the narrator is left wondering: 'We are coming into a century of flame' (251). This is a teasing novel, utilising the conventions of science fiction to revivify the ideas and atmosphere of Biblical apocalyptic.

There are several fictions which examine the cult of the Messiah, both before and after the holocaust. In Heinlein's *Stranger in a Strange Land* the Martian Michael Smith re-enacts the Crucifixion and the New Revelation of Fisterism plays a prominent part in the future evolution of mankind. The poor hero of Poul Anderson's gentle parable 'A Chapter of Revelation' (1972) has a harder time of it. Louis Habib, an Oakland mechanic, suggests on a TV show that what the world needs is a sign from God to encourage us to re-form the world and avoid the imminent nuclear war between the United States and China: 'If God would stop the Sun a while, maybe we'd get the idea. Because we sure can't understand a Sermon on the Mount any longer' (23). When such an event ensues, chaos erupts (unlike the negative vision of R. A. Lafferty): some people join the church, others join 'White Americans for Christ', others march on Washington, and Israel attacks her neighbours in confidence. Finally Habib himself is mauled to death by the mob demanding miracles. Only after this sacrifice does peace come again, and a young couple contemplate the future:

I do expect the great empires to fall, ours amongst them. Whatever civilisation rises on the ruins won't be like any the world has seen before. And that, however painful, may show us a new side of our souls. . . . When will we see that we've always lived in a miracle? (77–8)

Equally satirical, and without the gentle ending, is Gore Vidal's *Kalki* (1978), where the masses are gulled into thinking that the end is at hand. At a mass rally 'four billion or so bodies had been unceremoniously dropped by their owners' (190) – not caused by 'an atomic chain reaction' summoned by the new Messiah, but by the deadly fumes of the distributed lotus flowers. A more ambiguous Messiah figure is Andrew Sinclair's *Gog* (1967), a Second World War sailor wrecked on the Scottish coast, who makes a painful pilgrimage to London because 'Your reappearance was forecast by the Book of Revelations, before the end of the world and the coming again of Israel. . . . The first coming of Gog and Magog drove the first Israel from Albion and the last battle of Gog and Magog shall bring it back again' (22–4). Although the haunting figure of Magog, which torments Gog in various guises during his trip, prophesies the two atomic bombings ('I shall destroy a great city in the Far East. . . . The time of the final solution' [96]), the actual holocaust for Sinclair is the firebombing of London. When Gog arrives he finds

only the scorched globe and all that therein survives is left, and the survivors are equal under the fire and the hammer that falls to chasten and purge them and temper their eyes into seeing that men are men and no more than men, not set over each other, but condemned with each other to trial by survival in their inescapable flesh. (415)

Magog is identified with the mad scientist and destructive technology – 'and it's Etna and Vesuvius over the whole earth . . . Dresden and Hiroshima global, Day of Judgment and Night of Inferno. . . . Welling heat, molten metal, pea-soup gas, burning blindness' (452) – but he is also Gog's half-brother and they are 'condemned with each other'. The Bagman or prophet Wayland Merlin Blake Smith can fight more openly against Magog's forces, as he does in a radio interview:

Repent ye, London, for Gog is abroad in the land fighting against Magog his brother, and they are the signs and forerunners of the end of the world. . . . Ye shall surely be the third city caught up to the flaming heavens by the fiery fist of the Almighty. (457)

The interviewer replies urbanely, 'I'm sure the Royal Air Force will take care of that problem, Mr Smith. Anyway, the United States of America is our ally, and no other nation will have the know-how to make atom bombs for decades. We're perfectly safe . . .' (457). But Smith, unconvinced, is electrocuted trying to fight Magog's technicians. For Gog at the end of the novel the choice is a difficult one between the self and Albion, or the community and London/Magog: 'As Gog comes to the fork, sober yet unsteady on this August night, of victory and peace on earth, he does not know which way . . .' (474). Sinclair's novel, suffused with apocalyptic imagery and rhetoric, correctly locates the origins of modern apocalyptic in the Second World War (like the novels of Vonnegut, Dahl, MacLennan, etc.) and plays itself out in that interim period of warring and warning before the final judgment which must be imminent in our own age. His characters are like apocalyptic characters, symbolic yet sweatily real, and his tone is loquacious, enigmatic and remorselessly 'present'. His Everyman is drawn from intimate familiarity with the literature of England, but as in Blake's poetry he is also a global figure carrying with him our destiny. The final choice between individual retreat and salvation or throwing in one's lot with the complicated power struggles of the mass, is profoundly conceived and presented.

Sinclair's novel is an example of that tenacious, supple and intimate theological debate with God and his purpose for Man which is found in so much Jewish writing. It finds its way into the literature of nuclear disaster in a variety of ways including the black humour of *Dr Strangelove*. A good example of the specific religious debate is the duo of stories by Ward Moore, 'Lot' and 'Lot's Daughter' (1953–4). In the first story a long-suffering husband guides his prattling family out of Los Angeles and away from the horrific inferno. They are preoccupied with the mundane: finding washrooms and television, quarrelling, and admonishing the father when he ignores a traffic officer, at which point he protests, 'None of you seem to have the slightest initiative or ability to grasp reality. Tickets, cops, judges, juries mean nothing any more. There is no law now but the law of survival' (114). The son responds, 'You mean we can do anything we want now? Shoot people? Steal cars and things?' Not surprisingly the father abandons his family except for his daughter, and finds safety near the desert. In the second story the religious dimension becomes apparent. He ekes out a living while his daughter forlornly attempts to start the car. He mocks the fictional archetype ('the heroic fictional man (*homo Gernsbacchae*) would have found the house, rounded up the cattle, started all over'[33]) but maintains a civilised lifestyle – 'his had been the middle, sensible course as befitted a survivor and the prototype of survivors' (26). But in his self-absorption he ignores his daughter, save to father a son upon her, and one day he returns to find she has committed suicide. It is perhaps not entirely Lot's fault that his daughter should, like a pillar of salt, abdicate from life, but we are surely intended to rebuke him for his arrogance and maltreatment of those closest to him.

A similar charge may be levelled at the hero of Bernard Malamud's *God's Grace* (1983), but perhaps more tentatively. The novel begins with 'This is that story' and recounts the nuclear holocaust in a series of short formulaic sentences. Malamud is clearly adopting the apocalyptic voice, enigmatic and unoriginal, and a tone of foreboding wrestles throughout the novel with the desired release of tension in the black humour of a Jewish fable. Calvin Cohn is the sole survivor of a flood sent by God in rage at man's misbehaviour, chiefly his pollution and atomic war (epitomised in the unexploded missiles which Cohn discovers lying on the seabed like 'smoking turds'). Because he himself has survived, Cohn is uneasy about God's omnipotence, but resigns himself: 'Einstein said God doesn't dice with the universe; if he could believe it maybe I can. . . . Some had lived after Hiroshima; some had not. What comes will come' (7–9).

His discovery of Dr Bunder's chimpanzee Gottlob ('Praise God') is the beginning of the evolutionary debate. How can Cohn avoid the extremes of Bunder's Hitler-like belief in man's evolution towards an ideal, and yet continue the race? Cohn's attitude is symbolised when he changes the chimp's name to 'Buz', perhaps an allusion to the Old Testament tribe of Buzites which included Job's friend Elihu, who believed in God as a teacher of man who does not deliberately send suffering but who finally judges. Cohn never loses a sense of community, quietly saying Kaddish for one hundred souls named in the Manhattan telephone directory which is his 'Book of the Dead'. He tells the chimp stories about human history – 'Holocaust – that's a total pogrom and led directly to the Day of Devastation, a tale I will tell you on the next dark day' (55) – and human depravity, although 'man paid for what he was – maybe – to my mind – er – somewhat unjustly' (75). Cohn establishes a school tree for a tribe of chimps:

> I will go into the Historical Past in six lectures I have planned; and the Twentieth Century Up to Now, in another two, the second beginning with the Holocaust that I mentioned yesterday: all that Jewish soap from those skeletal gassed bodies; and not long after that, since these experiences are bound to each other, the U.S. Americans drop the first atom bombs – teensy ones – on all those unsuspecting 8 a.m. Japanese crawling in broken glass to find their eyeballs. I could say more but haven't the heart. (134)

He transcends the 'eschatological living trauma the Lord had laid on the world' (168) by mating with a female chimp, obeying the biological imperative at least, and leaving God to his mysteries: 'God is not love, God is God' (171). But his usurpation of Esau's mate prompts the chimp to indulge his lust for baboon flesh, and the monkey tribes disintegrate into cannibalising factions. Buz leads the chimps in destroying Cohn's monkey-daughter Rebekkah, he and Esau mount the mother in scorn, and finally Cohn is captured and executed. In this third holocaust, Cohn himself is the offering, but what does it mean? The narrative moves from the intimate dialogue of God and Cohn, to Cohn's bewilderment and the narrator's ('Let's see what happens now' [165]); we are teased with meaning, as when the blood spurts from Cohn's throat before the knife touches it, but meaning is not confirmed. The gorilla who had previously eaten Cohn's record of his father chanting the Kol Nidre, a prayer of atonement, is at the end chanting a Kaddish for Cohn's soul – but it is an empty, parroted travesty. Cohn utters the book's title only once, when he decides to mate with the chimp, but the last two chapters ('The Voice of the Prophet' and 'God's Mercy') are bitter parodies of meaning. Malamud's novel is a highly enigmatic, prismatic assemblage of views on the nature of Man and his relationship with the universe. From the initial flood, which reverses the Hebrew prediction of God's promise to send not flood but fire next time, the novel upsets our expectations for straightforward allegory. In the void of God's silence we must struggle with the question of how great our commitment ought to be to the continuation of this life and the species. Cohn's decision to help the evolutionary process rebounds in tragedy and death; we have broken our covenant with God but we can establish no covenant with the world around us. It is a bleak novel indeed, apocalyptic in framework but offering no new Jerusalem, not even the secular re-assurance that the life force will continue to function in the post-disaster world.

The relationship of theology and evolutionary theory (or necessity) which Malamud explores in a personal, 'Robinson Crusoe' way, is debated as a matter of public policy in Lester Del Rey's *The Eleventh Commandment* (1962). The narrator Boyd Jensen is an exchange student from Mars, here to study the effects of mutation after the accidental nuclear war of 1993. Roman Catholicism dominates in Europe and North America, while Africa has 'fallen to the muslims' and the 'Christian territory' – in the opinion of Blind Stephen, self-styled Moses to Boyd's Joshua – of Australasia is threatened by Asiatics. But the teeming hordes belong to Catholic countries since, while nursing the 'original sin' of mutation, they have been exhorted by the eleventh commandment to 'Go forth and multiply'. While the American Pope Bonaforte defends the world population of three times that before the wars by arguing that man must allow God time to reorganise his gene pool according to natural selection, Blind Stephen urges a genuine apocalypse:

> But to the seed of Adam who shall have dominion over all that moves upon the Earth, I cry from the darkness; Gird up your loins and go forth to war and the vengeance of the Lord!
> There was war in Heaven – even in Heaven was the war. And the great dragon, the yellow dragon that spreads its wings of sable and its fiery breath of iniquity across the earth, that old serpent, was cast out. . . . Woe to the

inhabitants of the earth and of the sea! For the devil is come down unto you, having great wrath, because he knoweth that he hath but a short time. (119)

The theological debate is forsaken in favour of a sentimental story about Jensen, who discovers that he has been sent down from Mars because he himself is mutant, sterile. But there are some vivid novelistic touches: panic in a restaurant when a 'bleeder' (haemophiliac) is discovered; flight across a devastated mid-West; the mutated language of the street kids – 'Him's dead. Tol'm an tol'm, grab 'n neck. Catch 'n back, turns 'n bites off 'n nose' (44). Jensen's meticulous cytological research into the yeast which maintains the food supply of krill and algae to the subhuman population is metaphoric of the Church's espousal of the detached methods of science which turn humankind into a genetic experiment.

The fictions of Moore, Malamud and Del Rey address the concerns of Chapter 4 in religious terms but Del Rey also explores the relationship of priest and scientist, the most common dramatic situation in the literature. In Edmund Cooper's *All Fool's Day* the Brothers of Iniquity lose out to the cynical advocates of secular progress ('We've got a new civilisation going. We're back to square one. Everybody wants to kill everybody else. It's quite exciting, really' [192]), while in Sterling Lanier's *Hiero's Journey* two religious bands struggle for supremacy. One of them, the Elevensers, proclaim an additional commandment, 'Thou shalt not despoil the Earth and the life thereon' (219); but they are tyrannical, and their military base is destroyed by the Metz (or Metis) monks. Unfortunately a future conflict with science is foreseen because they take with them three volumes of *Principles of a Basic Analog Computer* (342). These oppositions have their source in the ancient conflict between the sorcerer and the man of God, and the nuclear explosion would seem to offer triumphant proof that the scientist is indeed a servant of the Devil. Unfortunately the magnitude of disaster, as we have seen in previous fictions, also may cause the survivors to call into question God's guiding, caring plan for mankind. James Blish's two novels *Black Easter* and *The Day After Judgment* (1968 and 1971) are two daring explorations of these issues and form a suitable climax to this chapter.

Blish's Faustian figure is Baines, whose company Consolidated

Warfare Service is about to take over the running of the Sino-Soviet limited nuclear war. As a connoisseur of chaos, Baines wants to witness an even larger carnage, so he employs a master of black magic to let loose the forces of evil for one night. At a castle retreat Blish is able to carry on the philosophical debate, set off by copious quotation from Marlow and C. S. Lewis, reporting on the chaos which the experiment is causing the world but not getting absorbed by it. While Baines follows the radio reports gleefully ('There goes Rome'), Blish maintains an austere, theatrical atmosphere somewhere between a Platonic dialogue and a Jacobean melodrama. For the mundane world, Blish points out, cannot provide an appropriate setting for Armageddon: the destruction of Rome is learnt to 'a mixture of The Messiah, Mahler, and The Supremes' (155). By contrast, Blish's spokesman Adolph Hess is able to provide a setting not only for Baines's Manichean passions, but for Blish's novel itself:

> It happens about every thousand years. People start out happy with their gods, even though they're frightened of them. Then, increasingly, the world becomes secularised and the gods seem less and less relevant. The temples are deserted. People feel guilty about that, but not much. Then, suddenly, they've had all the secularisation they can take, they throw their wooden shoes into the machines, they take to worshipping Satan or the Great Mother, they go into a Hellenistic period or take up Christianity, *in hoc signo vinces* – I've got those all out of order but it happens, Baines, it happens, like clockwork, every thousand years. . . . We've got another millennium coming to a close now, and people are terrified of our secularisation, our nuclear and biological weapons, our computers, our overprotective medicine, everything, and they're turning back to the worship of unreason. (156)

The sequel *The Day After Judgment* is divided into four acts, each a station of the cross: 'The Wrath-bearing Tree' asserts the earthly presence of Satan as Baines's experiment gets out of hand; 'So Above' shows his encampment; 'Come to Middle Hell' documents the futile war waged by the military; 'The Harrowing of Heaven' shows Satan's triumph and defeat.

Apocalyptic echoes abound in the epigraphs and Father Domenico the white magician's inner debates. Yet until the end of the novel, the characters insist that what is happening, incredible as it may seem, is not the Apocalypse because there has been no Antichrist. In fact there is no need of such an evil agent because man has ably demonstrated his own depravity. Satan has merely established his Citadel of Dis on earth in order to conduct Judgment Day, but faced with the enormity of man's folly he gives up even this project and vanishes. Nevertheless Satan's manifestation may have been what is needed to regenerate fallen man; at least, this is the optimistic note on which the novel ends. The four principal characters 'attempt to state their cases but find that they cannot complete their sentences. However, their positions have changed. Father Domenico says 'I think' (not 'I believe'); Ware says 'I hope' (not 'I know'); Baines says 'I believe' (not 'I think'); and Ginsberg says 'I love' (not 'I lust'). Dante was kind to lovers, and Ginsberg has the last word.'[34]

Blish's novels are intended to provoke philosophical discussion. When the magician puts 'the centuries-old question of why a good and merciful God should allow so much pain and terror to be inflicted on the innocent' (63), or Satvje suggests that complete extinction, beyond Hell or Heaven, is 'the ultimate human achievement' (108), our minds are challenged. All this happens within a vividly realised context of supernatural happenings. Blish creates his fictional world by using the conventions we have already disclosed in apocalyptic and in early disaster stories. There is the distant point of view from the mountain top, aided only by malfunctioning TV cameras: 'The views from near the bombed areas were fragmentary, traveling, scarred by raster, aflicker with electronic snow – a procession of unconnected images, like scenes from an early surrealist film, where one could not tell whether the director was trying to portray a story or only a state of mind' (36–7). A clinical detachment highlights the grotesque horrors:

Rocket-borne Assault Infantry soldiers were being plucked first of their harness, then of their clothing, and then of their hair, their fingernails and toenails by jeering creatures with beasts' heads, most of whom were flying without even wings.

> The bodies, when there was anything left of them at all, were
> being dropped unerringly into the heart of the Pit. (133)

Here Blish draws on the visionary paintings of Heironymus
Bosch. When describing the Citadel of Dis itself, he uses the
dystopian image of a meticulous factory: 'a clean, well-lighted
city like an illustration from some utopian romance; it looked,
in fact, like a cross between the city of the future in the old film
Things to Come and a fully automated machine shop. It screamed,
hammered and roared like a machine shop as well' (150). Blish
exposes the literary, fictional basis of his construction by his
allusions to Dante, Blake, Wells, other science fiction writers,
and theologians. This serves only to reify his vision, however,
partly because technological man is essentially fantastic ('Many
of Baines's most lucrative ideas for weaponry had been stolen
bodily, through the intermediary of the Mamaroneck Research
Institute, from the unpaid imaginations of science-fiction writers'
[152]), partly because the military and computer minds which
also attempt to describe Hell are ludicrously prosaic. McKnight's
directive to the troops reminds them:

> It is anticipated that in combat the enemy will employ
> various explosive, chemical and toxic agents which may
> produce widespread novel effects. All personnel are hereby
> reminded that these effects will be either natural in origin, or
> illusions. (112)

And the computer of the Library of Congress concludes:

THE ASSUMPTION THAT THE CONSTRUCTION
IN DEATH VALLEY IS RUSSIAN CHINESE OR
OTHERWISE OF HUMAN ORIGIN IS OF THE
LOWEST ORDER OF PROBABILITY AND MAY
BE DISCOUNTED. THE INTERPLANETARY
HYPOTHESIS IS OF SLIGHTLY HIGHER
PROBABILITY, AN INVASION FROM VENUS BEING
COMPATIBLE WITH A FEW OF THE FACTUAL DATA,
SUCH AS THE IMMENSE HEAT AND ABERRANT LIFE
FORMS OF THE DEATH VALLEY INSTALLATION,
BUT IS INCOMPATIBLE WITH MOST
ARCHITECTURAL AND OTHER HISTORICAL

DETAILS IN THE DATA, AS WELL AS WITH THE
LEVEL OF TECHNOLOGY INDICATED. THE
PROBABILITY THAT THE DEATH VALLEY
INSTALLATION IS THE CITY OF DIS AND THAT ITS
INTERNAL AREA IS NETHER HELL IS 0.1 WITHIN A
5% LEVEL OF CONFIDENCE, AND THEREFORE
MUST BE ADMITTED. (52)

The one imaginative failure is Blish's attempt to dramatise
Satan himself, when he resorts to a Miltonic pastiche.

In his preface, Blish insists that his story 'is not a *vade mecum*,
but a *cursus infamam*' (8); his point is that the real diabolic
intent is found within man. The military in particular are
elated at the chance to employ their apocalyptic weapons in a
genuine apocalyptic showdown. They use Kahn's escalation
'nukespeak' to judge the progress of the war, ignoring objections
like 'Do you call atomising Denver "restrained"?' (31). After
all, the magician Ware is simply an instrument of the arms
dealer Baines who instigates the whole catastrophe for his own
amusement. Blish's enterprise is remarkable for the way it
assembles all man's historical devices for depicting the
apocalypse, only to remind us that these projections are just
that, and that we are really talking about our inward sense of
pride, sin and guilt.

We seem to be back where we began, with a fiction which
emphasises the personal and emotional aspects of the idea of
apocalyptic. The holocaust which burns a book, like the auto
da fé which burnt a heretic, is the twentieth century writer's
image for any mental tyranny which denies the individual
voice. One might think that a nuclear disaster would be the
ultimate stage-effect in the 'Repent ye!' sermon of the religious
fanatic, yet the fictions seem generally to discard the notion of a
post-disaster Church triumphant. Preachers in the waste land
generally appear as itinerant charlatans, playing on people's
newly awakened fear of mortality but rarely establishing the
new Jerusalem on earth except in grimly repressive regimes.
Certainly there is still a central place for the religious spirit;
the disaster at least solves the age-old conflict between
priest and scientist since the military–political–technological
establishment is discredited. But it was Einstein who said that
science without religion was lame, and religion without science

blind. In the post-disaster situation, a new kind of religious impulse must be reconciled with a new kind of scientific impulse. The disaster seems to mock the image of man as lord of creation, and likewise God as the supreme gardener. Instead, the survivors must seek some new relationship with creation, based on humility, scepticism and even bewilderment.

Fictions of nuclear disaster, supposing continued life beyond the apocalypse, are also at odds with the details of Biblical apocalyptic unless they imagine the waste land to be part of the thousand year interim before the final conflagration. But such Biblical eschatological calculations are beyond most characters and writers of these fictions. They are concerned to fashion a new attitude towards time itself, just as they must reassess their ideas of religion and science. The very concept of evolution, so fruitfully utilised and explored in the previous chapter, is called into question. Malamud's Cohn facing the chimps, or the monks in *Hiero's Journey* destroying the technological society but beginning to read computer textbooks, are symbols of this radical re-orientation. Many fictions look back in time to the Second World War, finding in Dresden, London and Auschwitz fitting emblems for the man-made holocaust which is merely confirmed or played out again in nuclear disaster. Time, then, is not important as chronology or prediction (as it was to the Biblical apocalypticists). In spiritual terms, the nuclear disaster is better imaged as Eliot's 'whimper' than as a 'bang'. A 'personalised' reading of apocalyptic, then, would seem most relevant to our reading of nuclear apocalyptic. Disaster is not so much imminent as immanent, the very possibility of man's genocide and destruction of the environment demanding reconsideration of man's morality and place in the scheme of things. The complicated edifice of Blish's novels supports the cry for a change of heart. Gog's pilgrimage has no goal except a deeper understanding of human nature. The attitude taken towards disaster is more important than the disaster itself, the most extreme anti-apocalyptic view, the absurd, being typical of the modern age:

> The current imagery of disaster, moreover, carries forward directly from the apocalyptic peerings of the earlier or prewar and prebomb generation, not to mention that of several still earlier generations. What has been added in recent years,

and again especially in fiction, is a pervasive sense of the preposterous: of the end of the world not only as imminent and titanic, but also as absurd.[35]

Again we come back to the special nature of fiction, which is not the sermoniser or speechmaker but the still, small voice of comradeship. Saul Bellow's fictional creation Herzog, himself a lover of letters (that epitome of the intimate communication) insists, 'We must get it out of our head that this is a doomed time, that we are waiting for the end, and the rest of it. . . . We love apocalypses too much, and crisis ethics and florid extremism with all its thrilling language. Excuse me, no. I've had all the monstrosity I want.' While fictions may utilise the imagery and techniques of apocalyptic, especially as portrayed in this chapter, their final message is like Herzog's – humane, sceptical, pacific. Ray Bradbury, author of a novel replete with bookburning and nuclear holocaust, ends with a community of walking, talking books, because 'the ability to fantasise is the ability to survive'.[36] R. B. Lewis sums it up: 'These apocalyptic visions indeed are offered as weapons for averting the catastrophe.'[37]

Two of the most outstanding works of nuclear disaster fiction, with a central theme of religion in the waste land, will not be considered here but in Chapter 7 as 'exemplary fictions'. *A Canticle for Leibowitz* and *Riddley Walker* set apocalyptic imagery within an evolutionary context to show how the imaginative structure of Christianity can be adapted or mutated to fit the new facts of the post-disaster world. But to illustrate the advance that fiction writers have made by feeling free to borrow from the apocalyptic tradition, one might compare two other stories, one by Edgar Allen Poe and one by Arthur C. Clarke.

Poe's story, 'The Conversation of Eiros and Charmion', simply recounts the end of the world brought about by collision with a meteor. The legendary figures picture 'the entire fulfilment, in all their minute and terrible details, of the fiery and horror-inspiring denunciations of the prophecies of the Holy Book. . . . Thus ended all'. Beyond the apocalyptic, daring for its time, the story has absolutely nothing in it to interest the reader. By contrast Clarke's *Childhood's End* (1954) soars effortlessly beyond Biblical apocalyptic, drawing from it but supplanting it with a newly coined version for the space age.

The alien Karellen and his 'Overlords' ban nuclear weapons and usher in the next stage of human evolution, a merging with the Overmind and the destruction of the world in a pillar of mental energy. As Earth gives up its 'hoarded energies' (188), a glow from inside begins to burn brighter and brighter; the stars fall down and Earth explodes like a bombarded atom in a glorious imaginative fusion of spiritual illumination and nuclear explosion. Clarke fully absorbs the evolutionary element into his apocalypse, passing beyond man as he is now and even beyond his present language. He utilises the apocalyptic convention of the prophetic voice ('Jan's'), but the secret manuscript of man as he was has now been superceded: 'Perhaps, lost in one of the still-intact cities, was the manuscript of some latter-day Gibbon, recording the last days of the human race. If so, Jan was not sure that he would care to read it' (180–1). There is even a tinge of sadness at the end of the novel, as if we have moved from Blake's *Songs of Innocence* to his *Songs of Experience* and lost something special – ourselves – in the process. Clarke's novel does not perhaps belong in a study of nuclear disaster, but it is a kind of negative example: only the interference of benign aliens will stop us from annihilating ourselves. Finally, though, the power of Karellen is the power of imaginations like Clarke's and our belief in them; like John's revelation, *Childhood's End* is just one more fiction to help us live more properly and more fully here and now. As Lucy Menger says, 'The universe is queer and cold. *Childhood's End* is comforting. We need our myths to keep us warm.'[38]

6 The Imagination of Disaster

> ... and a wish gestates
> For explosive pain, a punishing
> Demanded moment of mortal change,
> The Night of the Knock when none shall sleep,
> The Absolute Instant.[1]

Alain Robbe-Grillet described his 1976 novel *Topologie d'une Cité Fantôme* as a 'construction imaginaire par laquelle je nomme les ruines d'une future divinité.'[2] In this chapter I shall look at fictions which, while apparently describing some feature of the post-nuclear disaster landscape, are more importantly *naming* and giving expression to the fears and hopes of their authors for the future of this planet. While many of them still work with the conventional themes and images already established in this study – the waste land, religion and apocalypse, mutation and evolution, the place of the scientist and technology – I have separated them out like this because I feel that their most distinctive feature is their visionary quality. It is an uneasy distinction in the light of the visionary intensity of some of the fictions already explored, but I think there is a difference in kind between the work of extrapolation and the work of nightmare or dream. The fictions in this chapter seem, more insistently than those previous works, to be crying out for a change – now; as Auden puts it, an 'absolute instant' precisely to avoid the otherwise inevitable instant of nuclear destruction.

Particularly in Chapter 2, when I considered the appropriateness of scientific language and attitudes to an imagining of nuclear disaster and its aftermath, I have been keeping the question of an appropriate language, even the possibility of disaster fiction at all, at the forefront of my commentary. Before discussing these imaginative works, it may

145

'The Son of Man Among the Candlesticks', A Dürer, Apocalypse Series, Frederick van der Meer, *Apocalypse: Visions from the Book of Revelation in Western Art* (London: Thames & Hudson) p. 286.

be useful to expand that discussion, since the search for an adequate framework – plausibility rather than predictability – is a central concern to many of these writers.

Works like *Dr. Strangelove* and *Slaughterhouse-Five* make explicit the close connection in our communal imaginative experience between the Second World War and the possible Third World War. This is not simply a sense that we are 'in the middest', between wars as it were; the nuclear threat arose directly out of that earlier holocaust. The explosions at Hiroshima and Nagasaki provide us with the only empirical data on the effect of nuclear explosion on human populations, and the scientists who worked on the bomb during the War became leading figures in post-war developments (Dr Werner von Braun has provided a particularly sinister link between the Nazi worship of power and imperialism, and the contemporary nuclear threat, as satirised by Tom Lehrer and Stanley Kubrick). It is not coincidental that one of the monumental fictions of our time, Pynchon's *Gravity's Rainbow*, is 'about' the Second World War and the development of the V-bomb but ends by being about today. There is an even more powerful imaginative link to be made with the war through the Jewish Holocaust. Equally atrocious, equally destructive and equally implicating all of mankind, that experience offers a paradigm for writers attempting to encompass the nuclear disaster. Despite the wealth of appropriate symbolism from Biblical apocalyptic – the holocaust itself, the burning books, the crematoria, the whole Jewish tradition – the sheer possibility of describing that experience remains intensely debated. And if it is so difficult for an event which has, unwilling as we may be to grant this, been absorbed into history, how much more difficult must the task be to imagine adequately a holocaust which must by definition remain in the future?

Writers of the Jewish Holocaust, most of them Jewish themselves, feel compelled to discover a new kind of fiction, rejecting both the symbolic and the particular:

> The pietistic mode may be one legitimate response to atrocity, but I have chosen not to follow it here. The habit of finding old spiritual categories and vocabulary to sanctify the meaningless new deaths . . . has never seemed to me a fruitful way of entering the darkest recesses of that horror. . . . To

accept pure chance as the key to survival is to admit into the universe of atrocity a randomness that damages our precious image of the civilised mind.[3]

The writer, Lawrence Langer, attacks writers like Frankl, Bettelheim and even Ghandi (in a 1938 article he advocated non-violent action to European Jews so that 'the winter of their despair can in the twinckling [sic] of an eye be turned into the summer of hope'[4]) for placing the Holocaust or the threat of it within a humanistic frame of reference. For the Holocaust, says Langer, burst the verbal boundaries as well as moral ones, and our task is 'to create a language and imagery that will transform mere knowledge into vision and bear the reader beyond the realm of familiar imagining into the bizarre limbo of atrocity.'[5] Even the notion of character is inappropriate because there is no sense of becoming or continuity in the death camp situation; the victim, 'in the manner of his dying, violates every idea of human continuity that we have inherited from literature and history.'[6] Yet there are novelists of the Holocaust, the most successful being Elie Wiesel who has produced seventeen books about the inadequacy of language. His novels are about how one cannot express the truth: Moshe the Madman in *The Oath* resolves never to speak of the pogrom he has witnessed; the journal of a victim of a Stalinist purge finds its way to his mute son (in *The Testament*). By focusing on the survivors of the Holocaust and using 'the formidable resources of modernism',[7] Wiesel comes close to the experience he insists can never be described: 'There is no such thing as a literature of the Holocaust, nor can there be. The very expression is a contradiction in terms.'[8] Wiesel's image for that experience is the night or the wall of bodies higher than the sky, 'extending to infinity'.[9] Other writers attempt to recreate the abyss of the Holocaust through means other than memoir or factual history, such as D. M. Thomas in his collage, *The White Hotel*. Thomas may not be true to the millions who died (how can he be?) but he creates a reading experience which takes us into that hell, and out only by means of fantasy. This seems to me a legitimate form of art, for such fictions speak not to the dead nor even to the survivors, but to us the living, and our conscience. As I have argued elsewhere,

Bettelheim objects that we have used words like 'Holocaust' (literally 'burnt offering') to encompass an event we cannot comprehend. But the word is perfectly apposite to the best artistic treatments of the Jewish experience during the Second World War. These works of art are themselves burnt offerings, the presentations of sacred things, mutilated. We don't need Thomas's final section to confirm that for us, as readers, 'a part of her went on living with these survivors', because Lisa lives in us.

When Freud saw his books burnt in 1933 he remarked, 'In the Middle Ages they would have burnt me; nowadays they are content with burning my books.' His four sisters were to become burnt offerings in the death camps, but Freud was right to recognise the sophistication of Nazi thinking. People die in mystery, but case histories and novels carry a different flame.[10]

Case histories and novels are 'fabulations' which translate or gesture towards the unspeakable in terms of human experience. In the post-Auschwitz, post-Hiroshima age, the fabulators have kept the faith with remarkable resilience.

The career of H. G. Wells most vividly illustrates the twentieth century's abandoning of faith in God and science and finally art. From the utopian vision of *The World Set Free* we may move to the coalescing of private fears and public chaos in *The Shape of Things to Come* (1933), where the 'sibylline' dreams of Dr Raven are at odds with his public confidence; or more personally to *The Mind at the End of its Tether* (1945), written before Hiroshima but suffused with post-nuclear paralysis. To Wells it seemed that the human mind was now pursuing and contriving only 'endings and death' (30). He recognised, like so many other writers of the nuclear age, the lust for apocalypse:

We want to be in at the death of Man and to have a voice in his final replacement by the next Lord of Creation, even if, Oedipus-like, that successor's first act be parricide. (19)

Like the critics of Holocaust writing, Wells now felt that the fate of the Earth was beyond fiction. Yet he had shown (for example in the ending to *The Time Machine*) an ability to imagine a waste land of haunting power, and there have been many similar visions of the post-nuclear waste land which have a similar impact. One of the earliest and best was Jack London's novella *The Scarlet Plague* (1910) where, following a disaster caused by a variety of modern ills – pollution, explosion, moral decay – a group of young boys huddles round a camp fire and listens to old Granser's stories of the old times. He tells them how civilisation slid towards ruin, until now 'where four million people disported themselves, the wild wolves roam today, and the savage progeny of our loins, with prehistoric weapons, defend themselves against the fanged despoilers' (18). Granser, who used to be Professor of English at the University of California, refuses to pass on the old secrets such as 'a key to the alphabet' (59), though he knows that inevitably these secrets will be rediscovered, including the formula for gunpowder – and the whole cycle will begin again. London's vision is bleak and anti-humanist but it is conveyed poetically through image and through the idea of a story itself. For Granser it's 'the same old story over and over' (61), and only as he speaks does he rediscover the old language:

> [The boys] were very quick and abrupt in their actions, and their speech, in moments of hot discussion over the allotment of the choicer teeth, was truly a gabble. They spoke in monosyllables and short jerky sentences that were more a gibberish than a language. And yet, through it ran hints of grammatical construction, and appeared vestiges of the conjugation of some superior culture. Even the speech of Granser was so corrupt that were it put down literally it would be almost so much nonsense to the reader. This, however, was when he talked with the boys. When he got into the full swing of babbling to himself, it slowly purged itself into pure English. The sentences grew longer and were enunciated with a rhythm and ease that was reminiscent of the lecture platform. (20)

It was not until *Riddley Walker* that the possibilities of dramatising the change in human nature by the change in language was fully exploited, and Hoban's novel owes much to London's – even to the extent of a character called Granser, who rediscovers the fatal gunpowder.

Two other early short stories portray the waste land with a

similar poetic economy. Stephen Vincent Benet's 'By the Waters of Babylon' (1937), although proceeding from conventional explosives and gas warfare, has the priest Joh cross the 'River Ou-dis-sun' (Hudson) and enter the Dead Places of Manhattan Island. Here in the place of the Gods he finds the remains of a dead man still seated at his desk looking out over New York. When he returns to his homeland ready to rebuild civilisation he cannot communicate his experiences – 'How shall I tell what I saw?' (113). A similar reticence informs Walter Van Tilburg Clark's 'The Portable Phonograph' (1941), which moves Wells's group of informed after-dinner conversationalists into the nuclear waste land and under the shelter of Eliot's 'red rock'. The professor, 'priest of a doomed faith' as the author later described him,[11] has been reading *The Tempest* to his friends. The doctor wonders if he should read Shelley next, but is rebuked: 'That's more soul than we can use. . . . *Moby Dick* is better' (125). As the livid sun sets, the professor plays a Debussy nocturne on his phonograph while the musician listens and finally 'let his head fall back in agony'. The guests then depart leaving the professor to defend himself through the night with a piece of pipe – 'My brain becomes thick, like my hands' (124). Like *The Ancient Mariner*, *King Lear* or *Waiting for Godot*, Clark's story sketches the dimensions of human suffering, the cultured brought low and the victory of chaos. Despite the author's denial ('I had to be satirical. One cannot afford to speak seriously about the end of the world'), the story is powerfully symbolic; perhaps one had to wait until our own age for such invention to be seen as sombre possibility.

The desert forms an appropriate milieu for these mental landscapes of doom. Fritz Leiber's 'Night of the Long Knives' (1960) takes place in a Beckettian no man's land 'as if the maps had run'. Places called 'Nowhere, IT, Place' reflect the resignation of the imagination, as does the encounter between the male narrator and a girl. The impulse to rape vies with the impulse to murder, for the

> relief of wiping out one recognisable bit more (the closest bit we can, since those of us with the courage or lazy rationality to wipe out ourselves have long since done so) – wiping out one recognisable bit more of the whole miserable, unutterably disgusting human mess. (82)

But by way of a slow-motion striptease the 'High Noon' encounter converts to lovemaking and the couple murder the next stranger who happens along. Leiber cannot face despair, however, and after inventing Freudian pasts for the pair (he was one of the button-pushers, her father was killed by a gang) he has them reformed by an old man and we leave them carrying serum to plague-stricken villagers. However the story is notable for its emphasis on degenerate language – slang and obscenity litter the story – and vicious anti-cultural attitude (the narrator, although he quotes Swinburne and Arnold, distinguishes himself from the 'cultural queers who think they are the new Adam and Eve'). Leiber's world is also more believable than many of the more thoroughly worked out fictions because it is so disparate and fragmented: the waste land is populated by a multitude of crazy sects, 'radioactive blue gods and rocket devils of the Atomites', as people seek to incorporate nuclear disaster into their imaginative life.

Roger Zelazny's *Damnation Alley* (1969) is ostensibly a 're-cycled' Hells Angel myth, with the hero commissioned to cross the American waste land from west to east carrying a needed serum; but near the end there is a remarkably eloquent expression of the post-nuclear landscape:

> . . . those who respected no pacts between the basic elements, who smudged the heavens with a million pollutants and fear, filling the bottle above the air with the radioactivity of five hundred prematurely detonated warheads, aborted by a radiation level already raised to the point where it broke them apart with spontaneous chain reactions, troubling its still blue on those three days when the pacts were broken, so that within its still heights the clouds were torn apart and swept away before the wailing it raised up to protest this final too familiar familiarity, so that perhaps the word it cries is 'Rape!' or maybe 'Help!' or 'God!' even, and the fact that it cries at all may hold hope and the promise of an eventual purging, of land and the sea as well as the air, and then again, perhaps not, for it could equally be the banshee wail of doom near at hand, that rises from its round throat that swalloweth and spitteth forth again; and as it surges by, perhaps it takes fire from the hot spots where the cobalt bombs fell and, of course, perhaps not also . . .

It is this, more than anything else in the entire world, that demands regard.

A setting, nothing more – no plot, no characters.

Because of this nearness and this distance.

Put a frame around it if you would, and call it what you would, if you would.

But the winds will scream with the seven voices of judgment, if you're there to hear them, and may you never, and it just doesn't seem that any name will fit. (144–5)

There is also a fine sermon of doom punctuated by a tolling bell:

No wonder then that the Beast ——, with seven heads and ten horns —— them, rises up from the ocean, —— the seven seals have been broken —— the four horsemen out of the —— . . . (40–1)

Anna Kavan's *Ice* (1967) is a rare example of the projected 'heat-death' of the universe where, because 'man had destroyed the immemorial order' (158), humanity slowly dies out in the brutal lusts of an icy world. Generally in these visions the landscape simply becomes a nothingness, a territory whose lineage stretches from the Biblical Limbo through the mud of the Somme and the psychic signposts of Eliot and Beckett. The dissolution of mankind into factions and aimless, desperate prowling, is seen most vividly in the worlds of Leiber and Zelazny. One of the most fully worked out of these peopled landscapes, one where the intensity of the imagination and spareness of the images still suggest an imaginative vision rather than primarily an evolutionary extrapolation, is M. John Harrison's *The Committed Men* (1973). Dr Wendover (his name prefiguring the aimless wandering throughout the novel) surveys the remains of a futuristic super-highway, fenced in like 'the chicken-wire run of an experimental rat maze' (11), where spectacular multi-car collisions still occur in a weirdly soundless death-dance. The newspaper headlines – 'Soviets Accuse U.S.A.' – betoken the world crisis; Wendover's own rural village suggests the dislocation of technology and the eternal verities; and the desertion and death of his wife suggest the breakdown of what is so appropriately termed the 'nuclear' family. This prologue ends, 'At that time the motorway stretched away into the future'; thirty years later the highway, as the epigraph from Ambrose Bierce suggests, is derelict and has no destination. The village has become 'Tinhouse' where savages worship a geiger counter, Wendover has the 'sacrosanct air of the tribal shaman' (25) and his house is full of the useless detritus of the modern world: colour TV, a poster for vaginal deodorant, a photograph of J. G. Ballard, that master of post-technological landscapes. Attending a childbirth, Wendover is usurped by Holloway Pauce, a vaudevillean tribal leader dressed in a gold lamé suit with a mask to hide his skin cancer. The baby is taken away to be suckled by Morag, a destitute hag whose soul is fired by the pages of *True Life Romance* which she finds in an abandoned car.

Wendover begins wandering with a mutant dwarf called Arm and is progressively brutalised by the shocking new environment. During one beating he has a vision of 'an entomic Armageddon in which he participated as an armoured stick insect' (53). A degenerate civil service patrols the ruined city:

> It was the rags that gave him his first clue to their identity: here and there he saw the grubby sleeve of a black jacket, the absurd smear of a dirty white collar; and once, a pair of pinstripe trousers hacked off in tatters at the knee.
>
> The old hierarchy had hung on: intimately involved in centralisation, unable to deal with the problems presented outside the high-rise offices, a swarm of clerks had remained after the disaster. They lived out maggoty existences in the gutted buildings, the New Administrators, scavenging the dismembered corpse of the city.
>
> The regalia of a discontinued masonry – what meaning did it have for the starved remnants of urban man? (55)

A mutant called Senior Boardroom (with his assistant 'Personnel') rules, and Wendover is arrested and forced by the Ministry of Liability and Intent to sit an examination. He escapes to the desolate waste land, where a crazed nun leads a gang hunting down mutants and cannibalising them to the words of the Mass. Like Holloway, they see their mission as preserving the fragile purity of the human race, and a struggle ensues for the baby who has now joined Wendover's party. In a strange, haunting dénouement they surrender the baby to a mutant Queen who passes by on a unicorn. The epilogue introduces Nick Bruton, former political leader, now a wandering minstrel who will tell us this story. While the motivation of 'committed men' like Wendover is never examined closely, *The Committed Men* does give heroic dimensions to the ordinary, decent citizen's efforts to maintain some humanity in a crazy world. It is formally a rough book, alternatively stylish and grotesque, suiting the phantasmagorical world it describes. It moves from realism through the quest story (with the baby a kind of grail) to myth and focuses on the changing role of language and story. Written literature is a thing of the past, although Wendover tries to re-introduce poetry. One of his followers explores the ruined city and in a stream of consciousness Harrison interweaves fragments of political history where Nick Bruton (the minstrel at the end) has already become transmogrified into the Devil:

> Separated from a party of Tinhousers foraging for building material in the abandoned back gardens of the suburbs, he wandered into an area that had been devastated when the legendary Fifth Republic – under Hall, the last true Premier – had gathered its waning strength and wiped out Bruton's Situationalists, a year before its own defeat by entropy. He knew this only as a series of bedtime stories in which Bruton was cast as Old Nick and entropy as lack of paraffin. The event had taken place a year after his birth, and he was eleven . . . .
>
> Three or four acres of demolished streets surrounded him on all sides, isolated spurs of masonry fingering up from the rubble. *Nick Bruton brought up his Cadillacs, but Hall was wise to that.* The ragged skyline gave him a strange feeling of insecurity. Occasionally, he would come upon an almost intact row of houses, their windows starred and crazed, rotting curtains flapping in the wind. *Bit by bit old Nick's that.* At these times he walked jauntily in the middle of the road . . . (79)

Harrison alarms with the power of his vision and his stress on the rapidity of change: thirty years is all it takes for the shell of civilisation to disintegrate, for civil servants to become savages, and for politics to become a fairy tale.

Other fictions also try to suggest the waste land by linguistic means. David Bunch's series of stories *Moderan* (1959–70) is introduced by an editor who prides himself on his evolutionary superiority. He has discovered the tapes of a self-styled mechanical king who, with his android giants, established a kingdom of plastic and steel after the little human beings with their 'quaking oh-God-help-us fear' (22) had waged their Great Five Minutes War. Moderan is a machine society 'away from the mental clutter of the Moral Know' (103) but it too has decayed, and the final irony is that the editor, proclaiming his humanity, has to have his love affairs programmed for him by a 'Love Director'. The language of this partly successful series is rugged and full of technical jargon, to match the brave new world. Michael Butterworth attempts to escape this obvious linguistic ploy in his short fiction 'Post-atomic' (1969), a world full of electrified and obsolete sounds and pulsations which fly up in a parody of the missiles. 'Post-atomic' is itself a personification:

His face was a wide-open expanse of clinkered skin. His brain was layered, glazed levels of desert. His skull was uneven and thus deformed, pushed out at birth to make way for cancerous growth from the brain. The rest of him was imaginary. (80)

King Trash awaits like the Fisher King the restoration of the kingdom: 'At one stage things and people shat on one another. Then the rockets were called in. And I've got the legacy' (82). Mr Zero, by contrast, is a railway guard clinging to habit, tending his flowerbeds and writing to a nonexistent postman. Then there is Baby, an androgynous child in a deserted suburb where ghostly buses run but never stop, and her tears are the remnants of a domestic history. These surreal images and disjunctions, like those of Spike Milligan and John Antrobus in their play *The Bed-Sitting Room* (1970), sometimes have Beckettian power but too often run the risk of becoming Goon-ishly absurd, whimsical rather than catastrophic, endlessly fabricated without the cohesive force of an overall vision or plot. Nevertheless, the impulse to match the post-disaster landscape with a fiction which recognises, like Holocaust literature, the inappropriateness of conventional fictional elements like plot and unity, is understandable.

A counterpart of the waste land as an imaginative setting is the jungle, where what is stressed is not the evolutionary possibility of a return to animal-like behaviour as in some of the stories in Chapter 4, but rather the symbolic significance of the heart of darkness, a confusion where man has lost his way.

Richard Jefferies' *After London* (1895) presumes ecological and natural disasters – plagues of mice, meteors, technology – but has many of the attributes of the post-nuclear disaster landscapes of this century. In Jefferies' future England 'no one wants books' (30), and the truth about what happened is difficult to uncover: 'I must attribute the discrepancy to the wars and hatreds which sprang up and divided the people, so that one would not listen to what the others wished to say, and the truth was lost' (14). The author's misanthropy is fully dramatised in his picture of an England of putrid swamps, especially where London once was:

He had penetrated into the midst of that dreadful place, of which he had heard many a tradition: how the earth was poison, the water poison, the air poison, the very light of heaven, falling through such an atmosphere, poison. There were said to be places where the earth was on fire and belched forth sulphurous flames, supposed to be from the combustion of the enormous stores of strange and unknown chemicals collected by the wonderful people of those times. Upon the surface of the water there was a greenish-yellow oil, to touch which was death to any creature; it was the very essence of corruption. . . .

The earth on which he walked, the black earth, leaving phosphoric footmarks behind him . . . was composed of the mouldered bodies of millions of men who had passed away in the centuries during which the city existed. (206)

There is little to separate this from Wells's description of the aftermath of nuclear attack, or Philip Wylie's in *Tomorrow!*, or Hersey's in *Hiroshima*. But Jefferies also has a freedom of imagination which allows him to rediscover the pastoral beauty of Albion in the flora and fauna which are now covering these abominations; in the myth of Leviathan, London herself, corrupting in Hell; and in the Biblical apocalypse – as he describes the last days of London where men 'cast themselves into the flames of the burning houses, and their roasted bodies were eaten by the miserable creatures around. Others exclaimed that they saw armies fighting in the clouds . . .' (248). Jefferies' apocalyptic fervour is clearly stated in his introduction to the book: 'We must destroy the idea of our knowing anything. We must fully acknowledge that we know nothing and begin again' (xvi). His hero Sir Felix, although he has a secret book-horde, is unwilling to reveal his knowledge to a world where such learning 'was of all things the most despised' (47). But there is a nightmarish desperation in the novel which undercuts Jefferies' archaic diction, Biblical cadences and assertions of mediaeval chivalry under the greenwood tree. His world is unpopulated, and even the pastoral world seems almost to trip into its own kind of tangled chaos; as John Fowles notes, there is 'a faintly surreal quality, of the recorded nightmare, of a near-madness' (xix).

Brian Aldiss's *Greybeard* (1964) is set in the same territory, an internalised England. The eponymous hero and his wife Martha set off on a last adventure down the river Thames from Sparcot to the sea. Little by little the past seeps into the narrative: how in 1981 there was 'that deliberate act men called the Accident' (132) causing radiation sickness; then Britain and America detonated bombs in space which irradiated the globe and sterilised the human race; in 2005 a coalition assumed power in England and now, in 2030, various local despots like Croucher hold sway, cut off from neighbouring hamlets as of old by hedgerows, ferocious animals, mutant plants and flooded valleys. In short, 'of the seven ages of man, little but the last remained' (43). Aldiss creates a rich tapestry of English life in the communities on the river: the circus of Swifford Fair, the remnants of Oxford Colleges, the religious sects of Jingadangelow. These alternate with Greybeard's reminiscences, so that instead of progress down the river there is a strong sense of stasis, of an inward voyage, like Marlow's in Conrad's great story. Greybeard has to battle through the 'brain curtain' to relive the past; how he was involved in Operation Childsweep to kidnap the babies of the world, how he worked for DOUCH(E) – a clever acronym for the European Branch of the Documentation of Universal Contemporary History – to help the future generations 'construct a socially viable community' (149) and to leave a record for extraterrestrial visitors ('Maybe I read too much of my father's science fiction at too early an age'). Jingadangelow dispenses vitamin pills from his laboratory–skyscraper but Greybeard rejects his community – 'You carry the old rigmarole of mask-wearing into these simple days' (240). He thinks that the disaster has taught man to be simple and honest, 'more appreciative of the vital things, like life itself, like each other' (185), but no amount of rationalising can answer his wife's quiet lament, 'We would have had children and grandchildren by now . . .' (185). Aldiss's central concern here is to present the debate about human continuity itself, a debate which is simply highlighted by the apocalyptic setting: how much do we care for our children and the future? what value has the past for us? A preacher argues that God has taken away the generative function of Man as a punishment for his heinous crimes. Meanwhile groups pray for 'full wombs' and in the streets are hawked 'nursery-pornographic pamphlets':

> Little man Blue
> Come rouse up your horn,
> The babies all bellow,
> They aren't getting born! (196–7)

Aldiss fleshes out this world with marvellously realised invention, not only the sense of the English countryside but ironic details like the successful importing of Swedish reindeer (their horns aphrodisiacal) while mankind 'died in addled sperm' (66), colleges in Oxford firing mortars at each other, and a hairdresser complaining, 'I always used to say when we first heard about this radiation scare that as long as there were people around they'd still want their hair cut – as long as it didn't all fall out, naturally . . .' (109). The verbal and character richness of *Greybeard* make it unusually memorable, and a successful imaginative counterpart to those other fictions (*The Eleventh Commandment* – religion, 'Tomorrow's Children' – evolution) which focus on the continuity of the human race.

A richer but equally locatable pastoral world is the setting for a trilogy of novels by the American Edgar Pangborn. Like the revisionist historian in one of Pangborn's stories, his narrator sits 'snug down here in the cellars of the Ecclesia at Nuber among the ancient books that the Holy Murcan Church hasn't yet destroyed' and creates a vibrant oral history – 'For I shall one day be transfigured by a printing press into a book, and chew my way out clear through you' (172). In another story Pangborn explains clearly why he admires the post-disaster world:

Having never heard of Twentieth Century sociology, and possessing a small enclave so far only moderately oppressed by a developing feudal tyranny from above, the Donsil villagers were free to be pleasant folk. Somehow, at least in this one little spot of the world, after the long dark of the Years of Confusion when savagery ruled and most remnants of civilisation were forced to shelter behind wooden blockades relearning the primitive arts (and forgetting much) – somehow the sick money-greed of Old Time had diminished to a manageable intensity. Human beings were still as a rule greedy animals – of course. But the bloated hugeness of Old Time society, and its ghastly illusion of success, had favoured priggishness at every turn, often openly making a virtue of it. Not in Donsil. (84)

The first novel *The Judgment of Eve* (1966) is based on the legend of Pallas Athene. Eve lives on a farm with her blind mother and is visited by three suitors: clever Ken, lusty Ethan and musical Claudius. They each have adventures pursuing the secret of life which seems to involve the correct orientation towards time. We never discover who wins the hand of Eve but the correct orientation is embodied in the narrator himself with his freewheeling attitude towards the past and a vivid absorption in the present. He may be contrasted with the old woman who sits watching a dead TV, or the politician who says breezily, 'Bugger old time. This here is the progressive here and now is what it is' (144). The narrator is happy to recycle the myth, 'tidying up' some versions of history, adding 'a bit of exegesis here and there' (159). Truth lies not in historical fact but in interpretation and morality, so what is important about the nuclear disaster is the people's reaction: '"We were all guilty" –

no, that was never much more than a whine, a way of dodging responsibility by seeming to accept it' (21).

Davy (1964) is set in the year 338 after the Age of Confusion which ended Old Time in 1993. The twenty minute nuclear war has isolated the regency of Nuin (New England) in the 'Katskil' Mountains. The Holy Murcan Church allows brothels under its Doctrine of Necessary Evils, but forbids the manufacture of gunpowder 'or any other substance that may by competent authorities of the Church be reasonably suspected of containing atoms' (152). It has a new Messiah, Abraham, whose teaching is repressive and especially outlaws books, but the hero Davy declares on the first page, 'I say to hell with the laws that forbid most Old-Time books or reserve them to the priests' (7). He refers to the Book of John Barth, a fragment whose possession means death, which he intends to print as soon as he acquires a press and paper (51). This reference to the author and critic John Barth gives us a clue to Pangborn's intentions in *Davy*. Like Barth, he makes the novel a self-conscious genre and Davy a spokesman for reflexive postmodernism. Davy is oppressed by the impossibility of telling his tale:

> There were so many stories I could never be certain which I was telling, and it doesn't matter as much as I thought it did when I was bothering you and your Aunt Cassandra about varieties of time. It may be well enough to look at the enigma, the crazy glory and murk of our living-and-dying with a pen in your hand, but try it yourself – you'll find more stories than you knew, and you'll find mirth, tragedy, dirt, splendour, ecstasy, weariness, laughter and rage and tears all so intricately dependent on each other, intertwined like copulating snakes or the busy branches of a jinny-creeper – why, don't be troubling yourself about opposites and balances but never mind, take hold of one branch and you touch them all. (262)

He worries about his audience, since 'Misipan' (Mississippian) refugees suggest the world is wider than Nuin:

> Your nations were stricken by the same abortive idiotic nuclear war and probably by the same plagues. Your culture

showed the same symptoms of a possible moral collapse, the
same basic weariness of over-stimulation, the same decline of
education and rise of illiteracy, above all the same dithering
refusal to let ethics catch up with science. After the plagues,
your people may not have turned against the very memory of
their civilisation in a sort of religious frenzy as ours apparently
did, determined like spoilt brats to bring down in the
wreckage every bit of good along with the bad. They may not
have, but I suspect they did. (50)

Indeed, Davy sounds more and more like his literary ancestor
Tristram Shandy. He is concerned about the nature of time,
regards the reader as a travelling companion, has a mistress
(Nickie) to whom he often refers, ages as he talks and goes not
to France but to Neonarchos. Like *Tristram Shandy* also, the
book is unfinished. Davy's friends Dion and Nickie carry on a
dialogue with him in the margins and footnotes of the text, and
Davy himself sometimes steps behind the asterisks to explain
things (34). He is ignorant of his own birth and also impotent –
'My only children are certain thoughts I may have been able to
give you' (265).

Davy's view of humankind, like Sterne's, is critical but
indulgent. Although his society is class ridden and destroys
'muses' or mutants, he will defend it against raiders from the
northern states. He wonders whether man will ever be able to
restore 'the good of Old Time without the evil' (265), but feels
links with humanity in that his own battles are not 'ethically
smaller' than the nuclear conflict, and the human race *has*
survived if only 'by the merest happen-so' (12). Although
'words are not magic' (58) (he approves of Mama Maura's rage
at the fustian laws of English grammar – 'Bugger the buggerly
book!' [230] and retains a line from his troupe's abbreviated
version of *Romeo and Juliet* only because it may be a clue to
Galilean astronomy [236]), Davy writes his book to maintain
the human continuity – 'so long as one book survives anywhere
. . . Old Time is not dead' (134) – and loves it when his new
island is accurately *named* by Dion (75). Like the golden horn
which he carries, Davy's own prose style rings true and clear,
energetic and inventive, if perhaps too insistently drawn from
rural American slang (Pangborn glosses over this lack of
inventiveness by having Davy deliberately write the book in 'an

Old Time style'). Like Aldiss, Pangborn tries to give us a panorama of human responses to an extreme situation, and to clarify what is worth fostering in human nature. Like his hero, Pangborn understands the importance of telling tales to one another as an expression of solidarity and Sterne-like sentiment.

His third novel *The Company of Glory* (1975) tries to combine the two previous elements – the legend-telling of *The Judgment of Eve* and the personal history of *Davy* – to show an old storyteller, Demetrios, leading a motley band around the countryside performing plays. His position in the community is crucial, for 'in a time when literacy is rare the storyteller and newsbearer come into their own; and the memories of some listeners develop astonishing powers that an age of typewriter and newspaper must have lost or submerged' (8). Demetrios tries to preserve the real world by fashioning words anew ('All through history people have imagined that giving horror a pretty name makes it no longer horror' [14]); but the novel disappoints – lifeless, endlessly prolific but unfocused, merely a display of garrulous, verbal pyrotechnics.

There are other imaginary visions as fully fleshed as Pangborn's which are set neither in the desert nor the jungle or pastoral microcosm, but in the context of a continuing technological society. Again, these fictions are considered here rather than in previous chapters because their over-riding concern seems to me to be as a consciousness-raising exercise, to speak directly and urgently to a present audience, and to dramatise a view of human nature.

Janet Frame's *Intensive Care* (1970) is set in New Zealand, which has seemed to many writers (John Wyndham, Aldous Huxley, etc.) a paradise immune from the effects of nuclear war: not so for Frame, who lives there. The first two sections of the novel focus on the experiences of participants in the two world wars, reminding the reader that global conflicts have not spared New Zealand in the past and have left there, as elsewhere, deep psychological scars. In the third section the rest of the world (including the North Island of New Zealand) has been devastated and the government has passed the 'Human Delineation Act'. This draconian legislation requires every citizen to be investigated by computer and judged on Classification Day either fit to survive or 'animal' and destined to be processed into useful items. By looking back explicitly to

the Second World War, Frame reminds us that such a step is
not a brave new world fantasy but simply an extension of
various other final solutions already perpetrated in history.
Under the influence of behavioural psychologists, effective
propaganda, memory-erasing drugs and the enforcement by
American troops, the outrageous scheme goes ahead. Only
Milly Galbraith, an autistic woman whose misspelt journal we
read, maintains a humane viewpoint. Through her innocent
vision the nuclear war becomes even more horrific:

> Then the war came, the last war, and at first it was all right
> because nobody bothered and everybody went on just the
> same and then a few men went to phite and then they started
> putting people in jail because they didn't want to phite. . . .
> And then the men started coming home from the war and
> some had no faces and no hands and no feet and no skins
> and no nothing and there were men with blew faces like
> kidknees only it was the graffite writing on their faces and
> their bodies. . . .
>
> Then everyone gave up hope and the doctors got tired and
> only the doll-normills continued working, but soon ther was
> nothing to clean up because no one bothered, it was too
> much to bear, instead they prayed and prayed but God was
> not in the mood for listening to so much prayer ovatime. He
> said, why didn't you ask me before when I was not rushed off
> my feet with work. And when maw of the wounded men
> came home in the Bowing seven-oh-seven with the black nose
> and silva wings an ambewlants met them at the airport and
> they were taken to the hospittle and put in rows on the flaw
> like seed potatoes, and most went rotten and died . . . (263–
> 4)

She sees the townsfolk of Waipori City as 'ghosts walking in
the fires of hell' (267) but, bereft of companions, she must
invent Sandy, the Reconstructed Man built mostly out of gold,
who was wounded in the war:

> He was burned with the bomb that writes its name on you
> with graphite and with the other bomb that leaves a glare in
> the sky and blinds you, but not if you hide in concrete under
> the earth with air excluded and supplies for many days until

the bomb loses its deadly power and you come out on the earth and you have all the fresh air you have saved in containers, but the earth is razed into an unfamiliar desert and you have to start all over again the task of building the western world safe for democracy. (243)

Together they read Biblical apocalyptic – 'that's most of the Bible, Sandy, fire blud, gold garments, and desserlitt cities' (305) – and prepare for the day of judgment. Milly of course does not survive, but the final narration by one of the overseers of the experiment reveals that the guilt is proving intolerable to the survivors, and now the 'humans' are being eradicated as well. *Intensive Care*, then, is about 'care' and how far the state should intervene in the psychic disorders, often inherited from previous state-decreed wars, of its people. Bureaucracy and technology lead to the totalitarian state, particularly in the fearful climate following nuclear war. We need a new language with which to communicate our fears and heal our wounds, for 'even the alphabetical atom may be subdued by the hydrogen atom, unless those who work with language, unless people who speak, learn also to split and solve the alphabet' (166). Here Frame introduces a memorable image, one implicit in this study, that the new world requires a new language, and even the avoidance of the new world needs a fundamental change in the language we use now – away from the direction of 'nukespeak' towards frankness and feeling. As Patrick Evans says, there is need in Frame's novel for 'a virtuoso display of poetry, a performance from the edge of the alphabet'.[12] Frame does not fully achieve this in Milly's too sophisticated speech but the attempt to reach our imaginative centre is there and, as Milly herself reminds us, the novel is not prediction but parable:

If you think I paint a grim picture of what will happen, then I can only say that you who are reading this are lucky not to be living in the time I write of. Do not be deceived – you may be living in it and not know, because two times can live together and the one doesn't know that the other time is living because if you're in one time whatever would make you want to think there is another there . . .? (240)

The citizens of Bernard Wolfe's *Limbo '90* (1953) are equally mutilated and fearful. Dr Martine, like Wells's Moreau, has been lobotomising natives on a desert island and when he returns to a warring world he finds himself deified in a religion of prostheses. The people have turned his notebooks into a Bible, his cry 'Dodge the steamroller' being misinterpreted as a call to self-mutilation ('vol-ampism' or the amputation of limbs) in the search for wholeness and innocence. Martine protests desperately:

> I'll tell you what *won't* work! . . . Attacking the human organism with a scalpel won't work, that's sure! I can slice up the worst homicidal maniac's prefrontal lobes and give you a real lamb of a pacifist, sure, the best little basket case you ever saw – but he's not a human being any more, just a lump! Just like an amp! Ambulatory basket case! For good! No, no, the knife won't work, you shit, you swine! . . . There's only one thing that'll work, you pig, that has any chance of saving man before he's annihilated through his own masochism, it's to get behind his shows of violence and pound it home to him that 99 per cent of them are phony, masochistic in inception and masochistic in aim, born of death and striving for death. That'll work, and only that, all the rest is suicide disguised as science and humanitarianism . . . (368)

Martine realises that the nuclear war between America and Russia 'was a war of annihilation between twins.' Not only were they 'afraid of living with the impossible anguished tension of humanness' (414); they were also bound into their frustration and confusion because, 'their feet planted in the dazzling electronic-atomic realities of the twentieth century, their heads were still in the archaic clouds of nineteenth century semantics' (142). Language dooms mankind to war, and like Frame's novel *Limbo '90* tries to free up our ideas about words. Perhaps a playful attitude to language will break us out of the mind-trap of nuclear conflict. Language of course is powerful: the new religion is based on a pun – 'arms mean armaments, legs mean marching orders' (166) – while Martine combats it with another literary reference – 'We might call our brave new world Limbo' (215) (it is also an awful pun). Even Man can be defined in Joycean puns, as 'Dog-God' or 'Noyes man' (no-yes). Martine's asides are misheard and erected into dogma, like his 'too late for womb-leaving' which instigates a discussion of the virtues of 'loom-weaving' among Ghandi's Untouchables! Martine himself is a literary man styling himself on Joyce – 'Old myth-mother, old artificialer, stand me now and forever in not too bad stead' (142) – and Sterne, and like their novels, *Limbo '90* is a potpourri of current intellectual thought, from Korzysbki to Freud, Weber to Wiener, Nietzsche to Reich. Like his hero, Wolfe is half-exuberant, half-despairing. In an afterword he says he wrote this sprawling 'anatomy' of a book because he wanted to describe 'the overtone and undertone of *now* – in the guise of 1990 because it would take decades for a year like 1950 to be milked of its implications' (438). But at the same time as he argues for the moral virtues of extrapolation, Wolfe quotes Tolstoy on how a man, after he has acted, will 'supply in his imagination a whole series of retrospective reflections to prove his freedom to himself' (433). Certainly Martine ends the book by retreating to his island but he also writes a page-high 'YES' to life in answer to his earlier 'NO' to war. Wolfe's message seems to be that we must accept the whole of life, man's stupidity and capacity for self-mutilation and self-destruction as well as his nobility, if we are to avoid the reification of his worst fantasies. The most effective way to open up the imagination and keep it supple and alive is playing with language, and *Limbo '90*, for all its bombast, is a brilliant example of the verbal imagination at play.

Verbal pyrotechnics also mark Brian Aldiss's *Barefoot in the Head* (1969), where instead of nuclear war the weapons are mind-altering drugs: 'When the Acid Head War broke out, undeclared, Kuwait had struck at all the prosperous countries. Britain had been the first nation to suffer the PCA bomb – the PsychoChemical Aerosols that propagated psychotomimetic states, twilight ruptured its dark cities' (17). The anti-military, anti-Christian saviour Charteris takes advantage of this to advocate a new freedom of mind: 'weren't these lay songs and carnal fictions a brighter fire than any burning in a regulation grate blessed by clergy or a funeral?' (51) But although 'the bombs were only/In his head' (236) (as Charteris's epitaph reads), he does project a vision of nuclear war on film, and Aldiss shows here the power of language to evoke rather than to define, in a series of dazzling images:

There are sequences from old-fashioned wars, when the processes of corruption sometimes had a presynchronicity to moribundity, and a shot of a nuclear bomb detonated underground, with a whole sparse country rumpling upward into a gigantic ulcerated blister and rolling outwards at predatorial speed towards the fluttering camera. There are sequences in shuttered streets, where the dust lies heavy and onions rot in gutters; not a soul moves, though a kite flutters from an overhead wire; somewhere distantly, a radio utters oldfashioned dance music interspersed with static; sunshine burns down into the engraved street; finally a shutter opens, a window opens; an iguana pants out into the roadway, its golden gullet wide. (137)

Verbal invention also sustains the more overtly political vision of Suzy McKee Charnas in *Walk to the End of the World* (1979). Envisaging 'a society in which power is the crucial question, and the struggle of males is the central form that question takes',[13] Charnas creates a tightly-organised saga with prologue and epilogue and five chapters, each for a central character: Captain Kelmz, Servan di Layo, Eykar Bek and Alldera. After the 'Wasting', society survives in the city or 'Holdfast', brutally fascist and homosexual, where the young men are sodomised in the 'Boyhouse' and the 'fems', like Wells's Morlocks, slave in underground pits. Dead fems and fem-cubs provide food, processed on a conveyor belt: 'Some man must have designed the process; it was too beautiful, too efficient to be a product of the fems' own thinking' (75). The plot involves Eykar Bek's quest for his father. On the way to the Emerald City of Troi, Eykar falls in love with Alldera, and when he finds that his father rules a kingdom which has exterminated all women except for food, he strikes him down and tries to reshape the kingdom.

What might have been feminist rant is almost always saved by Charnas's vision and verbal skill. The oppressive locker-room atmosphere of thuggery and power provides a believable attitude towards everything, even the Bible:

The Book's religion, he said, had once been a fine and manly one, complete with armed battles against unbelievers and the burning of heretics under the auspices of a powerful and strictly organised hierarchy. The entire structure of early Ancient society, with its codes of honour, rigid class divisions, and the subjugation of whole races of the Dirties, had been based on that religion. The problem, he maintained, was that fems had infiltrated and perverted a fine, manly creed . . . (95)

While Alldera sings haunting songs about patience and fortitude, the people of Troi chant feverishly against their enemies:

Having just done the beasts, they were telling the names of the Dirties, those gibbering, nearly mindless hordes whose skins had been tinted all the colours of earth so that they were easily distinguishable from true men: 'Reds, Blacks, Browns, Kinks; Gooks, Dagos, Greasers, Chinks; Ragheads, Niggas, Kites, Dinks . . .'
They chanted the Freaks, commonly represented as torn and bloodied by explosions their own bombs had caused: 'Lonhairs, Raggles, Bleedingarts; Faggas, Hibbies, Families, Kids; Junkies, Skinheads, Collegeists; Ef-eet Ironmentalists', the last a reference to the softminded values of the Freaks, iron being notoriously less strong than steel.
Finally, the chant came to the fems, huge-breasted, doused in sweet-stinking waters to mask uglier odors, loud and forever falsely smiling. Their names closed the circle, for being beast-like ('red in tooth and claw,' as some old books said) they had been known by beasts' names: 'Bird, Cat, Chick, Sow; Filly, Tigress, Bitch, Cow . . .' (129)

In the sequel *Motherlines* (1981) Alldera escapes into the waste land beyond the Holdfast where two bands of women roam free, one of them, the Mares, reproducing themselves by copulation with the stallions which they ride and worship. The bizarre rite of the Gather is rendered eloquently and beautifully in images of unity and continuity: '[The Mares] were like some woven design in which each broad, clear thread could be traced in the image of each Motherline, repeated from individual to individual and from generation to generation' (55).
Although Charnas's novels arise out of a plausible post-disaster situation – the attribution of guilt to all women – they move towards an alternative, a vision of the new species of androgynous (wo)mankind. There is a desperate need for a

perspective on the holocaust, some kind of frame which goes beyond it. The progression of Doris Lessing's fictions of nuclear disaster shows a similar movement, from realism to vision to polemic.

The fourth and final part of *The Four-Gated City* (1969) ends with Martha the heroine deciding that any change must begin with herself: 'Here, where else, you fool, you poor fool, where else has it been, ever . . .?' (645) Outwardly the world is moving towards some kind of crisis, as predicted by Mark in his novel and his Memorandum to himself:

> 1. We are all hypnotised by the idea of Armageddon . . .
> 2. This prevents preparation, psychological and physical, for what is likely. . . . What will happen is a development of what is already happening and what has been accelerating, out of control, since 1914 and the green light for mass extermination. (605–6)

Lessing then appends several documents which take us beyond the holocaust, although the gesture towards realism is token only since the sixty pages of evidence were destroyed by Amanda Coldridge 'before the Northern National Area (formerly North China) was overrun by the Mongolian National Area' (647). They were destroyed, indicating one of Lessing's main themes: the difficulty of obtaining information, of knowing what is going on. She effectively abandons the novelist's privileged viewpoint to show us the desperate ignorance which both hastens and is the result of global conflict. In one letter Francis warns his stepdaughter not to provide the Preserver of Historical Studies (the Mongolian invader) with information, but to commit her thoughts 'to one of the Memories' (650). He himself documents the confusion of ominous events which led to the dissolution of society: North Sea leaks, stricken Russian submarines, nuclear accidents at Aldermaston, suicidal fighter planes, until 'No week passed then without forecasts of Armageddons or freshly minted Paradises' (680). Having escaped to a commune in Western Ireland, Francis and the mutant children try to absorb information telepathically:

> At first when we listened in (and this was true for months and months after the disaster) it was to a screeching, wailing,

howling bedlam of sound as if all humanity begged for mercy and help. And it is still too easy to plug into this band now. We had no idea, we still don't know, if the event in Britain had triggered off more wars elsewhere, and if perhaps there were now more than two sick areas. We did not know if we could trust the air that blew over us, the seas that surrounded us. (697)

The children offer hope but Mark is more pessimistic. For him the 'holocausts of the flesh in our lifetime' make it impossible for there to be 'any conversation between the shape of a face and the spirit' (709). The novel's final document, concerning Martha's special child, is both a promise of the Sufi epigraph about the next stage in evolution, and a threat that the new regime will destroy any possible spiritual growth. Lessing's imaginative vision hovers out of time between stasis and evolution.

In *Shikasta* and its sequels (1979–) Lessing continues to explore the psychological conditions of nuclear disaster in the imaginative freedom of outer space. The outer world with its official version is as distant from the inner world of experience as in Frame's *Intensive Care*, and the documents and reports which litter Lessing's fictions (here, students are directed to the 'History of Shikasta. . . The Century of Destruction, Twentieth Century War: Third and Final Phase' [355] and *Envoys of the Last Days: A Concise History*) contrast with Lynda Coldridge's subjective vision:

As I go along these roads I am sometimes alone with my faithful jaguar and dog but sometimes with others, and when talk starts about the awfulness, then it is as if people are not hearing. Not that they are not listening. Not hearing. They look vaguely at you. Blank. Do you know what I think. They can't believe it. Well sometimes I look back and it is such a little time, and I can't believe it. I think that dreadfulness happens somewhere else. I don't know how to say that. I mean, when awful things happen, even to the extent we have all just seen, then our minds don't take them in. Not really. There is a gap between people saying hello, have a glass of water, and then bombs falling or laser beams scorching the world to cinders. That is why no one seemed able to prevent the dreadfulness. They couldn't take it in. (361)

Doris Lessing goes to outer space in order to 'free up' the imagination in its attitude towards nuclear disaster. Many other writers are forced to similar extremes. Milly Galbraith suggested possible parallel worlds, and Robert Heinlein utilises the notion in *Farnham's Freehold* (1965). The novel begins as a conventional, realistic extrapolation, with the Farnham family safe in their shelter under the command of their partriarchal father:

> 'All the talk about the horrors of World War Three has been about atomic weapons – fallout, hundred-megaton bombs, neutron bombs, the disarmament talks and the pacifist parades have all been about the Bomb, the Bomb, the Bomb – as if A-weapons were the only thing that could kill. This may not be just an A-weapons war; more likely it is an ABC war – atomic, biological, and chemical.' He hooked a thumb at the tanks. 'That's why I stocked that bottled breathing. Against nerve gas. Aerosols. Viruses. God knows what. The communists won't smash this country if they can kill us without destroying our wealth.' (35)

Mr Farnham is particularly aggrieved that his library does not stock more fiction and Mark Twain. He seems eminently fit to lead the survivors, but when the family emerges it is to find they have been shocked into a parallel world, a pastoral paradise where the last war took place in 703 B.C. (Before the Great Change). However, they discover that they have only slipped back slightly in time, and that the nuclear holocaust will begin in one hour, giving them time to retire to a mine shaft and prepare to start it all again. For all its survivalist crudity the novel does have some insights: the new language will be based on Arabic, French and Swahili (184), and Farnham's account of the war is appealingly succinct:

> The bright boys made it possible, and the dull boys they worked for had not only never managed to make the possibility unlikely but had never really believed it when the bright boys delivered what the dull boys ordered. (191)

An equally imaginative parallel world is the basis of René Barjavel's *The Ice People* (1968). Scientists discover a frozen world beneath the Antarctic ice. It is Gondawa, victim of the third war which 'lasted for an hour' (99) and involved solar weapons – 'as if the sun itself were to fall' (170). Survivors are resuscitated and after some banal adventures with life elixirs and sexual encounters, the world seems to be headed for the same fate once more – 'They've achieved the same state of idiocy they were in before, ready to blow themselves up all over again. Great, isn't it? That's the human race!' (191)

In Norman Spinrad's *The Iron Dream* (1972) a kind of parallel Adolf Hitler who seems to have had nothing to do with the Nazis wrote a 1950s science fiction novel called *Lord of the Swastika*. His leatherjacketed motorbike riders of Heldon attack their neighbours and escape nuclear doom by cloning themselves and sending the purest of the race to colonise space: 'The seed of the Swastika rose on a pillar of fire to fecundate the stars' (243). There is not one female character in the book, and technology and power are the only dimensions of a sterile landscape, 'naught but reeling contaminated wildlands with astronomical geiger counts, while nothing could live besides stomach turning things resembling ambulatory carcinomas' (29). Ursula le Guin called the novel 'a flawless example of clean obscenity',[14] but Spinrad had another purpose, suggested by the critic's afterword which sees in Heldon Germany and in her enemy the Soviet Union. Another critic Whipple argues that the whole novel is the fantasy of a neurotic mind. In both interpretations we are reminded of the links we make between fiction and fact. Critics are only too willing to see the real world reflected in fiction, and at the same time we reject the wishful fantasies of powerful imaginations at our peril:

As a work of fantastic literature by a popular science fiction writer, *Lord of the Swastika* exists only in a fantasy world parallel to our own. In the real world, it was no fantasy. Nazism not only happened, it has happened and recurred with a ferocity which cannot all be understood through the economic and political explanations of conventional historians nor limited to the history of but one country. People have subjected themselves to a real Hitler and to other monsters, with alarming frequency.[15]

Like Lessing, Frame and so many other writers, Spinrad grounds his warning of future nuclear disaster in the recent historical past, and his fiction is far more provocative and intelligible than vague apocalyptic stirrings, as exemplified in John Cowper Powys's *Up and Out* (1957). Here the hero wakes up in a spiritual never-land after the bombs have fallen:

> The hydrogen bombs of both East and West had been dropped in one wild, mad, reckless orgy of universal destruction. . . . We found ourselves standing on a grassy plain the horizon of which stretched away into the sky in every direction. (19)

After a metaphysical journey and debate, the narrator appeals to the reader to enjoy the moment. His uncertainty about his audience ('I must have you, whoever you are, to hear my last words' [121]) is shared by a more articulate poet of private visions, William Burroughs – 'Listen to my last words anywhere' (*Nova Express*, 9). Burroughs's depraved imagination is eerily lit by the 'tower blasts from Hiroshima and Nagasaki' (79), but his apocalyptic terror – 'This is a burning planet – any minute now the whole fucking shit house goes up' (14) – results only in a cry of personal despair, without the fictive framework which helps us to cope with those fears.

Another historical perspective on Armageddon is given by Roald Dahl in *Sometimes Never* (1949). The first half of the novel is a realistic account of the Battle of Britain, except that the efforts of the fighter pilots are frustrated by a band of likeable, amoral and thoroughly real 'gremlins'. When the nuclear war erupts, the gremlins provide a new imaginative perspective. They look on in glee from their underground world: 'Better and quicker,' they chuckle as the mega-deaths mount, 'They're at it again . . . Hurrah . . . another million gone' (164). Having established in the reader's mind that the gremlins are immortal beings, Dahl powerfully conveys the nuclear horror ('it couldn't happen to us' becomes 'it couldn't happen to them') by having some unfortunate gremlins caught in the fiery hell of London:

> Stuffy was neither concerned nor anxious. He merely had it somewhere in his mind that Peternip and he should meet and talk and drink that afternoon; he had it vaguely in his mind,

and there it was. But where? Where was he now? Stuffy stood there in the street and looked at the many bodies lying on the ground.

Then he saw him. He knew him at once by the size and shape of his body and by the way he lay there on the ground. He knew for certain it was Peternip and he strolled slowly over to the body and stood beside it, looking down at it and seeing the way the hands were clasped together with the skin hanging loosely from them like two gloves half taken off, seeing the red–black face, the scorched and melted flesh upon the face, the empty eyes, the hair burnt off, and seeing now the knees drawn up close under the stomach and the grey suit half-burnt, half-singed, lying in fragments over the pale blue shirt which showed clean and untouched underneath. (159)

Undeterred, the gremlins emerge to take over the world, but their admirable utopia (founded on laws like 'There shall be no such thing as countries' [235]) soon fades because gremlins are dependent on the human imagination for their existence. The leader's hope, that 'what they saw would in time become a legend and a moral fable' (247), has nevertheless become true through Dahl's novel. The author has successfully taken us through the reality of nuclear disaster (although the detail is drawn heavily from the historical experience of the firebombing of London) without disrupting our realistic expectations. His novel simply makes explicit in the person of the gremlins the fictional device by which most of the authors considered here guide the reader both in and out of their visions.

We have moved from vividly realised landscapes, whether deserts or ruined cities, to vividly realised fictional strategies, where the framework of the novel is foregrounded in some way to give an acceptable perspective on disaster. These strategies are ways of coping with the inappropriateness of the fictional form which we discussed at the beginning of the chapter. What has happened is that writers have utilised earlier fictional forms: Lessing's letters reach back to Richardson, Davy echoes Sterne and Fielding, Wolfe copies Burton's *Anatomy*, Dahl the Brothers Grimm. In Robert Sheckley's *Journey Beyond Tomorrow* (1964) we are in the world of Voltaire's *Candide*. The hero Joenes was brought up on a Pacific island, but visits the nightmare world of North America and inadvertently instigates the nuclear holocaust. Half of America's missiles land on American soil, thereby setting off even more missiles. This inept confusion is prefigured in the picture of the Octagon (Pentagon) as a maze of bureaucratic muddle where the mapmaker has been shot and only a character called Theseus knows his way about. Joenes retreats to his island paradise with a beatnik called Lum who says, 'As soon as we get rid of all the damned metal, everything will swing' (182). Joenes is more cynical; he realises that the Pacific is pacific only because 'you ever try to build a atom bomb out of coral and coconut shells?' (185). He presents a puppet show where human beings are the dupes of the gods, and finally he disappears up a mountain with some maps of the old days, giving rise to a religion and stories of an old man, ghostly, sitting in a cave reading papers. The Pynchon-esque motif of mapmaking runs through this funny, wise novel, and at the end one feels that Sheckley's novel and others like it are the only worthwhile maps in a directionless age. Certainly Joenes will not be using the realistic maps he has been given. His subsequent deification (the book is composed of various transcriptions of the oral history of the Pacific Islands such as the Book of Fiji) is just one more satirical example of man's desperate quest for signposts in a bewildering world.

Several short stories attempt a satirical framework for the nuclear holocaust. In Robert Silverberg's 'When we went to see the end of the world' the dumb, illiterate thrill-seekers of a disintegrating world take up American Express's timetripping offer to witness the end of the world – as if they are not already there. In Philip José Farmer's 'The Making of Revelation Part I' God revivifies Cecil B. de Mille to help him make an epic about Revelation in order to convince his people. De Mille signs away his soul in order to get Satan to play himself, but, looking forward to Part II, God says, 'I can't break your contract with him . . . let's discuss the shooting of the new heaven and the new earth sequences' (91). In John Gloag's novel *Tomorrow's Yesterday* (1932) London's sophisticates go to a new art film which portrays the holocaust from the point of view of two cat-like descendents of the human race. Although one critic complains of 'an overdose of H. G. Wells during adolescence' (181) and a mother is most unimpressed –

TO-MORROW'S YESTERDAY

HAS BEEN CALLED

" BLASPHEMOUS,"

" OBSCENE,"

" SILLY,"

" UGLY,"

" UNNECESSARY,"

and described as :

" SOCIALIST PROPAGANDA,"

" POISONOUS IN ITS INFLUENCE."

etc.

WE DON'T AGREE. WE DO KNOW I HAPPENS TO BE GOOD ENTERTAINMENT, A LITTLE INTELLIGENT PERHAPS, BUT THEN EXPERIMENTS ARE ALWAYS NOVEL AL-THOUGH THEIR RECEPTION IS USUALLY THE SAME.

COME AND SEE WHETHER YOU AGREE WITH US OR THE CRITICS.

TO-NIGHT AT THE NEW CENTURY THEATRE

GOLDEN SQUARE, PICCADILLY CIRCUS

8.15 AND 9.55

source: J. Gloag, *Tomorrow's Yesterday* (London: George Allen & Unwin, 1932).

As a mother, I can only say how grateful I am for the warning about this terrible film. My little ones are as yet only tots, but had they been of age, I should have forbidden them to enter the doors of the theatre where their minds could easily have been poisoned for life (169)

– one reviewer calls it 'essentially a nightmare . . . worth a second visit' (172). The satiric point of the novel comes when war is actually declared, the art work is vindicated and its critics cruelly exposed.

Anthony Burgess, a tireless critic of apocalyptic literature, attempts not satire but what he calls an 'entertainment' with his musically inspired trio, *The End of the World News* (1982). Recalling a photograph of President Carter watching three television sets simultaneously, Burgess attempts a 'visual counterpoint' (ix) by exploring three principal sources of twentieth century apocalyptic thought: the theories of Freud, set in Nazi Germany; the life of Trotsky; and the impact of a meteor. For Freud the new world will be achieved when the mind is freed from the tyrannies of the subconscious: 'If I'm right, the world will come to an end and then start all over again – a new world. Men and women will know themselves for what they are, for the first time. It will be a terrible shock for the world' (94–5). For Trotsky, the Hegelian dialectic will finally achieve synthesis, 'the classless society. . . . The end. History comes to a stop' (337). Against these two intellectual, celebratory apocalypses is set the natural disaster of the contemporary story: an American president flies over the devastated ruins of New York after tidal waves and earthquakes have rocked the country, and commits suicide; Calvin Gropius the fundamentalist preacher warns about an approaching meteor; and Brodie the science fiction writer organises the construction of a space rocket. In the epilogue we see the children in the rocket being taught the legend of Brodie and his descendent Joshua who established the new religion – they have been brainwashed of any thoughts of 'Sike and Pol' (psychology and politics). Burgess's brave new world is the world of science fiction as prediction, the banality of Brodie's first novel which, as it happened, *did* actually describe the end as it finally came. Beneath Burgess's elegant playing with the idea of disaster is an immensely important theme, epitomised in Brodie's later and less well received novel *Fluke Fang*, where the human race met its end 'in a form that nobody had expected' (29). Just as Freud's new world was mocked by the Jewish Holocaust, and Trotsky's by his assassination, so the apocalypse of any fiction will be mocked by the final, real end, whatever it may be. Readers are desperate for myths, and Burgess fabricates one as suavely as any other science fiction writer, but it has nothing to do with 'reality'. The last line of the novel records the reaction of the children to the story that has just been told to them: 'They had forgotten the story already' (389). As Burgess's punning title suggests, the 'end of the world' news exists always just beyond the end of the 'world news'. Fiction, like the ideas of Freud and Trotsky, can appeal to the imagination, but history takes care of itself.

So far I have been examining, in the main, imagined communities after the holocaust; but the simplest, purest appeal to the imagination is embodied in the 'last man' theme. Thomas Hood expressed it vividly as early as 1826 in a sorry little poem:

'Twas in the year two thousand and one,
A pleasant morning in May,
I sat on the gallows-tree all alone,
A-chaunting a merry lay.

That same year Mary Shelley's *The Last Man* documented the dissolution of Europe in Biblical image and style: 'Under our very feet the earth yawned – deep and precipitous the gulph below opened to receive us, while the hours charioted us towards the chasm' (197). The hero Lionel has a sense that history has ended, time has no meaning: 'Arrived at the same point of the world's age there was no difference in us; the names of parent and child had lost their meaning; young boys and girls were level now with men' (231–2). Lionel makes a pilgrimage to a deserted Rome where he sets down his history:

I also will write a book, I cried – for whom to read? – to

whom dedicated? And then with silly flourish (what so capricious and childish as despair?) I wrote,

DEDICATION
TO THE ILLUSTRIOUS DEAD
SHADOWS, ARISE, AND READ YOUR FALL!
BEHOLD THE HISTORY OF THE
LAST MAN.

Yet will not this world be re-peopled, and the children of a saved pair of lovers, in some to me unknown and unattainable seclusion, wandering to these prodigious relics of the ante-pestilential race, seek to learn how beings so wondrous in their achievements, with imaginations infinite, and powers godlike, had departed from their home to an unknown country? (339)

Shelley's apparatus of the found document, indeed the Sybilline leaves themselves as discovered in a cave near Naples in 1818 (3–4), is by now familiar to us; so too the Biblical imagery and acute sense of human evolution. 'Last man' stories are often heavily moralistic, drawing on the archetypal pattern of Adam's fall from Eden. In Alfred Noyes's *No Other Man* (1940) biological warfare devastates the planet and the survivor prays for 'the heart which must break or turn to bronze' (141). Alfred Bester's story 'Adam and No Eve' (1941) has the survivor escape in a rocket while 'rain fell; cinder storms blew; light thrust down – together, alternately, and continually in a jig saw of black and white violence' (36). He descends by parachute and hallucinates as he crawls over the waste land in search of water. Like Lionel he has a nice, selfconscious sense of grandeur, as when he eats his last can of peaches and observes, 'Metabolism plays its last act' (37). Bester's conclusion pivots neatly on the dividing line between linear and cyclic views of history, since the last man floats in the sea and realises that his body cells will begin a new form of life: 'the mother of life rocked the last born of the old cycle who would become the first-born of the new.' A less benign end lies in wait for Eve, as R. C. O'Brien shows in *Z for Zachariah* (1975), whose title comes from the 'Bible Letter Book' kept by the girl diarist, in which she recorded 'Zachariah' as the last man. But the last man after the nuclear disaster appears in the flesh to terrorise

her on her remote farm. After nursing him back to health and
reading to him from Jane Austen, she is chased and shot at,
and in a grimly open ending she sets off on her own across the
radioactive waste land. This novel is a long way in mood as
well as time from Mary Shelley's stylised posturing; what
matters is not the fall of Rome but the terror of a young girl
alone in a world full of biological, psychological and sexual
menace.

In a way these 'last man' stories, like many imaginative
visions, are pleas for peace. It is appropriate, then, to conclude
a chapter whose desolation is redeemed only by the ingenuity
with which writers have met the challenge of the critics of
Holocaust fictions, with some fictions which appeal overtly to
'the heart which must break.'

As I have said before, some of the early stories of the 1940s
sketched out the parameters of nuclear disaster fiction with
admirable freshness and insight. Robert Heinlein's 'Solution
Unsatisfactory' (1941), written under the pseudonym Anson
MacDonald, was one such story. A Maryland laboratory
develops U235 into a bomb, and radiation, that 'devilish stuff',
kills the fish in Chesapeake Bay. The scientists realise that the
world will soon be like a room full of men each armed with a
loaded .45 pistol, each dependent on all the others to stay alive,
'all offence and no defence!' (65) This was an image which was
to be used repeatedly up to the present day to defend an arms
policy of escalation.[16] The scientists try to avoid the bind by
demonstrating the power of the discovery to the world; they
drop some of the aptly named 'K-O dust' on Berlin.
Unfortunately Russia retaliates and the Four Days War is won
by America only because 'we used a two-year dust' (82). The
American peace officer Manning becomes a reluctant dictator,
and a concerned editorial endorses Heinlein's dilemma: 'I don't
like anyone to have that kind of power. And neither does
Manning.'

R. Abernathy's 'Heirs Apparent' (1954) isolates an American
and a Russian in the Siberian waste land, trying to establish a
pastoral community after the holocaust. They are interrupte~'
in their task of 'beating part of a gun-mounting i~'
plowshare' (6) by the Russian authorities who clai~
community must be disbanded in case of American air a~
The Russian is killed objecting and the story highligʰ

plight of the individual against a totalitarian regime which is only confirmed in its power by war.

Theodore Sturgeon continues the examination of the scientist's morality in 'Memorial' (1946) where the inventor of nuclear fission proposes the creation of a Pit in the desert as a 'war memorial to end war, and all other war memorials. A vast pit, alive with bubbling lava, radiating death for ten thousand years. A living reminder of the devastation man has prepared for itself' (161). Sturgeon observes wryly that the scientist 'was probably as mad as any other man who, through his own efforts, moved the world' (62). His colleague betrays him to the military authorities who arrive and say, 'I understand you have a nuclear energy device on the Premises' (167). They accidentally knock the bomb to critical mass, and the ensuing explosion prompts the first and second nuclear wars, the Mutants War, and by A.D. 5000 the world is a rat-infested waste land where half-humans crawl about the legendary 'Pit' – 'after such history, there could only be peace.' A year later Sturgeon turned his powerfully symbolic talent on the military in 'Thunder and Roses' (1947). Young Pete, cowering in an army base as the nuclear conflict rages, is converted to pacifism by the pleas of Starr Anthim, a pop singer who visited the base for a final concert and who repudiates the nationalistic fervour epitomised in her name and profession by preaching as she dies, 'In the name of justice, if we must condemn and destroy ourselves, let us not condemn all life along with us. We are heavy with sins. If we must destroy let us stop with destroying ourselves' (87).

Some of these short fictions capitalise on Kahn's ladder of escalation to condense world history into a series of rapidly escalating chapters. Norman Spinrad's 'The Big Flash' has a rock band called 'The Four Horsemen' intoxicating the buttonpushers on a Polaris submarine by their video countdown to an orgastic zero. Poet George MacBeth reduces space as well as time to give an account of a feud over the back fence which rapidly escalates to the last rung, or 'Spasm' –

> Get out the hammer, son: we need our
> own walls now. I don't care if the whole
> block comes down. I'll get that maniac
> if it's the last thing I – Christ. Oh, Christ.[17]

And Joe Haldeman has written a wishful little parable 'To Howard Hughes: A Modest Proposal', where a millionaire places nuclear bombs in all the major cities of the world and holds the world to ransom until all nations disarm. The story, written in twenty-four sections to suggest one miraculous day, ends with a quotation from *The Encyclopaedia Britannica*, 2020: '1. World War II 2. "Cold War" 3. Treaty of Reykjavik' (278).

The Canadian Hugh MacLennan's 1980 novel *Voices in Time* also uses its structure to significant effect – not cumulatively, but as a system of Chinese boxes opening into the past and into wisdom. Set in the year 2030 after the nuclear holocaust, the novel uses the motif of the manuscript found in a box, in this case a box in the basement of a ruined building discovered by the re-builders of Montreal. During the social breakdown near the end of our century, novels had been destroyed 'as though they were carriers of a plague' (123) and most printed matter was converted into fuel. Now, as the new world rises from the ashes, the young are seeking the wisdom of the aged and of the past. John Wellfleet is asked to record and interpret the diaries and videotapes of his stepfather and other relations. Like so many nuclear disaster novels, *Voices in Time* proper begins with the Great War, and a German naval officer. His son Conrad Dehmel became an archaeologist and was lured back into Hitler's Germany by the promise of a job and the love of a Jewish girl. His friendship with Admiral Canaris, that enigmatic head of Hitler's *Abwehr* whom MacLennan regards as perhaps the tragic figure of our time,[18] allows him to join the Gestapo as a means of saving his beloved, but he is eventually caught. He survives the Holocaust and emigrates to Canada, where Wellfleet's cousin interviews him on television about the October crisis in Quebec during the late sixties. Timothy Wellfleet is a child of the information age, immaculate of history (his popular television show, *This is Now*, owes its title to his Jewish mistress's cry during orgasm), who irresponsibly reveals the truth of Dehmel's past, with the result that a Jewish survivor shoots him dead in the street shortly afterwards.

MacLennan draws parallels between these historical and personal holocausts, including the suggestion that the contemporary world is spiritually lost like the victims of Hitler's regime, in the '*Nacht und Nebel*' (287). Timothy imagines a play about communications with a vast backdrop of flickering images – newsmakers, advertisements, bombings – 'everything in the news which adds up to the vast war of shadows and images the world has become' (86). Overloaded by the chaos of the present, modern man succumbs to political paralysis, sensationalism or else the kind of terrorism and subterfuge practised by the Separatists and linked by MacLennan directly to the techniques of espionage developed during the last war. The novel is wedge-shaped, moving in ten sections from the 'present' through the immediate past (our present) to the events of the world wars, and back again to the present. At the centre of the wedge, in section 6, Wellfleet meditates on the effects of the Second World War in a passage which clearly (and this has been confirmed to me by the author) contains the essence of MacLennan's world view:

> According to Conrad, he [Admiral Canaris] had deliberately chosen to live in a maze of contradictions – on the one hand, to do what he could to prevent Hitler from winning the war, on the other to save Germany from the mindless vengeance of enemies who had come to hate her worse than any nation had ever been hated in human history. Double games, triple games, multiple games, I can see now that the work of all those intelligence agencies, plotting deceptions more complex than the chart of the world's weather systems, had a great deal to do with the *fin de siècle* into which I myself was born. The techniques developed during that war became endemic after it. They lingered and bred in the bloodstreams of the nations and no moral antibiotic was discovered to neutralize them. The deliberate murder of truth led to the murder of people. In our case it led to the self-murder of a civilization. (248–9)

MacLennan is unusual among nuclear disaster writers in imagining not a Big Bang but a slow slide into barbarity: oil shortages, money problems, moral decay, terrorist use of nuclear bombs, finally 'a collective nervous breakdown' (247) which triggers limited, but totally disruptive, war:

> For many years, indeed from before I was born, people had dreaded what we called the nuclear bombs. . . . Something profound and mysterious, something blessed and almighty in

the genes of humanity, had created a taboo against these
bombs. Trillions of dollars were spent on them, but no
bureaucracy used them. André Gervais will never understand
the genius of our scientists. They were sincere men, pure-
minded men, devoted to their countries and even to mankind.
They bypassed the taboo. They invented what were called
'clean bombs', which had a destructive power less than that of
the nuclears but nevertheless tremendous. These were the
bombs that did the trick. (247)

MacLennan's focus is on man as a moral being, and here he
captures the awful paradox of men wanting to destroy, but not
utterly. They are motivated by what Conrad, in his big speech,
describes as a 'screaming for release from freedom's slavery,
which means they are screaming for somebody to return them
to slavery' (295). Nuclear destruction is a secular version of
religious apocalypse, then, an insane quest for order and
authority, for regimented sameness, born out of a deep distrust
of one's fellow man manifested in the growth of espionage
during and after the last war.

One may disagree with MacLennan's analysis, but the
experience of reading his book is a powerful endorsement of his
argument for the personal voice. We rely on one person telling
us about another person, or the naked record on tape or diary
of one person's life. The novel ends with Wellfleet dying over a
letter addressed 'Dear——', a final call to a personal friend,
whether lover or reader. MacLennan is arguing that if we can
only listen to each other's voices, we might avoid the nuclear
disaster 'in time', and establish a responsible, free society on
Earth.

Voices in Time is just one example of the kind of novel which I
have been implicitly recommending throughout this study: a
novel which uses the resources of the art form of the novel,
foregrounding voice, structure, the reading process itself, to
offer a challenge to the imagined future disaster even as it
describes that disaster. It is no accident that the two fictions I
have chosen as exemplary are pre-eminently literary, concerned
with language both as a means of personal expression and as
custodian of man's history and aspirations.

Maggie Gee's *The Burning Book* (1983) is the most recent
imaginative vision which I have encountered (though so

ubiquitous is the nuclear apocalyptic consciousness that many more fictions will undoubtedly have appeared by the time this study is published). It attempts to look two ways, towards the realistic world of the Ship and and Lamb families (complete with family trees), and towards the world of the book. In the early part of the novel the narrator's self-consciousness is obvious and tedious. The narrator breaks off from the historical narrative, usually at the ends of chapters, to muse about Hiroshima and impending doom. The movement between world and book is schematic rather than organic, and Gee's meta-fictional debate leaves us in the dilemma of accepting the reality of her characters as succeeding generations live up to the present crisis (and thus rejecting the intrusions), or regarding the whole reading experience as a fiction and so losing the cutting edge of contemporaneity – London race riots, NATO tensions in Germany – which is essential to Gee's purpose, e.g.

> *Her hair was a burning bush*, but her body crackled like pork.
> They would find that all hair burned, and that metaphor is a lie. They would find all their talk had been chatter, while generals talked about death. Their griefs were refusals to mourn, their 'worries' fled from their worry. And while they evaded the issue, others made plans with hard edges. Just around the corner, just underground, just out of our depth, it was brewing. . . .
> And people whispered, of course, *But then, people like to be gloomy*. . . .
> Then suddenly something cracked, and the novel was torn to pieces. (39)

For much of the novel these irruptions are most effectively read as postmodernist exercises in exposing the fictionality of the text in order to create a genuine sense of crisis. When the narrator complains, '*But this is the language of novels, the architecture of novels. There are other and brisker languages, other lessons to learn*' (52), and the text breaks up into italicised fragments, the reader locates the true plot of the novel in the narrator's attempts to construct a fiction in the light and knowledge of Hiroshima. Gee successfully educates us in the truth so effectively put by Elie Wiesel, that there cannot be a novel about Auschwitz; if it is a novel, then it is not about that particular historical event.

So she objects, 'The bodies will cover the books, if it comes to the final violence. The bodies will have their revenge on the novels which left them out' (177). But for all Gee's protestations, something happens in the middle of the novel which compels the reader to become absorbed in the 'reality' of the story of Lorna and Henry Lamb and their children. Gee herself is aware of the temptation – 'I think it's because of Henry, perhaps, the fact that Henry rebelled. A little leak in the book and the ocean rushes in' (161). For in comparison with the shopkeeping ordinariness of Lorna's family, Henry and his father Frank are free spirits, and while Gee documents their pilgrimages excellently they have escaped from the shackles of the traditional novel of character – there is something potential, unmastered, in them. That volatility is inherited by Henry's children: Angela, who becomes involved in the Peace Movement, Guy the misfit who is beaten to death during a National Front march, and George who cares for them both and joins the army. Through Guy and the terrible racist bigotry of the butcher Big Ray, we understand some of the wellsprings of violence in loneliness and sexual ignorance. Through Angela we recognise the constant state of crisis for a thinking person living after 1945: 'It was hard to remember a time when the smoke of fear was not there. Ever since they explained to them at school about the bomber-planes in the War. After that whenever a plane came over she'd felt the same sick fear' (229). The sequence in school when Angela struggles to absorb the data of nuclear weaponry ('In her head, the whole world had just died' [241]) is particularly horrific.

The motivation for Gee's alienation techniques becomes increasingly unclear as the reader is drawn in by the traditional story-telling techniques. At one point Gee uses the 'fiction' image to suggest that all her characters are living lives of 'bad faith' in the shadow of the mushroom cloud:

> Rules of thumb didn't get you anywhere, learning to live didn't help you here. Smoke was erasing the triumphs of the characters, all they had learned was to live in a novel . . . learning to be 'human', learning to 'survive'. (250)

It is unclear just where the word 'here' refers to. At another point, Gee inserts the true story of American Defense Secretary

James Forrestall's suicide which took him 'falling past so many stories . . . he could have ended them all' (243). Here, the postmodernist concern with fictions has been reduced to a pun. Gee also uses the fiction framework as a familiar image for our powerlessness before the politicians: 'All of us live in a novel, and none of us do the writing. Just offstage there are grim old men, planning to cut the lighting' (202). All of these insertions are intriguing in their disparate ways, but the main force of the novel by the second half lies not with them but with the final stages in the story of Henry and Lorna Lamb.

After the difficult middle years of marriage, the Lambs have rediscovered each other, perhaps under the spur of increasing international tension. As the newspaper headlines of crisis litter the pages, they decide to visit Kew Gardens. This final chapter of the novel is a brilliant set piece. Kew Gardens is a memorial to the orderliness of man and Nature, and as the Lambs explore one pavilion after the other they are overwhelmed by the beauty of the world around them. At the same time, Gee subtly stitches in reminders of the archetypal features in the terrain of the nuclear imagination: a painting by Marianne North of Mount Fujiyama, the explosions of the 'Palm House Promenade Concert Firework Finale', a workman's radio broadcasting the news, an aeroplane flying into Heathrow, war memorials, a brilliant red Pagoda. Finally comes Armageddon as the Lambs gaze skyward in the Alpine House:

> They were in Kew Gardens   in each other's arms
>   skies flashed white and the day cracked open
> stories smashed as all became one   through the
> glass flaming for a split-second all was transparent,
>   the last light shone
>   glass became tears as the picture was taken (297)

The rupture is devastating in the narrative and mirrored by the appearance of three grey pages. But Gee remains true to her Janus-faced attitude towards fictions by reminding us that her apocalypse is a fiction and appending a short plea for peace, her words and ours becoming (literally) birds of peace on the last page. These foregrounded devices might sound obvious but in the context of the savage end of the Lamb family, and the author's consistent   metafictional   strategies,   I   think,   they   have considerable impact. Once again, as in Briggs, Vonnegut, Wolfe, Hoban and others, words must crack and reform to gesture towards the unspeakable, the unthinkable. The reading experience in *The Burning Book* is phoenix-like, for we live through an end to return to our middest, with Gee's final words in our eyes and ears like the orderly plants and birds of Kew Gardens, 'Always beginning again, beginning against ending.' (304) For at the last, Gee turns the tables on the nuclear disaster itself; it, and not her characters, becomes the fiction which we must disbelieve, even if it looms as '*a bigger and better fiction, closing down on my story. . .*' (287).

Two other themes make Gee's book a memorable study of the causes as well as the psychological effects of nuclear catastrophe. In one chapter, a discussion of Japanese swords leads into an account of the Japanese destruction of the city of Nanking, which is included so that we will not see Hiroshima as a parochial crime by the West. It is a brave move, and a profoundly disturbing one. And in Chapters 5 and 10, at one- and two-thirds of the way through the novel, Gee focuses on brothers: Henry and his brother George who was killed at the Front, and George and Guy, who meet unexpectedly in the London underground when Guy is beaten to death. In these chapters Gee suggests some of the causes of warfare, the reasons both noble and base for men taking up arms. They are also sympathetic, tender studies of brotherly love, and by their quiet placement and gentle exploration they suggest a feminist nuclear protest far more persuasive and tragic than the fashionable equations of missiles and penises.

I have presented in this chapter, then, some fictions which I believe surmount the difficulties which Jewish writers face in recounting the Holocaust. Their task is easier since they have no obligation to the dead or to the survivors, but nuclear holocaust writers face similar problems of finding an adequate language and form for their visions. These imaginative cities or constructions must also go beyond Auden's 'absolute instant' to inhabit a changed world for a time, a world which might not be fully fleshed as a utopia or dystopia but which must carry imaginative conviction, either from its imagistic force or from the beauty and ingenuity of the language and fictional structure. Sometimes, as with Mary Shelley's *The Last Man*, the effort seems to be itself genuinely apocalyptic, a desire and not only a vision. More often, whether intentionally or not, this splitting of the atoms of the alphabet, as Frame calls it, represents an alternative to the process of nuclear fission, a power to put up against the powers of destruction and the downward slide of contemporary history. I concluded with some overtly pacific fictions, but many others have also this effect, if only because any imaginative act re-affirms the value of the individual – however nightmarish or deathly the vision might be. Frederick Polak, a theorist about the future, is quite programmatic in his demands for visions of the future:

> A positive future-consciousness is an absolutely indispensable antidote against the mind-poisoning negativism and threatening ideologies now undermining the foundations of Western culture.
>
> If we do not want, like Toynbee, to depend on miracles, but are disposed to fight for survival, if we strain ourselves to search for a timely and adequate response to the grave challenge of the future, if we really aspire to regain control of human destiny – there is only one way open. A new elite will have to reflect seriously on and completely reorient themselves towards new and galvanising images of the future. Only images of the future which can depict a drastically changed but viable society can help to write the history of a better future.[19]

This amounts to a fascistic view of literature which reminds one of Frank Kermode's observation of the fascistic tendencies of apocalyptic literature. But the fictions presented in this chapter, even Spinrad's *Iron Heel*, represent liberation from a required way of seeing, kites flown in the wind, fictions of 'what if' whose very foundation is freedom from the slavery of any 'new élite'. Davy, the hero of Pangborn's novel, discovers a ball-point pen during his wanderings, and tells us in a footnote:

> That end has a tiny hole, out of which pops a wee metal whichit if you push the other end; push it again and the thing pops back. One of my philosophic advisers suggests it may have been used in the phallic worship that we assume was practised privately along with the public breast–belly– thigh cult of ancient America: I don't find this convincing. I believe you could use the gidget for goosing a donkey, but why wouldn't any Goddamn pointed stick do just as well? There is need for more research. (42)

The pen, Pangborn wittily suggests, is mightier than the sword; Davy's document, and Pangborn's, while perhaps not written with the requisite ball-point pen, carry on that tradition of the immortal, endlessly researching, personal voice.

'What motivated me to write,' says Tim O'Brien of *The Nuclear Age* (1985), 'was this desire to treat apocalypse as a startling fact of modern life. Not as biblical backlash or absurd theatre or *Dr. Strangelove.*'[20] O'Brien's 'personal voice' speaks out of the American mid-West in 1995 but frames us in the downward spiral of history. As he digs a shelter for his family in the back yard, William describes his childhood in Montana and the political challenges of the sixties. Even as a child he was impressed by the fact that 'Fission, Fusion, Critical Mass' (the sections of the novel) and the other jargon of the nuclear age are real, that 'uranium is not a figure of speech' (65). He built a shelter under the ping-pong table; he held a placard at university which read, 'THE BOMBS ARE REAL' (74); he dodged the draft and worked for the revolution. However his fundamental instinct for 'retrenchment' means that he cannot commit himself to the cause or to his ebullient girlfriend Sarah. Eventually he opts for Bobbi the idealised air hostess, and a fortune made by selling a uranium mountain. O'Brien, that is, shows us the psychological fallout of our age. William can choose calculated survival or fantasy, but the in-between world of moral responsibility and commitment has been rendered absurd by the nuclear threat which William has always felt so keenly. It is not a questiuon of insanity, he insists: 'If you're sane, you're scared; if you're scared, you dig; if you dig, you deviate' (200) – and besides, 'You can't shrink a warhead.' (106) The ambiguity of recent American history, no less than European history, is symptomatic of the nuclear age, for O'Brien. 'There was a dynamic at work' (110) which propels William to the framing scene where he prepares to destroy his family when Kansas finally burns.

But William's extreme experiment, like our experience of reading the book, is cathartic. Having visited the nuclear age in word and deed, we must knowingly retreat to the fiction of a happy ending. Imagined disasters keep us sane, and there is a sense of communal confession and affirmation as we join with William in acknowledging that even when it happens we 'will hold to a steadfast orthodoxy, confident to the end that E will somehow not quite equal mc^2, that it's a cunning metaphor, that the terminal equation will somehow not quite balance.' (312)

'The Great Angel and John Devouring the Little Book', A. Dürer, Apocalypse series, Frederick van der Meer, *Apocalypse: Visions from the Book of Revelation in Western Art* (London: Thames & Hudson) p. 295.

7 Two Exemplary Fictions

The apostle tells us that in the Beginning was the Word. He gives us no assurance as to the end.[1]

In his book *The Coming Dark Age*, Robert Vacca proposes that we set up monastic communities to preserve culture and civilisation through the incipient chaos.[2] If he had read either Walter M. Miller's *A Canticle for Leibowitz* (1959) or Russell Hoban's *Riddley Walker* (1980), he would be aware of the huge difficulties in such an undertaking. In both these novels of a post-nuclear disaster waste land, small bands of dedicated thinkers try to rise above the bestial conditions around them. Such is the trauma of the disaster that the major problem is not in maintaining civilisation but in re-discovering what civilisation was and even what the word means. For the wordsmith of such a world, the semiotic system of written and oral language is a teasing, enigmatic collection of signs whose references have been blasted to atoms and whose constituent parts have been mutated into strange new forms. Both novels foreground language as well as vividly realising a devastated landscape, so that – like the heroes – the reader lives in this maze of signs which beckon and frustrate, forever holding out the promise of continuity and humanity – and, finally, grace.

A Canticle for Leibowitz is 'heavily steeped in the gloom of the immediate post-Hiroshima age, expressing a confidence in catastrophic conclusions which is typical of later 1950s sf.'[3] It originally appeared in the form of three stories: 'A Canticle for Leibowitz' (April 1955), 'And the Light is Risen' (1956) and 'The Last Canticle' (1957) – all in *Fantasy and Science Fiction* magazine. Miller had previously written only short stories. 'Dark Benediction' (1951) has a hero challenged by a comet-born parasite to debate man's evolutionary possibilities with a priest and a scientist; in 'Crucifixius Etiam' (1953) a Peruvian worker on Mars learns in a 'desperate Gethsemane' to tolerate the dangers of constructing a habitable planet, recognising 'an eight century passion of human faith in the destiny of the race of Man' (113). Already in these stories one can see the intermixing of scientific and religious issues in the context of man's place in the vast cycles of Time, a preoccupation which gives Miller's novel its extraordinary power and breadth. Miller is at home with small, discrete units, short stories or 'canticles', but in *A Canticle for Leibowitz* he weaves them together to create something like a church service, its various moods and responses all circling around the central question of man's place in the universe. In the novel, the three sections are called 'Fiat Homo', 'Fiat Lux' and 'Fiat Voluntas Tua', suggesting a working towards enlightenment and humility which is more a quality of the reader's response than narrative momentum. The plot appears to be schematically optimistic: it moves in three six hundred year segments from around A.D. 2600 to around A.D. 4300, beginning with a nuclear holocaust and ending with a spaceship taking off for the stars; but the eighteen hundred year debate over the place of signs, that is knowledge, in man's existence, is not at all resolved by the end of the novel. Walker Percy captured the ambiguous tone of the novel when he called it 'an agreeable battle of co-ordinates' with 'the authentic oxymoronic flavour of pleasurable catastrophe. Shiva destroys, but good things come of it'.[4]

At the outset Brother Francis of Utah is enduring his Lenten fast in a desert setting owing much to T. S. Eliot's 'red rock' and to Beckett's *Waiting for Godot* (first performed in America two years before the stories began to appear). On a lonely road Brother Francis meets a Wandering Jew figure who points him to a keystone in the ruins which may help the monk complete his makeshift shelter but in fact discloses the entrance to a Fallout Survival Shelter. Earlier the monk resisted a stranger's offer of bread by hissing '*Apage Satanas!*'; is this new key a key to life or death, then? Brother Francis believes 'a fallout' to be a creature, half-salamander, born in 'the Flame Deluge' (44) and likened to those demons which afflicted Job. Yet a monk's curiosity takes him into the shelter where he discovers the blueprint of a circuit design; this becomes a holy relic which he spends the next few years laboriously reproducing, blue on white, in his cell.

Already Miller has established the parameters or 'co-ordinates' of his debate: religious superstition versus secular curiosity. The paradox is that in the post-disaster landscape, as in the Dark Ages, the monasteries are the preservers of science as well as of religion. This is because, as in so many post-nuclear visions, the men of learning have been exterminated because of their association with the bomb:

> In all parts of the world men fled from one place to other places, and there was a confusion of tongues. Much wrath was kindled against the princes and servants of the princes and against the magi who had devised the weapons. Years passed, and yet the earth was not cleansed. So it was clearly recorded in the Memorabilia.
>
> From the confusion of tongues, the intermingling of the remnants of many nations, from fear, the hate was born. And the hate said: *Let us stone and disembowel and burn the ones who did this thing. Let us make a holocaust of those who wrought this crime, together with their hirelings and their wise men; burning, let them perish, and all their works, their names, and even their memories. Let us destroy them all, and teach our children that the world is new, that they may know nothing of the deed that went before. Let us make a great simplification, and then the world shall begin again.* (52)

Here we see entwined the themes of earlier chapters in this book: masquerading as evolutionary purpose, the demand of the 'simpletons' is a forlorn attempt to regain Eden, to put the apple back on the Tree of Knowledge. Ironically, the nuclear physicist Leibowitz managed to escape and, as his own penance, founded an order of monks named after Albertus Magnus, patron of scientists. Their task is to 'preserve human history for the great-great-great-grandchildren of the children of the simpletons who wanted it destroyed' (53).

But by Brother Francis's time (six hundred years from now, if we suppose the destruction to be imminent) that knowledge has accreted into a superstitious dogma, obfuscating rather than enlightening: as the monk enters the shelter he chants the Litany of the Saints – 'From the place of the ground zero, *O Lord deliver us*. From the rain of the cobalt, *O Lord, deliver us . . .*' (15). For the monastery time has stopped, as it awaits patiently an investigation from New Rome; similarly, Brother Francis's interminable preparations for the priesthood result only in his wasting fifteen years copying out the circuit diagram. On his way to an audience with the Pope, he has his manuscript stolen by a mutant band who curse the past and the science which deformed them. Yet, to multiply the ironies, Brother Francis's manuscript is now a work of art and deserving, as such, of preservation.

But time marches on with the insouciance of a Forster novel: the manuscript is not restored, and Brother Francis meets a violent death on his way home. We need a more complex hero, and we find one in the next section in the form of Dom Paulo, master of the monastery, whose view of time and history is Spenglerian:

> Now a Dark Age seemed to be passing. For twelve centuries, a small flame of knowledge had been kept smoldering in the monasteries; only now were their minds ready to be kindled. Long ago during the last age of reason, certain proud thinkers had claimed that valid knowledge was indestructible – that ideas were deathless and truth immortal. But that was true only in the subtlest sense, the abbot thought, and not superficially true at all. There was objective meaning in the world, to be sure; the nonmoral logos or design of the Creator; but such meanings were God's and not Man's, until they found an imperfect incarnation, a dark reflection, within the mind and speech and culture of a given human society, which might ascribe values to the meanings so that they became valid in a human sense within the culture. (119)

Dom Paulo's monastery is part of that slow process of manifestation, sifting out the false as it sifted the relics. This process goes on more radically in the scientific experiments of Kornhoer who produces a dynamo and a lamp according to Thon Taddeo's principles. The Thon has pieced together earlier knowledge and encourages the monks to use the scientific method of measurement, rather than, for example, reckoning time by the amount of wear on the kitchen lintel. But the Thon's first creation is suitably symbolic and ambivalent: does he bring the light of Christ's wisdom or the dynamo of deadly power? Dom Paulo with his more sacramental view of history senses an adversary in Thon Taddeo, who also recognises in a reading from the Book of The Flame Deluge an antagonism to science:

> And a great stink went up from Earth even unto Heaven. Like unto Sodom and Gomorrah was the Earth and the ruins thereof, even in the land of that certain prince, for his enemies did not withhold their vengeance, sending fire in turn to engulf his cities as their own. The stink of the carnage was exceedingly offensive to the Lord, who spoke unto the prince, Name, saying: 'WHAT BURNT OFFERING IS THIS THAT YOU HAVE PREPARED FOR ME? WHAT IS THIS SAVOR THAT ARISES FROM THE PLACE OF HOLOCAUST? HAVE YOU MADE ME A HOLOCAUST OF SHEEP OR GOATS, OR OFFERED A CALF UNTO GOD?'
> But the Prince answered him not and God said: 'YOU HAVE MADE ME A HOLOCAUST OF MY SONS.'
> And the Lord slew him together with Blackeneth, the betrayer, and there was pestilence in the earth, and madness was upon mankind, who stoned the wise together with the powerful, those who remained. (153)

The reconciliation never comes; as the Thon leaves, Dom Paulo acknowledges 'mutual respect between foes' and laments, 'Neither infinite power nor infinite wisdom could bestow godhood upon men. For that there would have to be infinite love as well' (195). But the scientist Thon Taddeo fails, even as a scientist. The Wandering Jew figure sighs, 'It's still not Him' (177) and offers him a goat, saying, 'Crown him with the crown Saint Leibowitz sent you, and thank him for the light that's rising. Then blame Leibowitz, and drive him into the desert. That way you won't have to wear the second crown, the one with thorns, responsibility, it's called' (168). The Thon does not understand this symbolic warning and leaves the monastery unhumbled, unaware even that his visit is being used by a warlike tribe to investigate the monastery defences. The Thon even refers to an ancient text which suggests that men were replaced by robots; we – though not the Thon – appreciate the allusion to Čapek's *R.U.R.* and, again, the necessity for scientists to see themselves humbly and to accept moral responsibility for their inventions.

With power and wisdom still separated, the third section of
the novel whirls us into a world like our own filled with
rebellion, noise and confusion. The hero Dom Zerchi epitomises
the struggle to comprehend in his losing battle with a
berserk word processor which keeps writing in 'doudoubleble
sylsylabablesles' (204). The text of this section, unlike the
severely controlled, latinate measures of the previous two, is
similarly corrupted:

Hut two threep foa!
Left!
Left!
He-had-a-good-wife-but-he
Left!
Left!
Left!
          Right!
Left!
          Wir, as they say in the old country, *marschieren weiter wenn
alles in Scherben fallt.*
          We have your eoliths and your mesoliths and your
neoliths. We have your Babylons and your Pompeiis, your
Caesars   and   your   chromium-plated   (vital-ingredient-
impregnated) artifacts.
          We have your bloody hatchets and your Hiroshimas.
We march in spite of Hell, we do –
          Atrophy, Entropy, and *proteus vulgaris*, telling bawdy
          jokes about a farm girl name of Eve and a travelling
          salesman called Lucifer.
          We bury your dead and their reputations.
          We bury you. We are the centuries. (200)

While his servant attempts a desperate retreat from this
cacophony, Dom Zerchi muses on the entropic direction of
human history toward the 'colossus of the State' (231). The
monastic order itself is 'fissioning' (234) and a satellite begins
raining down nuclear bombs, enacting the Biblical apocalypse:
'How strange of God to speak from a burning bush, and of
Man to make a symbol of Heaven into a symbol of Hell' (235).
Dom Zerchi, like ourselves, is torn between Dom Paulo's belief
in cyclic history and a desire for this end to be the final end:

'Are we doomed to it, Lord, chained to the pendulum of our own mad clockwork, helpless to halt its swing? This time, it will swing us clean to oblivion' (217–18).

Everything in this final section foregrounds the ambiguity and paradox implicit in the previous sections: religion is custodian of science but cannot enter time; science is progressive but yearns for stasis. Ambiguity is personified in Mrs Grales, a two-headed woman (her name mocking the possibility of answer or 'grail') whose other head was animated by an explosion, just as she had been originally mutated by another explosion. Her *doppelgänger* is an innocent girl who administers last rites to the crushed Dom Zerchi – as with Malamud's novel, we ask if this is a sign or a travesty of God's grace. The Wandering Jew figure still waits in the form of old Lazar, but has he already been resurrected? For the third time there is a one-eyed character (in the first section Brother Francis was shot in the eye, in the second the cynical poet had a glass eye which became a holy relic), a boy with fatal radiation exposure. All three characters die violent, pointless deaths, yet all three have uniquely innocent visions of the world. Now all that is left is the political greed of the Asian invaders who wage war because 'an eye was taken for an eye' (254).

If Miller leaves us with a vision of no vision, he also leaves us with the pinnacle of progress, the spaceship, bearing with it to the stars the Memorabilia with its fatal key to knowledge. As in so many of the fictions considered here, the rainbow apogee of man's invention, the rocket, also carries his destruction – not a pot of gold. And so Miller ends with two sections: the first describes the successful launch, 'a new Exodus from Egypt under the auspices of a God who must surely be very weary of the race of Man' (239); the second leaves us back on the familiar terminal beach with a wrecked seaplane (itself a hybrid):

A wind came across the ocean, sweeping with it a pall of fine white ash. The ash fell into the sea and into the breakers. The breakers washed dead shrimp ashore with the driftwood. Then they washed up the whiting. The shark swam out to his deepest waters and brooded in the cold clean currents. He was very hungry that season. (278)

The terminal visions of Wells, Ballard, Bunch and many others are epitomised here. The great chain of being has been severed and the enigmatic shark has a tenuous future, for all his deadly power. Meanwhile Miller's exodus is heavily qualified by this final image and by the reference to a weary God. The debate is unresolved just as the Dom's debate about whether radiation victims should be allowed to take their own lives remains unresolved and epitomises the conflict between religious humility and secular compassion.

The greatest success of this memorable novel is the way these themes and debates are held in suspension in every line. Every event and thought, directly or indirectly, feeds the debate. Yet the pictured world is particular and intimately rendered, for Miller knows the difficulty of the global view: 'I doubt if a single completely accurate account of the Flame Deluge exists anywhere. Once it started, it was apparently too immense for any one person to see the whole picture' (153). Accounts require language, and while 'for the characters linguistic precision is an elusive art',[5] Miller writes with an acute sense of the history and echo of each word as if it were part of a chant. The novel is full of learned puns, chiefly religious or patristic, e.g. the 'lamedh' and 'adhe' which Francis finds scraped on the keystone are, the monks decide, the first and last letters of the name 'Leibowitz'; but they are also, as morphemes, the Hebrew for 'Learn, wise one'. 'Leibowitz' means fool or lover of jest, while Mrs Grales, a grotesque Eve figure, sells tomatoes which were also known as 'love apples'.[6] But for all this erudition, and the brilliant opening to the third section 'Fiat Voluntas Tua', the characters themselves generally speak in a flat kind of American English, reflecting little interaction between Latin (copiously quoted) and contemporary terms.

While this lack of verbal inventiveness illustrates the cultural isolation of the characters well, there is a regrettable thematic restriction of the novel to an almost totally male context – indeed the only woman in the novel is the mutant Mrs Grales. One is tempted to wonder (along the lines of Spinrad's *The Iron Heel*) whether part of the dilemma of Miller's characters results from the exclusion of female principles and a concentration on power, technical or insightful, rather than on Dom Paulo's 'infinite love'. Nevertheless, *A Canticle for Leibowitz* is a fine fiction, its free play of ideas and vivid dramatic realisation turning the waste land into an urgent debating ground in the reader's mind. Miller is certainly not, for all his deep knowledge, an apologist for the Catholic Church, and any reading on that assumption ('passages in the book reflect a certain defensive mentality found within pre-counciliar Catholicism'[7]) trivialises the book's effect and ignores the dialectical and tripartite structure.

Russell Hoban has always been interested in the power of fiction not only to express but to create what we are. 'We make fiction because we are fiction', he wrote, 'because there was a time when "it lived" us into being. Because there was a time when something said, "What if there are people?"'[8] Disaster fictions have been increasingly aware of the verbal texture of their created world (think of the titles *The Burning Bush*, *A Canticle . . .*, *Voices in Time*) and *Riddley Walker* (1980) has the richest texture of any novel considered here, a texture almost as rich as that of *Finnegans Wake*. The language, as Hoban said, 'carries in it the ghost of a lost technology';[9] but more than that, 'the language we speak is a whole palimpsest of human effort and history. The language of the debased and degraded future that Riddley lives in is bound to be full of uncomprehended remnants of what we have today'. No other nuclear disaster fiction has pushed this commonplace idea as far as Hoban has in this novel, which teaches the reader a dimly recognisable, mutated form of Cockney English even as he reads. In a world without information storage systems, stories also regain their central place in the life of the tribe. Lorna Elswint, 'our tel woman' (4), laments the fact that Riddley doesn't know the story of 'why the dog wont show its eyes': 'Thats what happens with peopl on the way down from what they ben. The storys go' (17). The art of telling stories becomes the main form of power for the tribe, and can be used politically (by Goodparley and Orfing) or shamanistically, as eventually Riddley learns to do. The people of southeast England, 2347 years after the nuclear disaster of 1997, have 'placed' themselves by piecing together a story of sorts of their own history, 'Hart of the Wood'. It is not a tale of Robin Hood ('thats a nother thing' [2]) but of a family of survivors of the 'Bad Time' who meet a 'clevver looking bloak' who teaches them how to make fire, in exchange for the roasting of their child. The parents sacrifice their offspring for the sake of survival and the knowledge of 'flint and steal' (as the clever man says, 'clevverness is gone now but littl by littl itwl come back' [4]). The parents fall asleep by their new fire and are consumed by it. In this opening story, then, the concerns of the book are established: the pursuit of knowledge and its perils, the attactions of power.

Riddley, the narrator, reveals himself as indeed a riddler or punster, highly conscious of the possibilities in even his rudimentary language. He connects this salutary tale with the 'aulder' tree, which is best for making charcoal, the fuel which the tribe spends its time excavating and which will become a component of gunpowder. He also learns metaphysics from Lorna Elswint (as well as the mysteries of dope and sex), particularly the notion of the life force – 'It thinks us but it dont think *like* us' (7). Riddley's father is accidentally killed and he has the chance to see destiny operating in his own life. He searches the old machine which his father had been excavating at the time of his death for some meaning, 'some kind of las word some kynd of onwith' (11). His instinct that the rediscovery of technology may be fatal leads him to puzzle over the central myth of the tribe, the Eusa story. This tells how Eusa (St Eustace, or perhaps the USA) wanted the secret formula, the magic number or alchemical password to the 'Master Chaynjis', in order to wage a final war using the '1 Big 1 . . . the Berstin Fyr' (30). A scientist tracks down the 'Littl Shynin Man' (the atom) in the Hart of the Wud (carbon), the process of sub-atomic physics being here translated into a pastoral quest. Ignoring warnings, Eusa creates the atomic bomb and like the sorcerer's apprentice unlocks the unstoppable devastation which consumes even his own wife and two children (a reference to the St Eustace story). Another example of Eusa's pride is the computer (Hoban, like other writers, sees the bomb as just one aspect of high technology which may also be manifested in computers or space rockets), which he claims will create 'Good Time. . . . You name it wewl do it. Pas the sarvering gallack seas and all that' (48). The story is presented in Biblical language and format:

13. Eusa wuz angre he wuz in rayj & he kep pulin on the Littl Man the Addoms owt strecht arms. The Littl Man the Addom he begun tu cum apart he cryd, I wan tu go I wan to stay. Eusa sed, tel mor. The Addom sed, I wan to dark I wan

tu lyt I wan tu day I wan tu nyt. Eusa sed, Tel mor. The Addom sed, I wan tu woman I wan tu man. Eusa sed, Tel mor. The Addom sed, I wan tu plus I wan tu minus I wan tu big I wan tu littl I wan tu aul I wan tu nuthing.

14. Usa sed, Stop ryt thayr thats the No. I wan. I wan that aul or nuthing No. The Little Man the Addom he cudn stop tho. He wuz ded. Pult in 2 lyk he wuz a chikken. Eusa screamt he felt lyk his oan bele ben pult in 2 & evere thing rushin owt uv him . . .

Then thay dogs begun to tel uv tym tu cum. Thay sed, The lan wil dy & thay peapl wil eat 1 a nuther. The water wil be poysen & the peapl wil drink blud. (32)

In performance, the story rouses the audience to fierce debate, the supporters of Goodparley (the 'Pry Mincer') claiming that the holocaust was the responsibility of politicians, Orfing the 'Wes Mincer' blaming the scientists and 'puter leat', or 'computer élite'.

As newly appointed 'connexion man' for the tribe Riddley explores man's place in the scheme of things, a metaphysical as well as an historical quest. At the outset he favours the quasi-religious view that 'EUSAS HEAD IS DREAMING US' (61), a way of escaping responsibility and remorse by seeing the whole post-disaster world as the God-scientist's grotesque fiction. But Riddley is led by the leader of a pack of wild dogs (their presence a vivid allusion to the wild beasts of Revelation) on a pilgrimage through the landscape of Canterbury, learning about the claims to power of the priests and the scientists. Both groups, ironically, are after the same symbol of power, the secret of the atom bomb: the Ardship of Cambry believes that when his flock gathers the formula will be revealed to them because 'the 1 Big 1 and the Master Chaynjis aint some thing you littl in to writing' (84), while Goodparley searches for a clue to the formula in the Eusa show itself. In the spectacular ruins of the nuclear power plant near Canterbury, Riddley is converted to science: 'How cud any 1 not want to be like them what had boats in the air and picters on the wind? How cud any 1 not want to see them shyning weals terning?' (100). But Riddley, being poetic and mystical by inclination, sees science in a spiritual way, identifying the atom as 'right doing' and confusing atomic power with spiritual power 'radiating' goodness.

This vivid, personalising attitude persists even as he traverses the waste land towards the Cathedral at Canterbury, a landscape full of 'the shape of the nite what beartht the day when Canterbury dyd' (157). In the bombed city Riddley has a further epiphany, perhaps a psychological response to the lingering radiation field:

> I knowit Cambry Senter ben flattent the werst of all the dead town senters it ben Zero Groun it ben where the wite shadderd stood up over every thing. Yet unner neath that Zero Groun I lissent up a swarming it wer a humming like a millying of bees it wer like 10s of millyings. I begun to feal all juicy wuth it. Juicy for a woman. Longing for it hard and hevvy stanning ready. Not jus my cock but all of me it wer like all of me wer cock and all the worl a cunt and open to me. The dogs begun running roun me all in a circel roun and roun with ther little heads up hy and ther hy sholders up. (159)

In the womb-like crypt of the cathedral Riddley discovers arches made of stone which look like growing trees: the pastoral pun in 'hart of the wud' is linked to the tree of knowledge and to the tree of crucifixion. Riddley transcends all these metaphors when he decides that 'hart of the wud' is 'the hart of wanting to be' (165), yet another pun on 'wud/would'. This yearning to be, for Riddley, involves a desire to give himself up to a larger life force, whether it be the power of God or the power of the atom:

> I fel down on to my knees than I cudnt stan up I cudnt lif up my head. The 1 Big 1 the Master Chaynjis it wer all roun me. Wood in to stoan and stoan in to wood. Now it showit 1 way now a nother. The stoan stoans. The stoan moves. In the stanning and the moving is the tree. Pick the appel off it. Hang the man on it. Out of the holler of it comes the berning chyld. Unner the stoan. See the bird boan. Thin as grass. Be coming grass. (161)

But the mystery is not yet unravelled. Riddley discovers the picture of a face overgrown with vines and draws on a wall St Eustace. Eustace, the English saint, was originally a supporter of Hadrian; but Hadrian stood for division (Hadrian's wall) and warfare, so Eustace dissociated himself from Hadrian's campaign and was martyred, having also lost his family. Into the shape of this ur-legend can be fitted the Christian and the Eusa stories, with Christ as the element of saltpetre (saviour–savour–saver–salt) crucified or split to release tremendous power. Along with the power resulting from division, however, goes the loss of family (the 'nuclear' family). Like Miller, Hoban centres his story on the re-interpretation of an ancient relic. Whereas for Miller the circuit diagram is an enigmatic, useless symbol of past technology, for Hoban the Eustace story provides a key to understanding both the religious and the scientific impulses. There is also the implicit pacific message that the truly religious sign is the relic of Eustace in the crypt, not the rocket-like assertion of power symbolised in the huge cathedral erected above him, and so completely destroyed.

That is not the end of Hoban's story. The waste land still needs a saviour, and in a coup Orfing becomes Pry Mincer, blinding Goodparley who then roams the countryside with Riddley for his Fool. At least Orfing has recognised, along with Riddley, that man is a spiritual being and will dictate his destiny according to his irrepressible need for power and knowledge; Goodparley, on the other hand, 'thot you cud move the out side of things frontways and leave the in side to look after its self. Which I think its the in side has got to do the moving' (203). So, fatalistically, Riddley watches the inventor Granser finally discover the secret formula of gunpowder, and blow himself up with it. As he observes, 'Some 1s got to happen it. If it aint me or you it cud wel be some 1 wersen us cudnt it' (199). In a coda to the novel we see Riddley teamed up with Orfing to perform their travelling puppet show before a hostile audience. Instead of the riddle-like Eusa show, they perform Punch and Judy. Like Eusa, Punch destroys his children and family in his desire to remain powerful, but the play says simply this, portraying man's basic aggression in comic form. Its view of man is as uncompromising as Riddley's at the end of his quest: life is a matter of 'sum tyms bytin sum tyms bit' (206).

As Miller utilised the forms and matter of Catholic church

ritual, so Hoban utilises the rugged energy of the traditional Punch and Judy show. The atmosphere and linguistic vigour of *Riddley Walker* owe much to old showmen like Jim Body:

> Old Jim was shy about it, like; he couldn't do it reglar, and as soon as he got a few shilluns he had to go and spend it on beer in the pub. And then we did have a time of it! When he was boozed he used to start swearin' if he couldn't git the dolls up quick enough. He used to swear something 'orrible – and all the people outside could hear him. I used to have to bang the curtains and say, ''Ere you shut up – we can hear everything you're saying inside.' And then he used to start banging about and nearly knock the show over. It used to rock about, and there was me 'olding on to it and 'im inside a-cussing 'orrible, shouting out that the dashed dolls wouldn't keep still, and talking to 'em, and telling 'em to keep still as if they was alive.[10]

Riddley's adventures, like Punch's, are picaresque, with many digressions. Hoban's language is superbly inventive, words like 'arga warga' for death occurring alongside technological ghosts like 'datter' and 'pirntow' (data and printout), 'party cools of stoan' and a 'some poasyum' (107). Like the Punch and Judy show, *Riddley Walker* appeals to the visual and auditory imagination (the mis-spelt text, while initially foregrounded, soon fades like the score of a musical performance), and the text is not so much a found document as a performance itself, a collection of voices and told tales.

Hoban has understood exactly the problems of an illiterate society. With records and precise complexity gone, the people communicate through image and symbol, and stories become more and more enigmatic as time passes. Lorna explains, 'Bint no writing for 100s and 100s of years til it begun agen nor you wunt never get a strait story past down by mouf over that long. Onlyes writing I know of is the Eusa story which that aint nothing strait but at leas its stayd the same' (20). The Eusa story yields what people want to take from it – a formula for gunpowder, an allegory of man's Fall. Everything must be interpreted, which is why the hero assumes the central tribal role of 'connexion man' or a man who talks in riddles. While his own story begins with the death of the father and a quest for

from Mod — P. Mod

truth, it ends with varieties of truth, an acceptance of multiplicity, and the bald antics of Punch. Everything in Hoban's world can be endlessly deconstructed, as exemplified in the story of Hangman's Hill, a name which may or may not have come from the terrifying 'Auntie', a copulating mincing machine which destroys human beings.

Like Miller, Hoban sees history as cyclic. His answer to the question of evolution is that sooner or later gunpowder and rockets will be re-invented. Both writers are obviously sympathetic with the quest of their heroes for a password into history, their attempt to get the show on the road again. What concerns them both is the spirit in which that step is taken. Miller's characters are polarised between the claims of God and Mammon, and at the end Miller skilfully balances the claims and blindnesses of both religion and science. Hoban goes a step forward (or is it backwards?), away from the outward institutions of the cathedral and the laboratory, to suggest the need for a personal re-orientation towards what is happening. Even while Granser is blowing himself up, Riddley is reaching his attitude of sceptical indifference, since it seems that any activity involves division, and division causes pain. While the 'Fiat Voluntas Tua' in Miller becomes an ironic, unanswered prayer, in Hoban it is an affirmation of life, embodied in the vigour of the text.

Because of its mastery of form, I think that *Riddley Walker* goes further than *A Canticle for Leibowitz* as a religious meditation. But both books are masterpieces, and show how even the deadly terrain of nuclear disaster can be turned into rich fictional pasture. Both authors are highly literate, and it is appropriate that *Riddley Walker* should be the last text to be studied in this book, since it alludes, in its climactic scene, to another fiction forty years on the far side of the nuclear debate. Jack London's *The Scarlet Plague* (1910), you may remember, featured the professor of English literature Granser, who ponders the mutation of language as he sits with the boys round the waste land fire, recalls the disaster, and concludes, 'Nothing can stop it – it's the same old story over and over.' In *Riddley Walker*, Granser mixes up the ingredients of gunpowder, and then there is an explosion:

I gone back inside the fents. That littl hump back hut where Granser ben doing the mixing it wernt there no mor it wer jus only sticks and sods scattert wide. Granser he wer like throwt away on the groun he lookit empty like when you take your han out of a show figger. His head wernt with the res of him his head wer on a poal. The gate a way from the rivver it had a hy poal on each side of it and Gransers head wer stuck on the poynt of 1 of them poals jus like it ben put there for telling. (194)

Both Hoban and Miller recognise that 'telling' is power. Miller assumes the mantle of 'teller' in his vast parable of human belief and evolution. Hoban assumes Miller's theme, that the quest for knowledge involves man in a cyclic destiny of invention and destruction, and focuses our attention on its articulation, its telling. It is at once a nuclear disaster fiction and a comment on such fictions, how necessary they are, how we must constantly be confronted with riddles and forced to contemplate our own destinies. Riddley, like Wells's bright-eyed story-teller at the beginning of *The World Set Free*, knows that the power of the bomb is ruled by the power of the word, and only by continual de-construction of the word will we avoid the destruction of the world. One critic of Hoban complains, 'If nothing is really separate, can we make any really meaningful statements?'[11] But this is to confuse Riddley's desire for epiphany (and the reader's) with Hoban's purpose of teasing us with the fiction of enlightenment while his vehicle, the verbal texture, continually dissolves into history and ambiguity. The worlds of both Miller and Hoban are worlds of fission not fusion, though both are acutely aware of a 'time was', an Eden when man was one with God and the World was with God rather than refracted into a Tower of Babel. The manmade patterns of religion and science shimmer like mirages on the horizon while immediate experience is raw, brutal and enigmatic. What one reviewer said of *Riddley Walker* could be applied to both books, that they are 'about voids and absences – about, that is, the character of experience minus the sedimentation of values'. Both books make many statements, but none of them are answers. As readers we are set loose in the shifting sands of a lexical playfield to consider the forked animal man, so that we might guess at, amongst other things, why he became a being with the capacity to destroy himself and his world. In an exemplary manner *Riddley Walker* does this; as Penelope Lively said of it, 'the matter of the book – for all its chilling supposition – is the human mind'.[12] More than any other fictions considered in this study, these two novels take us into a new 'mindscape'. As Dom Paulo says, meaning depends on the 'mind and speech and culture of a given human society', and in Miller's American desert and Hoban's English mud all three are utterly different from our own. Unlike many of the racy fictions I have studied, *A Canticle . . .* and *Riddley Walker* give a profound sense of time, having stopped, moving sluggishly and fitfully on. Both cultures are involved in painstaking archeological digs to restore the past but they are hampered because they have no sense of direction. Only questers like Thom Taddeo and Riddley try to put the pieces into a map, but the map can only have a meaning limited by their own culture except for the occasional, fortuitous breakthrough. By emphasising the fearful ignorance of society at large, the likelihood of misreadings and the difficulty of breaking out from a cramped oppressive, guilt-ridden mind-set, Miller and Hoban give us a reading experience which actually enacts an alien mind trying to get in touch with our own – a post-disaster mind trying to open itself to all the possibilities which we face right now. Besides being epic adventures, mystery stories and philosophical and theological debates, these fictions profoundly remind us of our privileged position, and the world which we might throw away.

the tenuous balance of past and future upon the fragile crux of the present.

Pg 183
130

'The Trumpets Distributed', A. Dürer, Apocalypse series, Frederick van der Meer, *Apocalypse: Visions from the Book of Revelation in Western Art* (London: Thames & Hudson) p. 293.

8 Conclusion Without Closure

The world needs a wash and a week's rest.[1]

One of the purposes of this collection of nuclear disaster fictions is to illustrate the huge range of responses to the threat of nuclear destruction made over the last seventy years (taking Wells's *The World Set Free* as the beginning of the imaginative epoch). While some of these responses may be bizarre or grotesquely inadequate, they only mirror and seldom surpass in banality or sheer ignorance the responses of men closely associated with the actual development of nuclear power. For example, General Groves of the Manhattan Project assured a Congressional hearing in 1945 that radiation death was a 'very pleasant' way to die,[2] and in June 1953 Winston Churchill, describing the British entry into the arms race, said, 'We had one and let it off – it went off beautifully.'[3] Even as late as 1960 W. C. Anderson, who witnessed the American nuclear testing in the Marshall Islands, could concoct a truly horrifying mélange of parochial responses in a book called *5,4,3,2,1,Pfft (or 12,000 Men and One Bikini)*. At the first explosion the author solemnly meditates, 'God had given men the key to His secret, and He undoubtedly meant for it be used. But for what purpose?'[4] After a momentary apocalyptic tremor ('Kinda makes you want to look at your hole card, doesn't it?') he finds comfort in the scientist as saviour: '. . . asking forgiveness for meddling in His business, and then I thanked Him in a postscript for guiding the brilliant minds of these incredible scientists, young and old, who could foretell with such accuracy the behaviour of His valence'.[5] But the dedication of the book is the most alarming, mingling patriotism and desire:

The beautiful, awe-inspiring, overpowering spectral of the H-

211

bomb as its symbolic shape climbs thundering towards the sky, will never replace the beautiful, awe-inspiring, overpowering vision of a soft American gal as her symbolical shape climbs eagerly into the sheets. To the men of Eniwetok . . .[6]

The recent claims by American servicemen for compensation for radiation exposure suffered at such testings render this odious passage grimly ironic, and not just an exposure of the phallic power worship identified by contemporary women campaigning against the bomb.

But Anderson's book is instructive in the sense that it reminds us that the adequacy or inadequacy of one's imaginative response to the nuclear threat is a measure of one's maturity, and possibly the maturity of the race. Gary Wolfe argues from two of the many fictions considered in this study which focus on juvenile heroes, that 'one could get the impression from *Rebirth* and *The Long Tomorrow* that nuclear holocaust is primarily a crisis of adolescence.'[7] Wolfe is correct to the extent that the nuclear capability places demands on the individual, the race and the human race as a whole to grow up or be damned. Of course there are those imaginative reactions which envisage either the end of everything or everything 'changed, changed utterly', and these may be classed as juvenile; Leslie Fiedler rightly railed against these 'drop-outs from history' in his essay on 'The New Mutants' in 1965. But the nuclear threat also challenges us to consider the value of human nature as it is, its moral or religious obligations and its possible evolutionary paths, and such a contemplation surely represents the mature liberal, and even conservative, mind. Indeed, the majority of the fictions I have discussed have been meditations of this type, just because they are stories about a time 'after'. James Blish reminds us of this essentially speculative, *engagé* attitude of these fictions when he says, 'Our modern apocalyptic literature, overlaid as it is with the mythologies of scientific humanism and technology triumphant, takes just as dim a view of chiliasm.'[8]

The challenge of nuclear disaster literature has been to remain fresh and original. Writers like Heinlein, Leiber and Poul Anderson sketched in broad outline the parameters of the meditation in those stories of the early forties. What has always been apparent is the inadequacy of ordinary ways of thought to comprehend the moral and eschatological challenges of the new predicament. In 1950 twelve American physicists presented to President Truman a document declaring, 'We believe that no nation has the right to use such a bomb [the H-bomb].'[9] The motivation is genuine and commendable, but what is the force or exact meaning of the word 'right'? Thirty years later Shelford Bidwell attempted to sum up the nuclear threat by saying that 'the present state of affairs is a genuine human tragedy'[10] – but what exactly can be meant by those last three words? Somehow the conventional language of humanism and humanist literature seems inadequate to the task. The writer of nuclear disaster fiction, then, is facing a double challenge: to imagine a new story and a new outcome; and to tell it in an appropriate language.

The response, as I have suggested in my arrangement of this book, was two-fold. First, there were the scientific extrapolations which dwelt on current knowledge of nuclear physics and weaponry to document events leading up to, during and immediately after the disaster; or which, in the longer vision, drew on the larger extrapolation of prediction or evolutionary notions drawn from biology, anthropology and genetics. Second, there were the visionary responses which saw disaster in terms of man's unconscious or nightmare world, or in terms of the readymade Biblical, apocalyptic framework. These, as I have stressed, tend to employ the literary strategies of imagery, framing, invention of new languages, mythic patterning and irony.

The first approach seems daily more and more justifiable. We live in an age when the Doomsday Clock in *The Bulletin of the Atomic Scientists* hovers around four minutes to midnight,[11] and in a world which contains more than three tons of TNT for every human being alive,[12] while the rate of accidents involving nuclear weapons (described in metaphor as 'broken arrows') is one a year since 1945.[13] We also live in a world of 'nukespeak' which has generated its own dictionaries and for the common person a 'miasma of words, numbers and acronyms' in Solly Zuckerman's terms.[14] We need a literature of informed explication of the present conditions in an accessible language. The stories examined in this book which come from the roughly defined realm of 'science fiction' are reminders of a tradition, within that much abused genre, of serious extrapolation. As Kingsley Amis wrote,

> One is grateful that we have a form of writing which is interested in the future, which is ready ... to treat as variables what are usually taken to be constants, which is set on tackling those large, general, speculative questions that ordinary fiction so often avoids. This is no less true when all allowance has been made for the shock and pain felt by some when they find these questions answered in a way that does much less than justice to their complexity.[15]

The concern and responsibility of many of these fictions is the reason for the disaffection of Dr Edward Teller, the nuclear physicist, from the genre. He laments, 'Today I do not read science fiction. My tastes did not change. Science fiction did. Reflecting the general attitude, the stories used to say, "How wonderful". Now they say, "How horrible".'[16]

The second approach is part of the tradition of imaginative literature and can be seen as an element of modernism in the arts generally. J. G. Ballard finds roots specifically in surrealism and justifies his technique by saying, 'The task of the arts seems more and more to be that of isolating the few elements of reality from this mélange of fictions, not some metaphorical "reality", but simply the basic elements of cognition and posture that are the jigs and props of our consciousness.'[17] The resistance to such a treatment of a 'scientific event' should by now be seen as clearly unjustified. E. R. MacCormac, in a book called *Metaphor and Myth in Science and Religion*, concludes that both languages have their roots in metaphorical systems.[18] Moreover, the nuclear event itself seems always to demand a fusion of the two cultures in order for comprehension to occur – from Oppenheimer's quotation of Buddhist scripture at the first explosion to his later, more considered opinion that 'In some sort of crude sense which no vulgarity, no humour, no overstatement can quite extinguish, the physicists have known sin; this is a knowledge which they cannot lose.'[19] And so the last three chapters of my book examined some of the ways in which nuclear disaster has been envisaged through the language of theology, psychology, mythology and, finally, the language of language itself.

Both these approaches, the scientific story-telling of *Fail-Safe* and the satirical vision of *Dr. Strangelove*, have produced works of art which successfully take us beyond the blankness of the atomic blast itself. Through them we can escape from the unbearable and unproductive contemplation of the one fact of the nuclear age which we know empirically, the bombings of Hiroshima and Nagasaki. Edita Morris's story about the birth of a deformed baby to a survivor of Hiroshima tears the heart, and we realise with the narrator that 'we survivors are victims of a war that has no end, a war that began with the *gembaku* and which might wipe out the future'.[20] To visit Hiroshima's memorials is to remind ourselves that we are part of that inescapable continuum, the long nightmare sleep of history. But to state the facts of radiation damage more than once, and in a heightened first person narrative ('Oh, Rag Doll, dearest Rag Doll, how much I have loved you all my life', ends Morris's *The Flowers of Hiroshima*[21]), is to risk sensationalism or sentimentalism. The trap of this kind of well-intentioned indulgence, or 'chic bleak' as H. B. Franklin neatly termed it, is to be avoided (as Jewish writers of the Holocaust discovered) only by creating special fictional patterns or documenting by indirection, calling on all the fictional resources of implication and silence. Many of these techniques, as I have shown, are derived from the Biblical apocalypticists. Other techniques, such as the disintegrating manuscript, the cartoon, the collage or the unfinished narrative owe much to modernism. The most successful fictions, I have suggested, are those which find solutions to the questions of point of view and a radically altered language.

If the creation of fictions about nuclear disaster is so difficult, one may ask, why bother? Such fictions are not to be valued for their predictive value, to be put away safely like Orwell's *1984* once the dread year is past. Nor are they essentially polemical, dire warnings for moral rearmament; fictions which do attempt these ends risk trivialising the very calamity they wish to warn against. No, their value lies in the notion of maturity discussed earlier. They are the means whereby an adolescent humanity – that is to say, unperfected, unfulfilled – can wisely consider the essential qualities of human-ness, under the most challenging conditions of personal and public crisis, in the grandest spiritual (good and evil) and secular (time past and time future) terms.

Although they are about endings and change, nuclear fictions have that sense of an ending, as Frank Kermode argues, which is of crucial relevance to us, people living in the 'middest'. Eric Rabkin puts the case most succinctly when he says,

> At one level, stories of the end of the world display the consequences of our social values; at another, the meanings of our wishes. The end that the world meets it meets as its end: the goal of world destruction is world creation, pro-creation, and re-creation for the citizen, for the child, and, most important, for the self. In the story, the world may end; the story of the end of the world goes on.[22]

Of course the danger of mind-numbing familiarity must always be stressed. Like violence on television, a ceaseless bombardment of nuclear disaster stories which give the reader no framework, no 'angle' beyond a sado-masochistic thrill or nihilism, may accustom the reader, at least in his dim imagination, to annihilation. An Australian poet Philip Neilsen has written a timely warning against this kind of de-sensitising in a poem called 'Tomorrow Loses Its Excitement':

> Returning from another pleasant Armageddon
> we are veterans already.
> Visiting all our friends, reading newspapers,
> we start to enjoy
> this living-room Angst. . . .
> We dig the grave with the shovels we made.[23]

These kinds of 'shovels' are certainly one kind of disaster fiction, and according to science fiction editor Robert Sheckley they are being mass-produced at the present time:

> As an editor, I get a lot of apocalyptic stories; that's very much in people's heads now. Unfortunately it's only one plot: a lot of writers are doom laden or doom haunted now. But for the purposes of there being a valid fiction, the dance must go on.[24]

For the purposes of there being a valid humanism, too, sophisticated disaster fictions must continue to be written and read.

To read these fictions is to place oneself imaginatively in a position of personal suffering and global despair, not in any chiliastic paroxysm, but in an attitude of calm enquiry. If nothing had prompted our forefathers, then Hitler's Holocaust at least has compelled us in the latter twentieth century to consider the nature of man *in extremis*. The nuclear threat now provides the most effective scenario for doing this. R. J. Lifton, who has evolved a philosophy out of his work with Japanese nuclear survivors, argues:

> What I am suggesting is that to 'touch death' and then rejoin the living can be a source of insight and power. This is true not only for those exposed to holocaust, or to the death of a parent or lover or friend, but also for those who have permitted themselves to experience fully the 'end of an era', personal or historical.[25]

I do not think we read these disaster fictions for 'power', but by permitting ourselves to experience fully the fictional world we may emerge with insight into the human condition. Lifton is in danger of slipping into the sentiment of 'chic bleak' and making doom-consciousness pragmatic, whereas the most common effect of such an experience, I have found, is to induce a feeling of profound humility and quietism before the vast forces of Nature, history and the mob. Nevertheless his general attempt not only to confront the nuclear facts but to turn them to account is similar to my own attempt in studying the fictions in this book. Lifton puts his case and mine more compellingly in terms of preparing ourselves for the burdens of mature living when he says later in the same study, 'We need Hiroshima and Auschwitz, as we need Vietnam and our everyday lives, in all of their horrors, to deepen and free that imagination for the leaps it must make. . . . The vision of total annihilation makes it is possible to imagine living under and beyond that curse.'[26] In the United States some critics are asking for more pragmatic effects. Considering disaster stories of the immediate post-war period Paul Brians says that 'Science fiction failed, by and large, to interpret effectively the new reality',[27] while H. B. Franklin in a recent anthology finds that 'relatively few stories have even attempted to suggest solutions.²⁸ I find it hard to imagine a disaster literature of 'effective solutions'.

This book has presented some of the answers given in fiction to the question of W. H. Auden quoted at the beginning: 'Do I love this world so well/That I have to know how it ends?'. The love is assumed, which is why many of the most harrowing reading experiences can also have a curiously uplifting effect as well. It is good to know that other people care. The debate about ends and means will continue; a nuclear holocaust, far from burning the books, will fuel the enquiry, for the answers are hidden not by the veil of the future but by man's humanity. In a strange way, fictions of nuclear disaster represent the first and most vital meeting place between the two cultures, between the scientist and the artist who together, in the words of Robert Oppenheimer, 'can make the paths which connect the villages of art and science with each other and with the world at large into the multiple, varied and precious bonds of a true and world-wide community'.²⁹ Fictions of nuclear disaster, as well as extending the horizons of fictional technique, call on the power of the word to de-fuse the power of the fused atom. Because we love the world we imagine its end and try to speak it so that we might not know it:

> Why is Punch crookit? Why wil he all ways kil the babby if he can? Parbly I wont never know its jus on me to think on it.

> Riddley Walkers ben to show
> Riddley Walkers on the go
> Dont go Riddley Walkers track
> Drop Johns ryding on his back

> Still I wunt have no other track.
>
> (*Riddley Walker*, 220)

Appendix: Nuclear Disaster Films

Perhaps the most well-known and memorable visual images of nuclear disaster are those in Stanley Kubrick's film *Dr. Strangelove*, itself adapted from a novel (as discussed in Chapter 3). Although my focus has been on literary fictions in this book, useful parallels might be made in the development of nuclear disaster films. At the time of writing there are at least two mass-release features, *Testament* and *The Day After*, and I am sure this is only the beginning of a vogue.

In 1946 MGM's *The Beginning of the End* focused on a young scientist dying from radiation after saving the bomb from premature detonation. In the final scene at the Lincoln Memorial, his voice-over hopes for the betterment of mankind.[1] The first survivor film, *Five* (Columbia 1951), isolates a microcosm of society on a Californian mountain top. Questions of militarism and radiation are swept aside as the hero and heroine restart the human race to the sounds of Revelation: 'Behold! I make all things new!'[2]

As fictions were becoming more subtle and complex by the late forties, so films began to transcend the all-American verities of Ray Milland's *Panic in Year Zero*. Alain Resnais's *Hiroshima, Mon Amour* (1959) uses the setting of Hiroshima as a vehicle for the exploration of a woman's past. The French actress who is in love with a Japanese architect engaged in rebuilding the city must come to terms (as do many nuclear disaster fictions) with the history, specifically, of the Second World War, and her affair with a German soldier. As she says to her new lover, 'You destroy me, you are good for me.'[3]

Cartoons depicting nuclear disaster include *A Short Vision* (1956) and *The Hole* (1962), the blackened screen at the end of the former paralleling the foregrounding techniques of such modern writers as Maggie Gee and Raymond Briggs, where the manuscript itself decays and mutates. A powerful treatment of the survivor theme was *Ladybug, Ladybug* (United Artists 1963), portraying the uncertainty and panic of teachers at a school after a nuclear alert. The reactions of the children are reminiscent of Golding's *Lord of the Flies*, until the easy moralising at the end. Still, as Jack Shaheen points out in his history of such films, these treatments were comparatively sophisticated considering the popular notions of atomic warfare in the fifties which ran to toy atomic bombs and cereal boxes promising 'a genuine atomic bomb'.[4]

Contrary to literary fictions, where imaginative vision generally outstrips journalistic accuracy in terms of effect, the film documentary of disaster – Freed's *The Decision to Drop the Bomb* (1965), *Hiroshima-Nagasaki* (1970) – has been most effective, culminating in Peter Watkins's *The War Game*. This forty-seven minute film, commissioned by the BBC in 1966 but never yet shown on television (it had a film release), portrays in searing detail – particularly facial makeup – the effects of a nuclear strike on Great Britain. By using *cinema verité* techniques as well as freeze frames, this record of the firestorms in particular established in many people's minds 'authentic ikons of a Hiroshima to come'.[5] The director's comments, considering the release of *The Day After*, may at last be obsolete:

> If I had made a film about nuclear war and people either laughed at it or had I made Britain's recovery from that war quite firm and the Union Jack fluttered on the non-radioactive breeze, I have no doubt the film would have been shown. I must emphasise that it was because there is a feeling of hopelessness at the end that the film was banned.[6]

Only by utter realism like Watkins's, or satire and symbolism like Kubrick's, can film adequately respond to the theme of nuclear destruction. Even so, such films can do little more than establish a few visual 'ikons' in the mind's eye. These may be 'fleshed out' (if the image is not too inappropriate) only by the medium of the printed word, which can insist on authenticity according to the tradition of the found document, or else liberate the mind to create the necessary fictions about an event whose central quality, unattainable in the medium of film, is that there is no privileged spectator status.

On the small screen, however, producer and viewer encounter problems of convention as well as realism. Susan Boyd-Bowman, analysing the differing responses of American and British audiences to *The Day After*, suggests that the deliberate mingling of a variety of opaque styles or 'generic discourses' (documentary, pastoral, disaster movie, etc.) may be objectionable to a non-American audience.[7] Bernard Levin complains that 'a vast panoramic shot of wounded and dying people waiting hopelessly for succour is lifted straight from *Gone With the Wind*'[8], but that kind of archetypal resonance may be deliberate, and powerful. An alternative to this 'national' viewpoint is the personal drama, such as Lynne Littman's *Testament* which follows the fate of one Californian family (is it an accident that some of the most powerful literary works in this vein – Helen Clarkson's *The Last Day* [1959] or Judith Merril's *Shadow on the Hearth* – should also be by women?).

The question of perspective clearly troubled Nicholas Meyer, director of *The Day After*: in an early scene at the museum, Marilyn tells her father that a Chinese landscape painter 'wants you to be in the landscape, a part of it, not out there looking at it'.[9] Fiction may more easily move from the psychological to the political dimension, but Michael Jackson in *Threads* (BBC, 1984) does well in conveying 'a mini-drama overtaken by a maxi-drama'.[10] News headlines on the screen elicit a shock of recognition in an audience accustomed to seeing global disasters reported in just this way (though the boy noticing the delivery of blankets in a schoolyard is an equally effective personal image of disquiet. It remains to be seen whether television can enlarge upon its powerful array of stock responses and find a new vocabulary as stunning as that of Stanley Kubrick, in film.

Notes

1: THE BOMB IN FICTION

1. W. H. Auden, *The Age of Anxiety* (London: Faber, 1948) p. 88.
2. H. Kahn, *On Thermonuclear War: Thinking About the Unthinkable* (London: Weidenfeld & Nicolson, 1962) p. 103.
3. F. Jameson, in *Science Fiction Studies* 1 (Fall 1974) p. 275.
4. See I. F. Clarke, *Voices Prophesying War 1763–1984* (1966) and *The Pattern of Expectation* (1979).
5. Ursula le Guin, in *SF at Large*, ed. Peter Nicholls (London: Gollancz, 1976) p. 32.
6. W. Wagar, *Terminal Visions* (Bloomington: Indiana University Press, 1982) p. 5.
7. Le Guin, p. 33.
8. P. F. Nowlan, *Armageddon 2419 A.D.* (New York: Avalon, 1962).
9. Brian Ash, *Faces of the Future* (London: Elek/Pemberton, 1975) p. 193.
10. Isaac Asimov, *Asimov on Science Fiction* (New York: Doubleday, 1981) p. 109.
11. D. Wollheim, *The Universe Makers* (New York & London: Harper & Row, 1971) p. 66.
12. G. Wilson Knight, 'The Sun-Bomb' in *Hiroshima* (London: Andrew Dakers, 1946) p. 29.
13. F. Kermode, *The Sense of an Ending* (London: Oxford University Press, 1967) pp. 17, 29.
14. O. Stapledon, *Starmaker* (London: Methuen, 1937) p. vii.
15. Brigadier General Thomas A. Farrell in *The Atomic Age Opens* (New York: Pocket, 1945) p. 30.
16. K. R. R. Gros-Luis, *Literary Interpretations of Biblical Narratives* (Nashville: Abingdon, 1974) p. 345.
17. Michael Seidel in E. Mendelson (ed.), *Pynchon* (Englewood Cliffs, NJ: Prentice-Hall, 1978) p. 210; E. Mendelson in G. Levine & D. Leverenz (eds), *Mindful Pleasures* (Boston: Little, Brown & Co., 1976) p. 192.
18. *The Effects of Nuclear War*, compiled by the Office of Technological Assessment (London: Croom Helm, 1980) pp. 8–9.
19. I. F. Clarke, *The Pattern of Expectations* (London: Cape, 1979) p. 293.
20. Wagar, pp. 67, 69.
21. In B. Aldiss & H. Harrison (eds), *SF Horizons* (New York: Arno, 1978) p. 53.
22. Susan Sontag, 'The Imagination of Disaster' in *Science Fiction*, ed. Mark Rose (Engelwood Cliffs, NJ: Prentice-Hall, 1966) p. 130.
23. L. Fiedler, 'The New Mutants', *Paris Review*, XXXII (autumn 1965) p. 508.

24. *The Sense of an Ending*, p. 95.
25. John Barth, 'The Literature of Exhaustion' in *The Novel Today*, ed. Malcolm Bradbury (London: Fontana, 1977) pp. 78–9.
26. J. O. Bailey, *Pilgrims Through Space and Time* (1947; Westport, Conn.: Greenwood, 1972) p. 10.
27. L. Jones (ed.), *The New SF* (London: Arrow, 1970) p. 8.
28. K. Amis, *New Maps of Hell* (1961; London: New English Library, 1969) p. 115.

2: THE SCIENTIST AND ARMAGEDDON

1. W. H. Auden, *The Age of Anxiety*, p. 92.
2. Robert Jungk, *Brighter Than a Thousand Suns* (New York: Harcourt Brace & World, 1958) p. 201.
3. J. R. Oppenheimer, *Science and the Common Understanding* (New York: Simon & Schuster, 1966) p. 98.
4. Review of W. Wagar, *TLS*, 18 March 1983, p. 256.
5. Perry Miller, *Errand Into the Wilderness* (Cambridge, Mass.: Harvard University Press, 1964) p. 232.
6. Ibid., p. 235.
7. Ibid., p. 239.
8. C. P. Snow, *The Two Cultures & A Second Look* (London: Cambridge University Press, 1964) pp. 13–14.
9. Ibid. pp. 98–9.
10. Ibid. p. 5.
11. J. B. S. Haldane, *The Inequality of Man & Other Essays* (1932; London: Pelican, 1937) p. 143.
12. Ibid., pp. 98–9.
13. q. Sir Solly Zuckerman, *Scientists and War* (London: Hamish Hamilton, 1966) p. 125.
14. J. W. Campbell, *The Atomic Story* (New York: Henry Holt, 1947) p. 295.
15. q. Paul Carter, *The Creation of Tomorrow* (New York: Columbia University Press, 1977) p. 251.
16. R. Heinlein, *The SF Novel* (Chicago: Advent, 1959) p. 29.
17. q. Carter, p. 25.
18. q. A. I. Berger, 'Love, Death and the Atom Bomb', *Science Fiction Studies* 8 (1981) p. 287.
19. Douglas Hill, *Encyclopaedia of Science Fiction* (London: Octopus, 1978) p. 43.
20. P. Parrinder ed., *Science Fiction* (London & New York: Longman, 1979) p. 93.
21. R. K. Emmerson, *Antichrist in the Middle Ages* (Seattle: University of Washington Press, 1981) p. 132.
22. S. Zuckerman, *Nuclear Illusion and Reality* (London: Collins, 1982) pp. 105–6.
23. Gary Wolfe, in F. N. Magill (ed.), *Survey of Science Fiction Literature* (Engelwood Cliffs: Salem Press, 1979) III, pp. 1244–5.
24. 'Historical Note' to *Nerves*, pp. 177–80.
25. F. Soddy, *The Interpretation of the Atom* (London: John Murray, 1932) p. 4.

3: THE DAY AND THE DAY AFTER

1. W. H. Auden, *The Age of Anxiety*, p. 22.
2. G. West, *H. G. Wells* (London: Gerald Howe, 1930) p. 199.
3. N. and J. MacKenzie, *The Time Traveller* (London: Weidenfeld & Nicolson, 1973) p. 299.
4. F. McConnell, *The Science Fiction of H. G. Wells* (Oxford: Oxford University Press, 1981) pp. 195–6.
5. *Hiroshima and Nagasaki: the Physical, Medical and Social Effects of the Atomic Bombings* (New York: Basic Books, 1981) p. 14.
6. Ibid., p. xlv.
7. R. J. Lifton, *Death in Life* (London: Weidenfeld & Nicolson, 1968) p. 49.
8. *Hiroshima and Nagasaki*, p. 598.
9. Iri & Toshi Maruki, *The Hiroshima Panels* (Tokyo: Denyen-Shobo, 1968) p. 7.
10. T. Shaheen, *Nuclear War Films* (Carbondale, Ill.: University of Southern Illinois Press, 1978) p. 49.
11. q. Julian Smith, *Nevil Shute* (Boston: G. K. Hall, 1976) p. 129.
12. *TLS*, 18 March 1983, p. 256.
13. Shaheen, p. 32.
14. John Gardner, *On Moral Fiction* (New York: Basic Books, 1978) p. 126.
15. Ibid., p. 6.
16. Ibid., p. 126.
17. Shaheen, p. 66.
18. K. Vonnegut, *Palm Sunday* (London: Jonathan Cape, 1981) p. 70.
19. A. Walker, *Stanley Kubrick – Director* (New York: Harcourt Brace Jovanovich, 1971) pp. 161–2.
20. Jack London, *The Bodley Head Jack London* (London: Bodley Head, 1963) p. 224.

4: THE POST-NUCLEAR SOCIETY

1. W. H. Auden, *The Age of Anxiety*, p. 122.
2. G. Dennis, *The End of the World* (London: Eyre & Spottiswode, 1930); K. Heuer, *The End of the World* (New York: Rinehart, 1953).
3. q. Heuer, p. 144.
4. q. Heuer, p. 148.
5. *Nuclear War: What's in it For You?* (London: Methuen, 1982) p. 71.
6. *PM* editorial quoted in *The Atomic Age Opens*, op. cit.
7. F. L. Polak, *The Image of the Future* (New York: Oceana, 1961) I, p. 53.
8. H. Kahn, *On Escalation: Metaphor and Scenario* (London: Pall Mall, 1965) p. 50.
9. R. Scholes, *Science Fiction* (London & New York: University of Notre Dame Press, 1975) pp. 41–2.
10. J. W. Davidson, *The Logic of Millennial Thought* (New Haven & London: Yale University Press, 1977) p. 297.
11. F. Jameson, 'Progress versus Utopia: or, can we imagine the future?' *Science Fiction Studies* 9 (1982) p. 151.

12. A. I. Berger, 'Love, Death and the Atomic Bomb: Sexuality and Community in Science Fiction 1935–55', *Science Fiction Studies* (Nov. 1981) p. 293.
13. I. F. Clarke, *Voices Prophesying War*, p. 200.
14. S. Orwell & I. Angus (eds), *Collected Essays, Journalism and Letters of George Orwell* (London: Secker & Warburg, 1968) IV, p. 10.
15. q. W. Steinhoff, *The Road to 1984* (London: Weidenfeld & Nicolson, 1975) p. 54.
16. W. E. McNelly in *Survey of Science Fiction Literature* II, 690.
17. F. Pohl, *Super Science Stories* (Jan. 1950) p. 97.
18. q. P. Carter, *The Creation of Tomorrow*, p. 242.
19. M. Clarke, *The Nuclear Destruction of Britain* (London: Croom Helm, 1982) p. 240.
20. *Unearth* 2, 3 (Summer 1978).
21. D. Wollheim, *The Universe Makers* (New York: Harper & Row, 1971) p. 62.
22. G. K. Wolfe, in *Survey of Science Fiction Literature* IV, p. 1758.
23. Ibid., p. 1756.
24. R. Thurston, introduction to D. Galouye, *Dark Universe* (Gregg Press, 1976).
25. C. B. Yoke, in *Survey of Science Fiction Literature* I, p. 478.
26. F. Jameson, 'After Armageddon: Character Systems in *Dr. Bloodmoney*', *Science Fiction Studies* 2 (March 1975) pp. 33–42; endorsed by Philip Dick in P. Nicholls, *Science Fiction at Large*, p. 213.
27. Jameson, p. 42.
28. R. B. Schmerl, 'The Two Future Worlds of Aldous Huxley', *PMLA* 77 (June 1962) p. 330.
29. E. Teller with Allen Brown, *The Legacy of Hiroshima* (London: Macmillan, 1962) p. 181.
30. E. S. Rabkin, M. H. Greenberg & J. D. Olander (eds), *The End of the World* (Carbondale: Southern Illinois University Press, 1983) p. 125.

5: APOCALYPSES AND REVELATIONS

1. W. H. Auden, *The Age of Anxiety*, p. 123.
2. D. Ketterer, *New Worlds for Old* (New York: Anchor/Doubleday, 1974) p. xi.
3. Brian Stableford, *The Encyclopedia of Science Fiction* ed. P. Nicholls (London: Granada, 1981) p. 433.
4. *The Atomic Age Opens* (New York: Pocket, 1945) pp. 17–18.
5. Ibid., pp. 39–40.
6. Ibid., p. 167.
7. Ibid., pp. 220–1.
8. Karl Rahner (ed.), *Encyclopedia of Theology* (London: Burns & Oates, 1975) pp. 16–17.
9. L. Morris, *Apocalyptic* (US: Erdmans, 1972) p. 35.
10. P. Grelot in *Encyclopedia of Theology*, op. cit., pp. 17–18.

11. H. H. Rowley, *The Relevance of Apocalyptic* (London: Lutterworth, 1947) pp. 25, 35–6.
12. D. S. Russell, *The Method and Message of Jewish Apocalyptic* (London: SCM Press, 1964) p. 297.
13. N. Frye, *The Great Code* (Toronto: Academic Press, 1982) p. 138.
14. D. H. Lawrence, *Apocalypse and the Writings on Revelation*, ed. M. Kalnins (London: Cambridge University Press, 1980) pp. 47, 54.
15. N. Cohn, *The Pursuit of the Millennium* (New York: Harper & Row, 1961) p. 74.
16. F. Kermode, *The Sense of an Ending* (London: Oxford University Press, 1967) p. 101. Commentators seem unwittingly to support Kermode's view: Rowley talks of the 'final great Assize' (p. 174) and W. A. Beardslee of 'a new and total solution to the human problem' (q. L. Morris, *Apocalyptic*, p. 36).
17. W. H. Oliver, *Prophets and Millennialists* (Auckland University Press/Oxford University Press, 1978) pp. 241–2.
18. B. Stableford in *The Encyclopedia of Science Fiction*, p. 495.
19. M. J. Laski, *Utopia and Revelation* (University of Chicago Press, 1976) pp. 285–6.
20. J. B. S. Haldane, *Possible Worlds and Other Essays* (London: Chatto & Windus, 1929) p. 264.
21. q. M. J. Laski, op. cit., p. 490.
22. M. Barkun, *Disaster and the Millennium* (New York & Yale: Yale University Press, 1974) p. 200.
23. Ketterer, p. 13.
24. D. Suvin, *Metamorphoses of Science Fiction* (New Haven, Conn.: Yale University Press, 1979) p. 4.
25. F. A. Kreuziger, *Apocalypse and Science Fiction* (California: Scholars Press, 1982) p. 173.
26. K. R. R. Gros Luis, *Literary Interpretations of Biblical Narratives* (Nashville: Abingdon, 1974) p. 345.
27. C. F. D. Moule, q. L. Morris, p. 45.
28. D. S. Russell, pp. 37–9.
29. W. Schneemelcher, *New Testament Apocrypha* (London: Lutterworth, 1974) II, p. 724.
30. Cf. Milton's description of Satanic weaponry in *Paradise Lost* (VII, ll. 482–90); Blake's vision in *America* (I, ll. 22–8, 157–82); Shelley's *Prometheus Unbound* (ll. 295–316); Tennyson's 'Armageddon' (ll. 14–24), etc.
31. D. H. Lawrence, *Women in Love* (1921; ll; London: Heinemann, 1971) p. 444.
32. B. Gillespie in *Survey of Science Fiction Literature* v, p. 2523.
33. Hugo Gernsback founded the first science fiction magazine, *Amazing Stories*, in 1926.
34. B. Rickard, '*After Such Knowledge*: James Blish's Tetralogy' in C. Chauvin (ed.), *A Multitude of Visions* (Baltimore: T-K Graphics, 1975) p. 27.
35. R. W. B. Lewis, *Trials of the World* (New York & London: Yale University Press, 1965) p. 184.
36. q. W. E. McNelly & K. Neilson, *Survey of Science Fiction Literature* II, p. 750.

37. Ibid., p. 235.
38. L. Menger, in Dick Riley (ed.), *Critical Encounters* (New York: Fred Ungar, 1978) p. 108.

6: THE IMAGINATION OF DISASTER

1. W. H. Auden, *The Age of Anxiety*, p. 42.
2. A. Robbe-Grillet, *Topologie d'une Cité Fantôme* (Paris: Les Editions de Minuit, 1976) p. 13.
3. L. Langer, *Versions of Survival* (Albany: State University of New York Press, 1982) pp. ix–x.
4. Ibid., p. 131.
5. Ibid., p. 12.
6. Ibid., p. 149.
7. B. Foley, 'Fact, Fiction, Fascism: Testimony and Mimesis in Holocaust Narratives', *Comparative Literature* 34, 4 (Autumn 1982) p. 348.
8. Quoted in A. H. Rosenfeld & I. Greenberg, *Confronting the Holocaust: The Impact of Elie Wiesel* (Bloomington: Indiana University Press, 1978) p. 4.
9. Ibid., pp. 45–6.
10. David Dowling, 'Burnt Offerings from *The White Hotel*', *Comment* 16 (Aug. 1982) p. 5.
11. W. van T. Clark, in T. E. Sanders (ed.), *Speculations* (New York: Glencoe, 1973) p. 598.
12. P. Evans, *Janet Frame* (Boston: Twayne, 1977) p. 184.
13. Quoted in *The Feminine Eye*, ed. Tom Staicar (New York: F. Ungar, 1982) p. 60.
14. U. le Guin in R. D. Mullen & D. Suvin (eds), *Science Fiction Studies* (Boston: Gregg, 1976) p. 156.
15. I. A. Berger, *Survey of Science Fiction Literature* III, p. 1065.
16. J. W. Campbell refers to it specifically in *The Atomic Story* (1947); F. Brown's 'The Weapon' builds on it; even *A Canticle for Leibowitz* has the image of 'a child who knows what a loaded pistol is supposed to do, but who never pulled a trigger before' (227).
17. James Sallis (ed.), *The War Book* (London: Panther, 1969) p. 150.
18. Letter to the author, 9 Dec. 1983.
19. F. E. Manuel (ed.), *Utopias and Utopian Thought* (Boston: Houghton Mifflin, 1966) p. 295.
20. T. LeClair & L. McCaffery, *Anything Can Happen* (Urbana: University of Illinois Press, 1983) p. 271.

7: TWO EXEMPLARY FICTIONS

1. George Steiner, *Language and Silence* (London: Faber & Faber, 1967) p. 30.
2. R. Vacca, *The Coming Dark Age* (New York: Doubleday, 1973) p. 73.
3. J. A. Sutherland, in P. Parrinder (ed.), *Science Fiction* (London & New York: Longman, 1979) p. 178.
4. W. Percy, in *Contemporary Authors* (Detroit: Gale, 1975) pp. 352–3.

5. T. J. Morrissey, 'Armageddon from Huxley to Hoban', *Extrapolation*, 25, 3 (Autumn 1984) p. 207.
6. R. Griffin, 'Mediaevalism in *A Canticle for Leibowitz*', *Extrapolation* 14, 2 (May 1973) pp. 112–25.
7. H. Rank, 'Song out of Season: *A Canticle for Leibowitz*', *Renascence* 21 (1969) p. 221.
8. Introduction to *Grimm's Tales*, quoted in *Isis*, 2 June 1977, p. 28.
9. 'John Haffenden Talks to Russell Hoban', *The Literary Review* (Nov. 1982) pp. 27–8.
10. G. Speaight, *Punch and Judy* (London: Studio Vista, 1970) p. 113.
11. D. J. Lake, 'Making the Two One: Language and Mysticism in *Riddley Walker*', *Extrapolation* 25, 2 (Summer 1984) p. 168.
12. Review of *Riddley Walker*, *Encounter* LVI, 1 (June 1981).

8: CONCLUSION WITHOUT CLOSURE

1. W. H. Auden, *The Age of Anxiety*, p. 22.
2. R. Jungk, *Brighter Than a Thousand Suns* (New York: Harcourt, Brace & World, 1958) p. 228.
3. John Cox, *Overkill: the Story of Modern Weapons* (Harmondsworth: Penguin/Kestrel, 1977) p. 27.
4. W. C. Anderson, *5,4,3,2,1,Pfft* (New York: Ace, 1960) p. 82.
5. Ibid., p. 149.
6. Ibid., p. 7.
7. G. Wolfe, *The Known and the Unknown: the Iconography of Science Fiction* (Kent: Kent State University Press, 1979) p. 137.
8. W. Atheling (James Blish), *The Issue at Hand* (Chicago: Advent, 1973) p. 59.
9. Jungk, p. 288.
10. S. Bridwell (ed.), *World War Three* (1978; London: Hamlyn, 1980) xvii.
11. Ground Zero, *Nuclear War* (London: Methuen, 1982) p. 71.
12. S. Zuckerman, *Nuclear Illusion and Reality* (London: Collins, 1982) p. 18.
13. L. A. Berès, *Nuclear Catastrophe and World Politics* (University of Chicago Press, 1980) p. 36.
14. Zuckerman, pp. 41–2.
15. K. Amis, *New Maps of Hell*, p. 134.
16. E. Teller (with A. Brown), *The Legacy of Hiroshima* (London: Macmillan, 1962) p. 81.
17. J. G. Ballard, 'The Coming of the Unconscious', in *The Overloaded Man* (London: Panther, 1967) p. 144.
18. E. R. MacCormac, *Metaphor and Myth in Science and Religion* (Durham North Carolina: Duke University Press, 1976).
19. Cox, p. 11.
20. E. Morris, *The Seeds of Hiroshima*, p. 93.
21. E. Morris, *The Flowers of Hiroshima*, p. 187.
22. E. S. Rabkin, M. H. Greenberg & J. D. Olander (eds), *The End of the World* (Carbondale: Southern Illinois University Press, 1984) p. xv.

23. Philip Neilsen, *We'll All Go Together* (Brisbane: Queensland Community Press, 1984) p. 21.
24. Robert Sheckley interviewed in *Dream Makers* by Charles Platt (New York: Berkley, 1980) p. 23.
25. R. J. Lifton, *The Life of the Self* (New York: Simon & Schuster, 1976) p. 115.
26. Ibid., p. 281.
27. Paul Brians, 'Nuclear War in Science Fiction, 1945–59', *Science Fiction Studies* 11 (Nov. 1984) p. 253.
28. H. Bruce Franklin (ed.), *Countdown to Midnight* (New York: Daw, 1984) p. 27.
29. Jungk, pp. 333–4.

APPENDIX

1. Jack Shaheen (ed.), *Nuclear War Films* (Carbondale: Southern Illinois University Press, 1978) p. 9.
2. Ibid., p. 14.
3. Ibid., p. 22.
4. Ibid., p. 56.
5. Ibid., p. 115.
6. Ibid., p. 114.
7. Susan Boyd-Bowman, '*The Day After*: Representations of the Nuclear Holocaust', *Screen* 25, 4–5 (July–Oct. 1984) pp. 71–97.
8. Bernard Levin, *The Times*, 10 Dec. 1983.
9. Boyd-Bowman, p. 95.
10. Ibid., p. 77.

Bibliography

Abernathy, R., 'Heirs Apparent', *Fantasy & Science Fiction* (June 1954).
Aldiss, B., *Barefoot in the Head* (1969; London: Corgi, 1971).
——, *Greybeard* (New York: Harcourt Brace, 1964).
Anderson, Poul, 'A Chapter of Revelation' in *The Day The Sun Stood Still* (New York: Thomas Nelson, 1972).
——, *After Doomsday* (1963; St. Albans: Panther, 1975).
——, 'Disintegrating Sky', *Fantastic Universe* (Aug./Sept. 1953).
——, 'Progress', *Fantasy & Science Fiction* (Jan. 1962).
——, *Vault of the Ages* (New York: Holt, Rinehart & Winston, 1952).
——, & Waldrop, D. N., 'Tomorrow's Children' in R. S. Silverberg (ed.), *Mutants* (London: Abelard, 1974).
——, *Orion Shall Rise* (New York: Timescape, 1983).
Anderson, W. C., *5,4,3,2,1,Pfft or 12,000 Men and One Bikini* (New York: Ace, 1960).
Anthony, Piers, *Sos the Rope* (1968; London: Faber & Faber, 1970).
Antrobus, J. & Milligan, Spike, *The Bed Sitting Room* (Surrey: M. & J. Hobbs, 1970).
Asimov, Isaac, 'Hell Fire', *Fantastic Universe Science Fiction* (May 1956).
Asterley, H. C., *Escape to Berkshire* (London: Pall Mall, 1961).
Ballard, J. G., *The Overloaded Man* (St. Albans: Panther, 1967).
——, *Low Flying Aircraft* (London: Jonathan Cape, 1976).
Balmer, E. & Wylie, P., *When Worlds Collide* (New York: F. A. Stokes, 1932).
Barjavel, R., *The Ice People*, trs. C. L. Markmann (1968; London: Rupert Hart-Davis, 1970).
Bax, M. *The Hospital Ship* (London: Picador, 1977).
Benet, S. St V., 'By the Waters of Babylon' (1937) in T. D. Clareson (ed.), *A Spectrum of Worlds* (New York: Doubleday, 1972).
——, *Selected Works* (1942; New York: Holt, Rinehart & Winston, 1969).
Bennett, M., *The Long Way Back* (New York: Coward-McCann, 1965).
Benson, R. H., *Lord of the World* (1907; New York: Arno, 1975).
Best, H., *The Twentyfifth Hour* (New York: Random House, 1940).
Bester, A., 'Adam and No Eve', *Astounding Science Fiction* (Sept. 1941).
Blish, James, *Black Easter* (1968; New York: Avon, 1980).
——, *The Day After Judgment* (1971; New York: Avon, 1980).
Blumenfeld, Y., *Jenny: My Diary* (1981; Harmondsworth: Penguin, 1983).
Brackett, Leigh, *The Long Tomorrow* (1955; New York: Ballantine, 1974).
Bradbury, R., *Fahrenheit 451* (1954; St Albans: Panther, 1977).
——, 'The Highway', *The Illuminated Man* (New York: Doubleday, 1951).
——, *The Martian Chronicles* (1946; New York: Doubleday, 1958).
Briggs, R., *When the Wind Blows* (London: Hamish Hamilton, 1982).

Brown, F., 'The Weapon', *Astounding Science Fiction* (Apr. 1951).

Bryant, E., 'Jody After the War' in *Among the Dead* (New York: Macmillan, 1973).

Bryant, P., *Red Alert* (New York: Ace, 1958).

Bunch, D., *Moderan* (New York: Avon, 1971).

Burdick, E. & Wheeler, H., *Fail-safe* (London: Hutchinson, 1963).

Burgess, A., *The End of the World News* (London: Hutchinson, 1982).

Burroughs, W., *Nova Express* (1966; London: Panther, 1972).

Butterworth, M., 'Post-atomic', in L. Jones (ed.), *The New SF* (London: Arrow, 1970).

Calder, N., *Nuclear Nightmares* (London: BBC, 1979).

Camp, L. S. de, 'Judgment Day', *Astounding Science Fiction* (Aug. 1955).

Campbell, J. W., *The Atomic Story* (New York: Henry Holt, 1947).

Čapek, K., *The Absolute at Large* (1927; Westport, Conn.: Hyperion, 1974).

——, *Krakatit* tr. L. Hyde (London: Geoffrey Bles, 1925).

——, *War With the Newts* tr. M. & R. Weatherall (London: Allen & Unwin, 1937).

Carter, A., *Heroes and Villains* (London: Heinemann, 1969).

Cartmill, C., 'Deadline', *Astounding Science Fiction* (Mar. 1944).

Casewit, C. S., *The Peacemakers* (New York: Avalon, 1960).

Charnas, S. McK., *Walk to the End of the World* (1974; London: Hodder & Stoughton/Coronet, 1981).

——, *Motherlines* (1978; London: Hodder & Stoughton/Coronet, 1981).

Childers, E., *The Riddle of the Sands* (London: Smith & Elder, 1903).

Christopher, J., *The Prince in Waiting* (London: Hamish Hamilton, 1970).

Clark, W. van T., 'The Portable Phonograph', (1941), in T. E. Sanders (ed.), *Speculations* (New York: Glencoe, 1973).

Clarke, A. C., *Childhood's End* (1954; London: Pan, 1963).

Clayton, B. C., *Life After Doomsday* (New York: Dial, 1980).

Collier, J., *Tom's Acold* (London: Macmillan, 1933).

Cooper, E., *All Fool's Day* (New York: Walker, 1966).

——, *The Cloud Walker* (London: Hodder & Stoughton, 1973).

——, *The Lost Continent* (London: Hodder & Stoughton, 1970).

Coover, R., *The Public Burning* (Harmondsworth: Penguin, 1978).

Coppel, A., *Dark December* (1958; London: Herbert Jenkins, 1966).

Dahl, R., *Sometimes Never* (London: Collins, 1949).

Darlton, C., *Mutants vs. Mutants* (New York: Ace, 1972).

Del Rey, L., *The Eleventh Commandment* (1962; New York: Ballantine, 1976).

——, *Nerves* (1956; New York: Ballantine, 1977).

Desmond, Shaw, *Ragnarok* (London: Duckworth, 1926).

Dick, P., *Dr Bloodmoney* (New York: Ace, 1965).

Disch, T., *100 and 2 H Bombs* (London: Roberts & Vintner, 1966).

——, *Genocides* (London: R. Whiting & Wheaton, 1965).

——, 'I–A', *New Worlds* (April 1968).

Divine, D., *Atom at Spithead* (London: Hale, 1953).

Duncan, R. L., *The Day the Sun Fell* (New York: Pinnacle, 1970).

Duncan, R., *The Last Adam* (London: Dennis Robson, 1952).

Ellanby, B., 'Chain Reaction', *Galaxy* (Sept. 1956).

England, G. A. *Darkness and Dawn* (1914; Westport, Conn.: Hyperion, 1974).

Farjeon, J. J., *Death of a World* (London: Collins, 1948).

Fitz Gibbon, C., *When the Kissing Had to Stop* (London: Cassell, 1960).

Flammarion, C., *Omega: The Last Days of the World* (1894; New York: Arno, 1974).

Flecker, J. E., *The Last Generation* (London: New Age, 1908).

Frame, J. *Intensive Care* (New York: G. Braziller, 1970).

Frank, P., *Alas, Babylon* (1959; New York: Bantam, 1977).

——, *Mr. Adam* (London: Gollancz, 1947).

Galouye, D., *Dark Universe* (London: Gollancz, 1961).

Gee, M., *The Burning Book* (London: Faber & Faber, 1983).

George, P., *Dr. Strangelove* (London: Corgi, 1963).

Geston, M., *Out of the Mouth of the Dragon* (1969; London: Sphere, 1972).

Gloag, J., *Tomorrow's Yesterday* (London: George Allen & Unwin, 1932).

Graham, D., *Down to a Sunless Sea* (London: Pan, 1979).

Graham, P. A., *The Collapse of Homo Sapiens* (London & New York: G. P. Putnam, 1923).

Graham, R., *Utopia 239* (London: Heinemann, 1955).

Greenaway, Peter van, *The Crucified City* (London: New Authors, 1962).

Griffin, B. C. & Poynka, B., *The Nuclear Catastrophe* (Port Washington, N.Y.: L. Ashley, 1977).

Griffith, G., *Olga Romanoff* (1894; Westport, Conn.: Hyperion, 1974).

Griffith, J., *The Survivors* (London: Collins, 1965).

Ground Zero, *Nuclear War: What's In It For You?* (London: Methuen, 1982).

Hackett, General Sir J., *The Third World War* (1978; London: Sphere, 1979).

——, *The Untold Story* (London: Sidgwick & Jackson, 1982).

Haldeman, J., 'To Howard Hughes: A Modest Proposal', in *Study War No More* (New York: St Martin's, 1977).

Harrison, H., *In Our Hands, the Stars* (London: Faber & Faber, 1970).

Harrison, M. J., *The Committed Men* (St Albans: Panther, 1973).

Harting, P., *Anno Domini 2079* trs. A. W. Bikkers (London: W. Tegg, 1871).

Hartley, L. P., *Facial Justice* (London: Hamish Hamilton, 1960).

Haven, T. de, *Freaks' Amour* (New York: William Morrow, 1979).

Hawthorne, M., 'A New Adam and Eve' in *Mosses from an Old Manse* (1843; Columbus: Ohio State University Press, 1974).

Heinlein, R., 'Blowups Happen', *Astounding Science Fiction* (Sept. 1940).

——, *Farnham's Freehold* (1965; London: Corgi, 1979).

——, (Anson MacDonald), 'Solution Unsatifactory', *Astounding Science Fiction* (May 1941).

Hersey, J., *Hiroshima* (1946; Harmondsworth: Penguin, 1982).

Hoban, R., *Riddley Walker* (London: Jonathan Cape, 1980).

Holm, S., *Termush* trs. S. Clayton (London: Faber & Faber, 1969).

Hoover, H. M., *Children of Morrow* (1973; London: Methuen, 1975).

Hoyle, F. & G., *The Inferno* (London: Heinemann, 1973).

Huxley, A., *Ape and Essence* (London: Chatto & Windus, 1949).

Ing, D., *Pulling Through* (New York: Ace, 1983).

Jakubowski, M., 'Just Another End of the World' in *After the Fall* ed. R. Sheckley (London: Sphere, 1980).

Jameson, M., 'The Giant Atom', *Startling Stories* (Winter 1944).

——, *The Giant Atom* (New York: Bond-Charteris, 1945).

Jane, F. T., *The Violent Flame: A Story of Armageddon and After* (1899; New York: Arno, 1975).

Jefferies, R., *After London/Wild England* (1885; London: Oxford University Press, 1980).

Jenkins, W. F., *The Murder of the U.S.A.* (New York: Crown, 1946).

Keyes, D., *The Contaminated Man* (1971; St Albans: Mayflower, 1977).

Knight, D., 'Not With a Bang', *Fantasy & Science Fiction* (Winter–Spring, 1950).

Kornbluth, C., 'Two Dooms' in F. Pohl (ed.), *The Best of C. Kornbluth* (New York: Ballantine, 1976).

Kuttner, H., 'Atomic', *Thrilling Wonder Stories* (Aug. 1947).

——, 'I Am Eden', *Thrilling Wonder Stories* (Dec. 1946).

Lafferty, R. A., *Apocalypses* (Los Angeles: Pinnacle, 1977).

Lanier, S., *Hiero's Journey* (London: Panther, 1976).

Leiber, F., 'Appointment in Tomorrow', *Galaxy* (June 1951).

——, 'Coming Attraction', *Galaxy* (Nov. 1950).

——, 'The Night of the Long Knives', *Amazing Science Fiction* (Jan. 1960).

Lem, S., *The Futurological Congress* (London: Secker & Warburg, 1974).

Lessing, D., *The Four-Gated City* (London: MacGibbon & Kee, 1969).

——, *Memoirs of a Survivor* (1974; London: Pan, 1983).

——, *The Summer Before the Dark* (London: Jonathan Cape, 1973).

——, *Shikasta* (London: Jonathan Cape, 1979).

Lightner, A. M., *The Day of the Drones* (New York: Norton, 1969).

London, J., *The Scarlet Plague & Before Adam* ed. I. O. Evans (1910; London: Arco, 1968).

MacBeth, G., 'Crab-Apple Crisis' in J. Sallis (ed.), *The War Book* (London: Panther, 1969).

MacLennan, H., *Voices in Time* (1980; Harmondsworth: Penguin, 1983).

Mailer, N., 'The Last Night' in *Cannibals and Christians* (London: Sphere, 1969).

Maine, C. E., *The Tide Went Out* (London: Hodder & Stoughton, 1959).

Malamud, B., *God's Grace* (London: Chatto & Windus, 1982).

Martel, S., *The City Underground*, trs. N. Smaridge (New York: Viking, 1964).

Merle, R., *Malevil*, trs. D. Coltman (New York: Simon & Schuster, 1973).

Merril, J., 'That Only a Mother', *Astounding Science Fiction* (June 1948).

——, *Shadow on the Hearth* (New York: Garden City/Doubleday, 1950).

Miller, W. M., *A Canticle for Leibowitz* (1959; London: Corgi, 1979).

——, 'Crucifixius Etiam', *Astounding Science Fiction* (Feb. 1953).

——, 'Dark Benediction', *Fantastic Adventures* (Sept. 1951).

Minot, S., *Chill of Dust* (New York: Doubleday, 1964).

Mitchell, J. L., *Gay Hunter* (London: Heinemann, 1934).

Moorcock, M., *Before Armageddon Volume One* (London: Wyndham, 1976).

Moore, D. A., *Mirrors of the Apocalypse* (Nashville & London: Charter House, 1978).

Moore, W., 'Lot', *Fantasy & Science Fiction* (May 1953).

——, 'Lot's Daughter', *Fantasy & Science Fiction* (Oct. 1954).

Morris, E., *The Flowers of Hiroshima* (New York: Viking, 1959).

——, *The Seeds of Hiroshima* (New York: G. Braziller, 1965).

Nation, T., *The Survivors* (London: Weidenfeld & Nicolson, 1976).

Nicolson, H., *Public Faces* (1932; Harmondsworth: Penguin, 1944).

Niven, L. & Pournelle, J., *Lucifer's Hammer* (1978; London: Futura, 1982).

Norton, A., *Star Man's Son* (New York: Harcourt Brace & World, 1952).

Nowlan, P. F., *Armageddon 2419 A.D.* (New York: Avalon, 1962).

Noyes, A., *No Other Man* (New York: F. A. Stokes, 1940).

Noyes, P. B., *The Pallid Giant* (New York: Fleming H. Revell, 1927).

O'Brien, R. C., *Z for Zachariah* (London: Gollancz, 1975).

O'Brien, T., *The Nuclear Age* (New York: Knopf, 1985).

Orwell, G., *Nineteen Eightyfour* (1949; Harmondsworth: Penguin, 1967).

Owen, D., *End of the World* (New York: Ace, 1962).

Padgett, L., 'The Piper's Son', *Astounding Science Fiction* (Feb. 1954).

——, *Mutant* (New York: Gnome, 1953).

——, *Tomorrow and Tomorrow* (London: World, 1963).

Palmer, D. R., 'Emergence', *Analog* (Jan. 1981).

Pangborn, E., *The Company of Glory* (New York: Pyramid, 1975).

——, *Davy* (1964; New York: Ballantine, 1982).

——, *Judgment of Eve* (London: Rapp & Whiting, 1966).

——, *Still I Persist in Wondering* (New York: Dell, 1978).

Pape, R., *And So Ends the World* (1961; St Albans: Panther, 1963).

Piper, H. B., 'Day of the Moron', *Astounding Science Fiction* (Sept. 1951).

—— & McGuire, J. J., 'Null-ABC', *Astounding Science Fiction* (Feb. 1953).

Powys, J. C., *Up and Out* (London: Macdonald, 1957).

Priest, C., *Fugue for a Darkening Island* (London: Faber & Faber, 1972).

Pynchon, T., *Gravity's Rainbow* (New York: Viking, 1976).

Rayer, F. G., *Tomorrow Sometimes Comes* (London: Horne & van Thal, 1957).

Reed, K., *Armed Camps* (New York: E. P. Dutton, 1970).

Reynolds, P. *It Happened Like This* (London: Eyre & Spottiswode, 1952).

Rose, F. H., *The Maniac's Dream* (London: Duckworth, 1946).

Roshwald, M., *Level 7* (New York: Signet, 1959).

——, *A Small Armageddon* (New York: Signet, 1962).

Schell, J., *The Fate of the Earth* (London: Picador, 1982).

Seymour, A., *The Coming Death of the U.S.A.* (London: Souvenir, 1969).

Shanks, E., *The People of the Ruins* (London: Collins, 1920).

Shaw, R., *Ground Zero Man* (London: Corgi, 1971).

Sheckley, R. (ed.), *After the Fall* (London: Sphere, 1980).

——, *Journey Beyond Tomorrow* (London: Gollancz, 1964).

Shelley, M., *The Last Man*, ed. H. J. Luke (1826; Lincoln: University of Nebraska Press, 1965).

Shiel, M. P., *The Purple Cloud* (London: Gollancz, 1963).

Shiras, W. H., *Children of the Atom* (New York: Gnome, 1953).

Shute, N., *On the Beach* (1957; London: Pan, 1982).

Silverberg, R., 'When we went to see the end of the world' (1972) in *Future Pastimes*, ed. G. Edelstein (Nashville: Aurora, 1977).

——, *Vornan-19* (1968; London: Sidgwick & Jackson, 1970).

Simak, C., 'Lobby', *Astounding Science Fiction* (Apr. 1944).

Sinclair, A., *Gog* (1967; Harmondsworth: Penguin, 1970).

Sinclair, U., *The Millennium* (1924; London: T. Werner Laurie, 1929).

Spinrad, N., *The Iron Dream* (New York: Avon, 1972).

——, 'The Big Flash', in *No Direction Home* (1969; New York: Pocket, 1975).

Stacy, Ryder, *Doomsday Warrior* (Toronto: General, 1984).
——, *Doomsday Warrior No. 2: Red America* (Toronto: General, 1984).
Stapledon, O., *The Last Man in London* (London: Methuen, 1932).
Stewart, G., *Earth Abides* (New York: Random House, 1949).
Strieber, W. & J. Kunetka, *War Day* (New York: Holt, Rinehart & Winston, 1984).
Strugatsky, A. & B., *Prisoners of Power*, trs. H. S. Jacobson (London: Colliers/Macmillan, 1978).
Stuart, D. A., 'Atomic Power', *Astounding Stories* (Dec. 1934).
Sturgeon, T., 'Memorial', *Astounding Science Fiction* (Apr. 1946).
——, 'Thunder and Roses', *Astounding Science Fiction* (Nov. 1947).
Sutphen, V. T., *The Doomsman* (1905; Boston: L. Gregg, 1975).
Sutton, J. *The Atomic Conspiracy* (New York: Avalon, 1963).
Svevo, I., *Confessions of Zeno* (1923; London: Putnams, 1930).
Tenn, W., 'Null-P', in *Spectrum I* (London: Pan, 1961).
Tracy, L., *The Final War* (London: C. A. Pearson, 1896).
Train, A. & Wood, R. W., *The Man Who Rocked the Earth* (1915; New York: Arno, 1975).
Tucker, W., *The City in the Sea* (New York: Rinehart, 1951).
——, *The Year of the Quiet Sun* (London: Hale, 1970).
Van Mierlo, H., *By Then Mankind Ceased to Exist* (Ilfracombe: A. H. Stockwell, 1960).
Vidal, G., *Kalki* (London: Heinemann, 1978).
Vonnegut, K., *Cat's Cradle* (1963; Harmondsworth: Penguin, 1980).
——, *Player Piano* (1953; London: Panther, 1969).
——, *Slaughterhouse-Five* (New York: Delacorte, 1969).
Waterloo, S., *Armageddon* (1898; Boston: L. Gregg, 1976).
Wells, H. G., *The Mind at the End of Its Tether* (London: Heinemann, 1945).
——, *The Shape of Things to Come* (1933; London: White Lion, 1973).
——, *The World Set Free* (1914; London: Corgi, 1976).
Williams, J., *The People of the Ax* (New York: Dell, 1975).
Williams, N. B., *Atom Curtain* (New York: Ace, 1956).
Williams, R. M., *The Day They Bombed L.A.* (New York: Ace, 1961).
Wilson, A., *The Old Men at the Zoo* (London: Secker & Warburg, 1961).
Wolfe, B., *Limbo '90* (London: Secker & Warburg, 1953).
Wright, F., *Deluge* (London: F. Wright, 1927).
Wylie, P., *Tomorrow!* (New York: Rinehart, 1954).
Wyndham, J., *The Chrysalids* (1955; Harmondsworth: Penguin, 1973).
Zeigfreid, K., *Atomic Nemesis* (New York: Badger, 1962).
Zelazny, R., *Damnation Alley* (1969; London: Sphere, 1973).
——, *This Immortal* (London: Rupert Hart-Davis, 1966).
Ziemann, H. H., *The Explosions*, trs. J. Neugroschel (London: New English Library, 1978).
Zola, E. *Work*, trs. E. A. Vizetelly (London: Chatto & Windus, 1901).

Index

236